Dear Reader:

The book you are about to read is the latest bestseller from the St. Martin's True Crime Library, the imprint *The New York Times* calls "the leader in true crime!" Each month, we offer you a fascinating account of the latest, most sensational crime that has captured the national attention. St. Martin's is the publisher of Tina Dirmann's VANISHED AT SEA, the story of a former child actor who posed as a yacht buyer in order to lure an older couple out to sea, then robbed them and threw them overboard to their deaths. John Glatt's riveting and horrifying SECRETS IN THE CELLAR shines a light on the man who shocked the world when it was revealed that he had kept his daughter locked in his hidden basement for 24 years. In the Edgar-nominated WRITTEN IN BLOOD, Diane Fanning looks at Michael Petersen, a Marine-turned-novelist found guilty of beating his wife to death and pushing her down the stairs of their home—only to reveal another similar death from his past. In the book you now hold, DANCING WITH DEATH, award-winning journalist Shanna Hogan details the life of a former stripper who was convicted of murdering one of her many husbands.

St. Martin's True Crime Library gives you the stories behind the headlines. Our authors take you right to the scene of the crime and into the minds of the most notorious murderers to show you what really makes them tick. St. Martin's True Crime Library paperbacks are better than the most terrifying thriller, because it's all true! The next time you want a crackling good read, make sure it's got the St. Martin's True Crime Library logo on the spine—you'll be up all night!

Charles E. Spicer, Jr.
Executive Editor, St. Martin's True Crime Library

Praise for *Dancing with Death*

"Headless corpse, topless dancer, endless suspense! Author Shanna Hogan bursts on to the scene with a noir tale that's both seductive and delicious. After reading *Dancing with Death* you'll remember why Mom and Dad warned you about those seedy little places." —Kevin Flynn, author of
Wicked Intentions, *Our Little Secret* and *Legally Dead*

"Shanna Hogan tells a chilling, intricate story of a world full of sex, greed and deceit, with significant aplomb. She leads the reader through the twists and turns of the horrific event with great attention to detail. It is a ride true crime junkies won't want to miss." —Amanda Lamb, author of
Deadly Dose, *Evil Next Door*, *Love Lies*

"Shanna Hogan hits her debut true crime book right out of the park! Keep an eye on this writer . . . if *Dancing With Death* is any indication of her talent, she's a rising star in the this genre." —Anthony Flacco, author of *The Road Out of Hell:
Sanford Clark and the True Story of the Wineville Murders*,
A Checklist for Murder, and *Tiny Dancer*

"A gripping story of greed and betrayal, *Dancing With Death* takes off full-throttle with the discovery of a dismembered corpse and plunges into a disturbing world where nothing is as it seems. Hogan gives a chilling account of a woman convicted of a crime as diabolical and cold-blooded as she is glamorous." —Phyllis Gobbell, co-author of
An Unfinished Canvas and *A Season of Darkness*

DANCING
WITH
DEATH

**THE TRUE STORY OF A GLAMOROUS SHOWGIRL,
HER WEALTHY HUSBAND, AND A HORRIFYING MURDER**

Shanna Hogan

St. Martin's Paperbacks

DANCING WITH DEATH

Copyright © 2011 by Shanna Hogan.

For information address St. Martin's Press, 175 Fifth Avenue, New York, NY 10010.

EAN: 978-0-312-53228-4

Printed in the United States of America

St. Martin's Paperbacks edition / June 2011

St. Martin's Paperbacks are published by St. Martin's Press, 175 Fifth Avenue, New York, NY 10010.

10   9   8   7   6   5   4   3   2

To the memory
of my beloved Great Aunt,
Phyllis White

AUTHOR'S NOTE

This is a true story, though some names have been changed.

CHAPTER 1

October 23, 2004

A putrid stench hung above the desert floor on the outskirts of Phoenix, Arizona. The heavy stink draped over the brambles of the brittle brush and prickly cacti to the edges of the asphalt roadways that quarantined the chunk of desert. The barren landscape was illuminated by the blinding afternoon sun. A towering saguaro cast a lengthy shadow on homicide investigators scouring the area amid the foulness stinking in the chill autumn air. At the center of their attention: a large blue Rubbermaid tub wrapped in thick black plastic.

Detective David Barnes sensed an almost eerie quiet amid the faint sounds of passing traffic as he crossed the yellow police tape. Suddenly he was struck, his nose assaulted by the rancid stench that permeated the horrific scene. Even to a rookie the smell of death was unmistakable.

Slowly, Barnes approached the tub to investigate the origin of the odor. Holding his breath, he peered down into its contents. The detective instantly recoiled, wincing with revulsion. Entombed inside the large plastic container was the body of a male who appeared to have been deceased for quite some time. Immediately Barnes realized two things: The man had been murdered, and his body had been brutally dismembered.

In the tub, covered by crumpled black trash bags and clear plastic sheeting, was a disemboweled partial torso. The headless, limbless corpse was severed above the belly button and below the knees. What remained of the body was clothed in a pair of bloody denim shorts held up with a brown leather belt. It was stewing in blood, bone chips, hair, debris, and other bodily fluids.

This was an extraordinarily gruesome murder for the quiet Phoenix suburb. Already theories were flying through the detective's mind. *Could this be part of some sort of satanic ritual? A mafia hit? Or possibly a drug deal gone bad?* Little did Barnes know, the truth would be more bizarre than any initial theory.

A gray plastic lid lay adjacent to the tub with tape still stuck to it. On the other side of the tub was a three-inch piece of jagged glass. Part of the plastic sheeting, wet with bodily fluids, had been pulled from the container and lay on the ground near a partially smoked cigarette.

Looking down into the tub, Barnes noticed that part of the corpse's abdomen was visible. A coiled-up electrical cord lay on top of the body, along with a slimy piece of orange and black rope. Barnes took a notepad from his pants pocket and scribbled down his preliminary observations. The victim's torso appeared to belong to an overweight, white male in his forties. Barnes stopped writing. Without an ID, head, fingerprints, or any other means of identification, it was impossible to determine much else about the man. *This was brutal*, Barnes thought. *What did he do to deserve this?*

Detective Barnes was a nine-year veteran of the Phoenix Police Department and considered an up-and-comer on the force. Nine months prior, he had been promoted to the coveted homicide division and was eager to prove himself as a capable and keen investigator. In his mid-thirties, tall, with a square chin supported by a powerful jawline, Barnes had a brawny build that filled out the polo shirts he typically wore with plain khaki slacks. He had short cropped hair, warm brown eyes, and ears that protruded ever so slightly.

An hour earlier, Barnes had been at home spending time with his children when he got the call from his sergeant: A body had been discovered in the desert. Moments later, he was in his cruiser racing toward the crime scene. By the time he arrived, officers had already cordoned off a large area of land surrounding the body. Barnes was assigned as the lead detective. So far most of his homicide cases had been routine. When he agreed to cover the on-call shift for a fellow detective, he hardly expected to be assigned to such a ghoulish murder.

It was a Saturday at about two p.m. A recent rain had strewn small puddles across the desert floor, which glistened in the sunlight. Barnes stepped away from the body and scanned the scene. The vacant swath of desert where the tub had been dumped was east of the intersection of Tatum and Dynamite Boulevards, about thirty miles from the bustling region of downtown Phoenix. Bordering the desert along the east side of Tatum Boulevard was a barbed-wire fence with a large gap wide enough for a vehicle to pass through. A dirt road cut diagonally across the southwest corner of the intersection; at the entrance, a small sign read STATE TRUST LAND, NO TRESPASSING.

The vacant desert parcel was blocked on two sides by housing developments. Rooftops could be seen to the west and north, while the areas to the south and east were open desert. Unlike the densely populated downtown region of Phoenix, where many of the city's 1.5 million inhabitants lived and worked, the surrounding neighborhoods consisted of peaceful suburbs, occupied by affluent young residents. Families spent summers here swimming in backyard pools, couples walked their dogs in the evenings, and children rode bikes along the roadways after school.

Undeveloped patches of land among the walled-in subdivisions were common in this part of the Valley. The recent boom in the housing market had pushed construction to the edge of the city limits, where homes cropped up like tumbleweeds. Suburban sprawl metastasized outward into the desert, endless concrete and asphalt razing the natural Sonoran splendor. In the surrounding developments, new tract homes were built uniformly, in a limited variety of designs and painted one of half a dozen shades of beige. The sporadic empty desert plots were a constant reminder of what lay underneath the strip-malls, gas stations, and grocery stores—an oasis of oblivion.

Investigators fanned out along the stretch of desert to collect evidence. Detective Barnes and Officer Barry Giesemann placed protective covers on their shoes and did a walk-through of the area while a crime scene specialist took photographs.

"Where's the rest of him?" Giesemann asked.

"Who knows?" Barnes glanced back at the tub. "Maybe we'll find the head somewhere around here."

The plastic tub had been dumped about fifty feet from the street, north of a widened area in the dirt road that was just large enough for a vehicle to turn around. On the ground, there appeared to be a faint trace of weathered tire tracks. A slight amount of soil, small pebbles, and dead plant material were scattered to the north side of the tire impression as if dropped by the right wheel when the car pulled ahead. By the time investigators arrived, the tracks were too eroded to identify anything about the vehicle that had been used to dump the body.

A few hundred feet from the corpse, clear sheets of crumpled plastic were found tangled in the desert shrubs. All of the other evidence was near the fifty-five-gallon plastic tub. It was covered by a dingy white futon mattress and a tan section of carpet, which did not do much to mask the dirty tub and its grisly contents. Part of the blue tub could be seen from the roadway by any passing motorist. This discovery, however, had been made by a wandering pedestrian.

A little after noon, a transient named Robert Aime left

the construction site where he was living to grab a six-pack of Bud Light from the gas station. On his way back, he cut across the desert and sat down on the mattress to have a beer and a smoke. That's when he noticed the carpet wrapped around a large tub. With curiosity, the man removed the futon, unwrapped the tub, picked up a broken piece of glass from the bottom of a bottle and cut away at the tape sealing the tub's lid shut. He was hoping he had found something of value, something he could pawn for a few bucks.

As he ripped away the black trash bags and pulled out the plastic sheeting, a foul odor started to eat away at his nostrils and an awful taste tickled the back of his throat. He shrank back in horror. The cigarette fell from his lips. Aime ran back to the gas station to call the police. The man was still visibly shaken a few hours later when Barnes approached him for questioning.

"I saw the belt buckle and the jeans and the belly. It was hairy," Aime said, his voice trembling. "That's how I realized it was human. Because there was a belly button."

The first person to discover a body was often considered a suspect, but Barnes could tell right away that this man was simply an unlucky witness. The jagged piece of glass and partially smoked cigarette near the tub all seemed to confirm Aime's story. Barnes took down the man's contact information and allowed him to leave.

For the next few hours the otherwise peaceful Saturday was buzzing with detectives documenting dozens of pieces of evidence. At around 5:40 p.m. the medical examiner, Dr. Alex Zhang, arrived. A slight Asian man in his late forties, Zhang spoke with a thick accent. He placed the lid back on the tub, zipped the entire container into two black body bags, and took it back to his office for an autopsy. Other evidence found at the site was escorted to the police station to be cataloged.

As Barnes drove away from the crime scene that evening, his mind was reeling. This was a savage murder. *Who could do that to another human being?* he wondered. *What kind of person cuts up a body?*

Two days after the discovery of the torso, on October 25, Dr. Zhang performed the autopsy. Carefully, he placed the corpse on the metal table and began sorting through the contents of the tub. At the bottom of the box, covered by crumpled trash bags, he discovered a spent .38 caliber bullet. Inside the victim's pockets was $459.10 in mixed bills, a small bottle of contact lens solution, and a key ring with eleven keys.

During the autopsy, Zhang discovered that the decomposition of the body was uneven and the deep skeletal muscle tissue was relatively fresh. Because of the condition of the body, he determined that it had been frozen for an extensive period of time before being thawed and hacked into pieces. Bone dust in the wounds also indicated that the dismemberment had not been executed by some lunatic who'd gone berserk with an ax, but by a cold-blooded butcher who had used some sort of an electric saw to slice the corpse with chilling precision.

At approximately 3:25 p.m., after the autopsy was complete, the medical examiner released the tub and other evidence to Detective Barnes, who escorted it to the main police station drying room. Everything was wet with blood and reeked of death. The smell stuck like fly paper to Barnes's clothes and hair, and days later he would still detect it in the leather of his shoes and belt.

Barnes spent the remainder of the afternoon cataloging each piece of evidence found with the body and hanging it out to dry. That evidence provided a strong start to the investigation. The tub itself was an impressive lead. On the container was a UPC sticker, which could be instrumental in tracing who purchased the victim's plastic casket. Additionally, the bullet was an important indicator of how the man likely met his fate and could later possibly be matched to a murder weapon.

Barnes fished the car keys, which were covered in a thick molasses syrup of blood, fat, and bone fragments, from the tub, and hung them up in one of the drying room bays. A couple of hours after he started working, Barnes received a page from the violent crimes' night supervisor.

The piercing odor had permeated the adjacent office spaces and other detectives were getting sick from the smell. The night supervisor instructed Barnes to take the evidence elsewhere. Inadvertently, that order would prove to be an important jumpstart to the investigation. Barnes brought the tub to the basement of the homicide impound lot and was hanging up the wet plastic sheeting when he ran into a fellow detective who had heard the tantalizing details of the torso discovery.

A wiry man, bald with a sparse physique and round-framed glasses, Detective Tommy Kulesa had grown up in Chicago, where his father worked as a cop. For more than two decades Kulesa had been with the Phoenix Police Department working in the organized crime unit and the homicide squad. Most recently, he had been assisting another detective on a perplexing missing persons investigation.

"What do you know about the vic?" Kulesa asked Barnes.

"Not much. All we know is the torso belongs to a white male, maybe in his forties," he replied.

"Really?" Kulesa was intrigued. "You know I've been assisting on this missing persons case involving a white male in the same age range."

Kulesa's missing person was a wealthy forty-five-year-old arts dealer named Jay Michael Orbin. The man's wife, Marjorie Orbin, said he'd never returned home from a recent business trip. However, her callous behavior and apparent lack of concern had investigators suspecting foul play. Since reporting her husband missing, Marjorie had been liquidating his assets and going on shopping sprees, buying a new grand piano, electronics, and thousands of dollars in clothes and furniture.

Even more suspicious, the police discovered Marjorie had been engaged in an illicit affair with a sixty-year-old body builder named Larry Weisberg. Unbeknownst to her husband, the man had been living in the Orbins' home while Jay was away on business.

"I doubt this guy will be found alive," Kulesa opined, as he recounted the details of the case.

Earlier that day, Kulesa continued, detectives had discovered the man's Ford Bronco. The vehicle, which had also been reported missing, was located in the parking lot of an apartment complex that was just a few miles from Barnes's crime scene. That last detail piqued Barnes's interest.

"You know, we found a set of keys in the victim's pockets," Barnes said as he fumbled through the keys, two of which were car keys. "Where's the Bronco?"

"Right over there." Kulesa pointed to a forensic cage in the basement, a few yards from where they were standing.

"Let's try them out!"

On what would turn out to be an incredible hunch, Barnes separated the two car keys, wiped them clean of blood and approached the vehicle. Slowly, he inserted one key into the door and turned it; with his other hand he pulled the latch on the Bronco. It opened.

Incredible.

"Unbelievable!" Kulesa exclaimed, seemingly reading Barnes's thought.

Barnes tried the key in the ignition, to be sure. No surprise this time: It started the Bronco. The two detectives were investigating the same case, although Kulesa's missing persons case had now officially escalated to a homicide.

Early the following morning, on October 26, Barnes met with Detective Jan Butcher, the lead missing persons detective who had been investigating Jay Orbin's disappearance. In her mid-thirties, Butcher was petite with soft, delicate features and wavy, shoulder-length honey-blond hair.

Butcher handed Barnes a copy of her case file. As they spoke, Barnes flipped through the pages on the man's background. At first glance it seemed Barnes's homicide victim was not some sort of con man, rapist, or convicted felon who had double-crossed the wrong man. Jay Orbin was a regular guy who lived a quiet middle-class life in the suburbs. He owned his own business. He had a loving family. And, sadly, he was the father of an eight-year-old boy.

Barnes came across a photograph of the man that had been provided to detectives by the family. He picked it up and examined it closely. Staring back at him was a husky, blue-eyed man with round cherubic cheeks, thinning dark hair, a neatly trimmed beard, and a wide, joyful grin. As Barnes studied the photograph, his mind flashed back to the macabre image of the mutilated torso in the blue tub. Barnes closed his eyes and slowly shook his head. It was hard to imagine that the grotesque dismembered corpse was the remains of this seemingly happy-go-lucky guy.

"When we first found the body, I had no idea which way this case was going to go. I'm thinking in the back of my mind, 'Is he a kidnap victim? A dope dealer? A child molester? Does he owe people money? Who is he and why is he out here dumped in the desert?'" Barnes recalled years later. "It all unraveled so quickly and I started learning about who this guy was. It turns out Jay Orbin did nothing to deserve such a thing. He was a great father, a great brother, a great son."

Butcher told Barnes that for his business Jay took frequent trips across the country selling Native American art and jewelry out of the back of a large white cargo truck. On August 28, he left Phoenix for a business trip to Florida and was scheduled to return three weeks later. But his trip was cut short and on September 8, he called his parents to say he was on his way home to Phoenix. In another unusual twist, September 8 was the man's forty-fifth birthday.

"That was the last time anyone heard from the guy," Butcher paused, "except the wife."

Marjorie told Butcher that Jay never came home and instead decided to continue on a detour trip. But the detective wasn't buying her story.

"I think she offed him," Butcher said. "She's definitely hiding something."

"You think the boyfriend could be involved?" Barnes asked.

"Possibly." She shrugged. "He's got a temper."

Butcher explained that Marjorie's boyfriend, Larry Weisberg, had been exhibiting suspicious behavior in the days following Jay's disappearance. In one encounter, he had even attacked a team of SWAT officers.

After speaking with Butcher, Barnes spent what remained of the afternoon buried in the missing persons case file. The information provided an extraordinary start to his homicide investigation. With so little remaining of the body, Barnes had worried it would take months to identify the victim. Instead, just a few days into his case, he had a name and two viable suspects.

Someone had killed this man and dismembered his body, leaving a piece of him to rot under the desert sun. It was about as cold blooded as you can get. *Was it possible that such a vicious murder was committed by the man's wife?* Barnes pondered. *Could her boyfriend be the killer?*

The ensuing investigation would not be so simple. Over the next four years Barnes would follow a series of twists, turns, and gruesome clues. Before it was over, he would uncover a scandalous murder mystery riddled with sex, lies, money, greed, and unspeakable betrayal.

CHAPTER 2

Jay Orbin didn't live a day past the age of forty-five. He was murdered on September 8, 2004—his forty-fifth birthday. More than a month later, a decaying chunk of his body would be discovered in the Phoenix desert. It was a sudden and violent end to his joyful and fulfilling life. By all accounts Jay was a kind, compassionate, hard-working businessman. An average, ordinary guy, Jay perhaps had an average, ordinary character flaw—a weakness for beautiful women.

It would turn out to be his fatal flaw.

Born on September 8, 1959, in Phoenix, Arizona, Jay Michael Orbin was the second son to Jake and Joann Orbin. His older brother, Jake Orbin Jr., was born six years earlier in Canonsburg, a tiny coal mining town in Pennsylvania with a population of just over 8,500. Jake and Joann were both born and raised in small Pennsylvania towns and married in Canonsburg. There, like most of the town's work force, Jake toiled in the local steel and coal mines, while Joann held various odd jobs.

When Jake Jr. was three, the Orbins relocated to Arizona for the same reason as many of the state's early settlers—the boy suffered from severe asthma. In the early 1900s, Arizona became a drawing point for people suffering from lung ailments such as asthma and tuberculosis. The hot, dry climate of the Sonoran Desert was thought to be an effective treatment for respiratory problems. Many western gunslingers, including Doc Holliday, migrated to the southwest after being diagnosed with consumption.

The two-square-mile town of Canonsburg was covered by soot and gray skies. As a toddler, Jake Jr. began having breathing problems and needed an inhaler several times a day. Joann turned to her doctor for advice. To ease Jake Jr.'s asthma, the doctor said, they needed to live somewhere with clean air, like Arizona.

"Literally, my dad took it to heart," Jake Jr. said years later. "The next week he packed everything in the back of a little Buick station wagon and headed out west. Later on we asked the doctor, 'Why did you say Arizona? Why not California?' It wasn't till many years later when he said, 'I just said Arizona as an example. You could have gone anywhere.' That's how we ended up here."

In 1956, the Orbins purchased a small home for about $8,000 in a northeast Phoenix suburb known as Alta Vista. They struggled to make the $78 mortgage payment and both parents worked several jobs. Jake took various odd jobs, working in the stockyard and washing dishes at restaurants, before landing a position in the post office, a career he would maintain for thirty years. Joann became an assembly line manager for Honeywell, a military and aerospace parts manufacturer.

The Orbins were a blue-collar, middle-class Catholic family. Like many hardworking families, they scrimped and saved to get by. Three years after they moved to Arizona, Jay Michael Orbin was born.

The Orbins were exceptionally close—warm and inviting. Birthdays were celebrated together; Sundays were spent in church. Jay's childhood was wholesome. Jake and Joann taught their boys values and morals. Above all else, family was most important. After his brother's murder, Jake Jr. wistfully recalled fond childhood memories—from Little League to pool parties. "We had a nice life. We lived in a neighbor-

hood where everyone was happy-go-lucky, friendly," he recalled. "Back then, in those days, we were always doing stuff
outdoors—riding bikes, playing sports, and building forts."

In the late '50s, Phoenix hardly resembled the booming
metropolis it had become at the time of Jay's death. Sparse
housing developments were checkered with farmland and
vacant parcels of desert. The population was 439,170; in four
short decades, it would more than triple, making Phoenix
the fifth most populous city in the United States.

In the summers, swamp coolers did little to relieve the
scorching 100-degree-plus temperatures, and most homes
were built with backyard pools. The Orbins' small pool became a gathering place for parties. The neighborhood boys
would spend the summer vacations swimming, while Joann
made lunch. Jake coached his son's Little League team, and
when Jay was twelve, he took them all the way to the Little
League playoffs. Sports were a big part of life for the Orbin
family. Because of their history in Pennsylvania, it was a
family tradition to root for the Pittsburgh Steelers. As a boy,
Jay became a diehard Steelers fan. Jay looked up to his big
brother. "When he was real little, he was always my little
brother who tagged along with everybody," Jake Jr. recalled.
"He wanted to hang out with me and my friends."

In his teens, Jay was tall and slim; he wore a mustache
and his thick, dark hair feathered with oversized, square-
frame glasses. As an adult, Jay grew into a bear of a man
with a crooked smile, striking blue eyes, thinning dark
brown hair, and a full beard he wore most of his life. He
was six feet tall and by his mid-20s his weight fluctuated
between 230 to 260 pounds.

Friendly, outgoing, and ambitious, Jay was a natural
born salesman driven from a young age to become a self-
made entrepreneur. When Jay was a teenager, he got his
first job working nights and weekends in the garden shop
at FedMart, a discount department store. At the time Jake
Jr. was working as a store manager and recommended his
brother for the job.

People gravitated toward Jay, and through his job at the garden store he ended up getting side work doing landscaping and gardening at construction sites. One of his biggest clients was a model home developer; Jay landscaped many of their new developments. "His gift of gab and his business management is actually something that got him moving forward in his life—he was able to talk to people easily," Jake Jr. said years later. "After a few months I noticed Jay was making more money doing landscape work two days a week than I was making in a full, forty-hour work week."

After graduating from Cortez High School in 1977, Jay started doing landscape work full time. He formed a company called Landscape Matters and asked his brother to be his partner. Jake Jr. happily accepted. He later said it was one of the proudest moments in his life. Jay ran the crews and Jake Jr. handled the clerical work. They worked the jobs together. Both brothers bought large four-by-four trucks for their tools and equipment. Together they took Landscape Matters from a small lawn maintenance business to a large licensed company that handled landscape work for every Motel 6 across the state.

In 1978, shortly after graduating from high school, Jay bought his first home with his brother at Dobson Ranch in Mesa, a suburb of Phoenix. That same year the Pittsburgh Steelers won the Super Bowl. Ecstatic, Jay got in his truck and drove around the neighborhood celebrating. "He had a Pittsburgh Steelers flag and stuck it out the window and he's driving around the streets, honking his horn, cheering," Jake Jr. recalled.

By the mid-80s, the landscaping business started to slow. Jake Jr. got married and took a job as a horticulturist for the city of San Diego Balboa Park, and Mission Bay Parks and Recreation. It was his dream job and a career he would stay in for the next two decades. Jake Jr. always credited that position to his start in the landscaping business with Jay.

After Jake Jr. moved, Jay used the profits from the landscaping business to invest in a comedy club called Chuckles in central Phoenix. It was a classy two-story pub that hosted several high-profile acts. Jay befriended many of the comedians, including a stand-up named Richard Belzer. Years later, Belzer would become famous for his role as Sergeant John Munch on the shows *Homicide: Life on the Streets* and *Law & Order: Special Victims Unit.*

After a few years, Chuckles closed. Jay then transitioned into sales, which would turn out to be his calling. He started a business called Spectral Kinetics, selling novelty static electricity orbs to bars and nightclubs. The company specialized in unique globes that could be customized with a brass eagle or a cut-out of a golfer inside. The globes were considered cutting edge at the time and Jay had a house full of demos on four-foot pedestals. Within a year, however, manufacturers in China began making a smaller retail version. Soon, the static electricity orbs went from cutting edge to a fleeting fad.

When that fell out of fashion, Jay found himself on the verge of bankruptcy. Around that time he met a wealthy businessman named Jim Rogers, who was making good money selling jewelry and Native American decor at local markets and craft fairs. Jim was immediately impressed by Jay's consummate work ethic and they became partners in business together for several years. Even after they went their separate ways and became competitors, they stayed close friends.

After venturing out on his own, Jay launched Jayhawk Trader and sold jewelry and Native American art. The business started small, with Jay renting booths at local swap meets to sell his merchandise, including Kachina dolls, Native American pottery, rugs, and jewelry, which were very popular in the southwest. Mostly, Jay sold at outdoor swap meets where he would rent a twenty-foot tent and set up a booth to display his merchandise.

Within a few years Jay went from contemplating bankruptcy to making over six figures annually. As the business grew, Jay transformed Jayhawk Trader into Jayhawk International and took the company on the road. He rented a warehouse in Phoenix, bought a large white cargo truck, and became a wholesale dealer for manufacturers and retailers. Jay was an undeniable success.

The bigger the business grew, the more time he spent on the road. Soon he was traveling more than half of the month to cities across the country, returning to Phoenix only long enough to fill customers' orders and restock his truck. It was difficult being away from home, but Jay loved being self-made and independent.

Wholesale jewelry dealers at the time were known as ruthless, cutthroat businessmen who were constantly undercutting each other to retailers to make a deal. Jay, however, ran his business honestly, which made a lasting impression on his clients. His customers described him as trustworthy and dependable.

Jay was a consummate businessman, but he was also sensitive and genuinely concerned about other people. Perhaps because making money came so easily to him, he was also very generous. One of his customers recalled an instance where they owed Jay a lot of money. Jay told him not to worry about it. "If he felt he was financially well enough off to help people out, then he did," one of Jay's customers recalled. "He was just that kind of guy. All of his customers were friends, as well as customers."

At the peak of his business Jay had over 2,800 customers. Meticulous and regimented in his business as well as his personal habits, Jay followed a precise routine. He wrote lists and followed schedules to the letter. Gary Dodge, Jay's friend and business supplier, described Jay as "an unbelievably hard-working guy." With Jay it was always business. He loved his job, he loved his work, and he hardly ever took a vacation. "He was a hell of a nice guy; he did things for people and did not expect nothing in return," Gary recalled.

Although he was financially successful, Jay was never

far from his blue-collar roots. Casual and frugal, he wore open-collar shirts with sneakers, jeans with a large metal belt-buckle, and a cowboy hat. His idea of dressing up was to polish his cowboy boots. "Jay wouldn't spend a dime on himself," one friend said. "As casual as you can get."

The things Jay enjoyed in life were simple. A staunch Republican, Jay was intensely interested in politics. Every-day he listened to Rush Limbaugh's radio program. He had a large collection of memorabilia and valuable collectables and he watched sports on television and attended Arizona State University football games.

For all his dedication to hard work, Jay was equally fun loving. He had a sharp sense of humor and a real zest for life. Gregarious and clever, Jay attracted a large network of loyal friends. One of the things people remember about Jay was his constant smile—broad and carefree. Jay always seemed like the happiest person in the room. "He was the person who, when he entered a room, you knew it," recalled family friend Carol Rita, who had known Jay since he was in grade school. "He had this booming, loud voice—I just loved that about him. He was always happy, always smiling. He was just so full of life."

Mario Olivarez worked in the same business as Jay. Short in stature, with a thick tuft of dark hair and small narrow eyes, Mario was unapologetically outspoken and boisterous. He had a vivid recollection of the night he first met Jay.

"Twenty-five years ago I met him in a bar and he couldn't stand me," Mario laughed, "'cause I'm loud." Not just any bar, Mario admitted. A strip bar called Cheetah's Gentle-man's Club. Jay frequented strip joints across Phoenix and often ran into Mario at these same clubs. Over time they became close friends. Jay worked hard and played hard. He enjoyed going to bars and meeting new people.

Jay was known for his good sense of humor and out-rageous practical jokes. Mario recalled how Jay was always pulling pranks. Jay and Mario would often golf together. On the course, one of Jay's favorite jokes was to unbuckle the back of their friends' golf carts, so when they drove away their clubs would fall off the back. Mario, who Jay often jokingly called "Munchkin" because of his height, also remembered how they used to play games with their friends at the bars. Jay would order shots, having already requested from the bartender for his to be a mixture of soda and water. Meanwhile, he would pass out tequila shots to the rest of the group. "They'd get messed up and wonder how he would stay sober. It was all in fun," Mario laughed. "He just enjoyed life. That's why a lot of people were attracted to him."

As a salesman, Jay was confident, charismatic, and persuasive. That charm, which helped him to profit in business, also helped him succeed with women. Perhaps Jay wasn't a conventional ladies' man, but there was an allure about him that women found appealing. Although he was good looking, it was his personality that made him especially attractive to the opposite sex, and he was never without a gorgeous woman on his arm.

Throughout the '80s and '90s, Jay was a regular at Arizona strip joints including Bourbon Street Circus, Babe's Cabaret, and Skin Cabaret. A couple of times a week, Jay would go with his friends. Other times he went alone. Everyone—all the dancers, all the managers—knew Jay. Jay met most of his buddies at strip joints. "He wasn't so much a guy who went and picked up strippers to keep a score card, everyone was just friends," Mario recalled. "Jay just liked having fun, not having a commitment."

Throughout his twenties, Jay lived a freewheeling bachelor life. He loved women unabashedly, but also respected and appreciated them. The girls he dated had tight bodies, beautiful faces, and large breasts. Many of these women were exotic dancers Jay had met at the topless clubs. The strippers knew Jay as a big spender who lavished them with cash and expensive gifts. He often saw these women outside the club, and more than one became his girlfriend. "There were so many girlfriends I can't remember all their names," Jake Jr. recalled. "He was having fun, he was making a lot of money, and he dealt in cash. That's probably how he met all the girls in the topless clubs."

Around 1984, Jay bought a house on over an acre in a quaint south Phoenix neighborhood. With a backyard pool and an outdoor volleyball court, it was the ultimate bachelor party pad. On weekends, his friends and many of the strippers would come over for barbecues and pool parties. Jay was famous for his twice-a-year volleyball parties, which dozens of dancers, strip club bouncers, and club managers attended. On one visit from San Diego, Jake Jr. remembered stopping by his brother's house and being impressed by all the beautiful women in bikinis. "I came into this place and it was like a little mini Hugh Hefner mansion," he recalled. "The girls from the clubs were all over there. It was like a huge party at Jay's house. I thought, 'Hey, my little brother's doing okay.'"

Unfortunately, Jay's love of beautiful women may have blinded him in his relationships. At the exotic clubs, Jay often got involved with dancers who were in a financial bind or a bad relationship. Generous and genuinely kind, Jay was always willing to help with money or anything else. But a few of these women only seemed interested in Jay for his wealth and took advantage of his generosity. Consequently, his relationships were often casual and short-lived, lasting just a few weeks or a few dates. But Jay never seemed bothered. He was on the road most of each month, which made relationships difficult. He didn't seem interested in a serious, committed relationship.

For years, Jay enjoyed the bachelor lifestyle. But that all changed for him one night in 1985. While at the Bourbon Street Circus, he would have a chance encounter with a beguiling blond dancer whom he would later describe as "the love of his life." Her name was Marjorie Marqui.

CHAPTER 3

Parading topless in a smoke-filled Phoenix strip joint was hardly where Marjorie imagined her life would take her. As a girl she dreamed of dancing on Broadway and performing with the ballet. But along the way her life took an X-rated detour, and by 1985 the only dancing Marjorie did was on a stripper pole. The journey that brought her to the stages of a seedy strip joint began twenty-four years earlier and 2,000 miles away from Jay's hometown in Phoenix.

Marjorie Ann Kroh was born on October 29, 1961, in Miami, Florida, to William and Janelle Kroh. Her only sister, Colleen, was born five years earlier. By the time Marjorie was three, William and Janelle had divorced. Janelle later remarried an air-conditioning repairman named Peter Garrett, who Marjorie always considered to be her father. They were a normal, upper-middle class family. Marjorie's mother was a kindergarten teacher who worked a second job to pay for her daughters' piano and ballet classes. From an early age, Marjorie's mother taught her to be a proper lady, educating her in etiquette and manners.

When Marjorie was young, the family moved to Altamonte Springs, Florida, a peaceful northern suburb of Orlando. Located in one of the more affluent areas of Central Florida, Altamonte Springs was a quiet community with homes nestled in lakeside and tree-shaded neighbor-hoods.

Marjorie's stepfather was Methodist and her mother was Jewish. Neither parent was deeply religious; Marjorie only attended church and temple on rare occasions. She did, however, learn a lot about the Jewish faith from her grandmother. Studying the Torah with her had a deep impact on Marjorie's life. She grew up believing in the Jewish faith.

From the age of six, Marjorie danced. Classically trained in ballet, jazz, and tap, she grew up with ambitions of becoming a professional dancer and choreographer. In the mid-seventies, she recalled playing dress-up with her cousins and watching variety shows like *Donnie & Marie* and *The Sonny & Cher Show.*

Marjorie was a bright, intelligent child who grew into a beautiful woman. She was statuesque, with long legs and a lean and curvaceous figure. A natural blonde with captivating brown eyes and a sultry smile, Marjorie was simply gorgeous.

She attended Lake Brantley High School, one of the most prestigious schools in the Orlando area, where she used her dance background to become a majorette. At Lake Brantley the majorette squad consisted of five girls in red, white, and blue sequined leotards and white patent knee-high boots. Twirling batons and flags, Marjorie would march along with the school band at parades and football games. Her classmates nicknamed her "Marching Marjorie." In her skimpy uniform, Marjorie would flaunt her figure. She liked to flirt, but she didn't date many high school boys. Marjorie preferred mainly older men.

When she was just fifteen, Marjorie got her first job working as a hostess at a steakhouse. While juggling her work and school responsibilities, she also danced part-time on the weekends at a dinner theater called Once Upon a Stage.

For the next three years, she held jobs as a hostess and waitress at various Orlando-based restaurants. During one shift she met an attractive older gentleman named Mitchell

Marqui. Tall, with dark hair and a mustache and beard, Mitchell vaguely resembled a young Barry Gibb from the pop trio the Bee Gees. Mitchell was about ten years older than Marjorie and also quite successful. While working a variety of jobs, Mitchell was able to put together enough money to launch a motorcycle shop called Cycle Riders. He frequented the restaurant where Marjorie worked and they began dating.

At age seventeen, Marjorie learned devastating news. During a routine gynecological visit the obstetrician told her she had endometriosis, a medical condition in which the tissue that normally lines the uterus grows in other areas of the body, causing menstrual pain and irregular bleeding. Her condition was so severe that Marjorie was infertile— incapable of ever having children. It was a tremendous disappointment; she had always believed that one day she would have a baby. Marjorie was left with a sense of emptiness that would haunt her for most of her adult life. It took a long while for her to come to terms with the fact that she would never be a mother. Ultimately, it altered the way she lived her life. "After that, I think the decisions I made in my life were pretty much that I was really living as though the only person I was ever going to have to be responsible for is myself," Marjorie said years later. "So if someone came into my life and I had feelings for them, I went into it with my whole heart, maybe too fully, maybe too often."

Often impetuous, Marjorie leaped into relationships. She and Mitchell became very serious, very fast. She was flattered that an older man would be interested in a teenager. All her spare time was spent with Mitchell. After she graduated from Lake Brantley in 1980, Marjorie moved to Orlando with Mitchell and took a job as a dancer and cocktail waitress at a massive entertainment venue called the Church Street Station. During the '80s, Church Street Station was one of Orlando's top tourist attractions. Spanning both sides of Church Street, the venue housed four separate clubs, each with a different theme.

At the time there was a disco bar, which catered to younger people, and a Dixieland jazz club, which was popular with an older crowd. Across the street was the Cheyenne Saloon, a huge country bar designed like a southern opera house, where Marjorie worked as a cocktail waitress and dancer. She and the other waitresses would serve drinks and five or six times a night they would all put down their trays and perform a choreographed dance number.

For the next five years, Marjorie worked various jobs at the Church Street Station. It was there that she would meet a wealthy restaurateur who would appear continuously in her life story. His name was Michael J. Peter.

Known across Florida as the "strip club king," Michael J. Peter was widely credited for his role in transforming seedy strip joints into upscale gentlemen's clubs. Short in stature but large on personality, he stood just five foot six and was a fast talker who tended to speak about himself in the third person. Swarthy, with a dark complexion and a strong, sharp chin, Michael was handsome with a lecherous sex appeal. His intense, piercing eyes and dark, wavy hair complemented the thick mustache that took up most of the width of his face.

Growing up in Ithaca, New York, Michael got his start in the entertainment industry in New York, where he studied at the prestigious Cornell University School of Hotel Administration, falling just short of a master's degree. In 1973, he moved to Orlando and took a job managing the Dubsdread Country Club, a hangout for Orlando's blue bloods. The country club was losing money, but Michael knew he could turn it around. He brought in loud music, late-night concerts, and a battery of waitresses with low-cut blouses. He also hired six beautiful women to model in bikinis during lunchtime. Soon business was booming, and in five months the club went from eighty-eight to 700 members. The club's owners liked the money but not the method. The management saw Michael as a con-man and in six months he was fired.

Soon afterward, Michael was driving along Orlando's Orange Blossom Trail, the city's informal red light district, when he saw a sleazy bar called the Booby Trap. It was just three in the afternoon but the parking lot was packed with expensive cars. Intrigued, Michael went inside. The club was nearly pitch dark. On stage, topless women were staggering around in a raunchy fashion. Michael grimaced. He thought the women were hideous—fat, unattractive, and sloppy. This was typical of strip joints in the '70s, Michael said years later. "The girls hadn't shaved in three days," Michael told a Florida newspaper. "They had no teeth, dirty fingernails, no makeup. They were fat and ugly and barefooted."

Still, Michael noticed the place was packed with professional-looking men in suits and ties throwing around money. Suddenly, Michael was struck with an idea that would revolutionize the strip-club industry. If he hired gorgeous, classy dancers, who had manners and poise, Michael knew he'd be a success. He set out to apply the principles of upscale club management to topless clubs.

In 1973, Michael launched the business concept which would eventually earn him his moniker. He bought a cheap bar for $13,000 and renamed it Thee DollHouse, the first in a series of similarly named clubs. Thee DollHouse was well-lit, carpeted, and painted pink and purple. The bouncers wore tuxedos with bow ties, and the dancers were required to take etiquette lessons, wear ball gowns, and have their hair and make-up professionally done. Within six months, the club was grossing $65,000 a week. The concept exploded across south Florida and by the time he was thirty, Michael had built a budding strip-club empire.

His success, however, infuriated the local motorcycle

gang who, up until that time, ran the south Florida strip-club business. One night a group of incensed bikers arrived at Thee DollHouse threatening to burn it to the ground. But Michael refused to be intimidated. He arranged a meeting with the gang's leader and warned them of his mafia connections. Michael later claimed it was an empty threat, but it forever after spawned rumors of mob ties. Regardless, it worked and the bikers backed off.

While Michael was revered for his business success, he was also despised as a licentious sex peddler by Orlando's conservative establishment. They viewed Michael as a threat to the city's moral values and attempted to close down his business by creating ordinances and rules directed at the clubs. Michael's legion of lawyers effectively challenged each rule. In time, Michael came to control the Orlando strip-club scene. He described it as a "topless Disneyland." By 1980, Michael J. Peter was on his way to becoming a legend.

Around this time, Michael was conducting a business meeting with some associates at the Church Street Station. He was a regular at the club, and because he was considered a high profile patron, the managers always assigned their best waitress to his table—Marjorie. Although he was fifteen years her senior, Michael was enamored with Marjorie's natural good looks, long legs, and flawless figure. She embodied everything he had built his empire around—beauty, glamour, and poise. But he was most impressed by her professionalism and strong work ethic.

With her formal dance training, Marjorie was one of the most skilled performers at Church Street Station and soon the managers had her choreographing routines at all of the clubs. She created line dance, jazz, and clogging routines. After a little less than a year, at the age of nineteen, Marjorie was promoted to manager of the Cheyenne Saloon.

There Michael and Marjorie began a friendship that would later blossom into a love affair. For the next three decades, he would be a fixture in Marjorie's life.

* * *

Before the age of thirty-four, Marjorie would marry seven times. Her relationships were always brief and often chaotic. Marjorie spent her entire adult life searching for someone to fill the hole in her heart left by her inability to have children. She longed for stability and a family of her own, but she also had impossible expectations. She wanted and needed a perfect love.

For the next fifteen years, Marjorie would live perpetually in the honeymoon period of a new relationship. When the initial passion dampened, she became dissatisfied and moved on to her next lover. Always, she had to have a man in her life, and many of her liaisons inevitably overlapped. She rarely left one relationship without choosing her next lover.

Men were initially drawn to her looks, but she was much more than just a pretty face. It was intoxicating to be around her. She made others feel special, attractive, and desired. But the warmth, love, and compassion she often showed were feigned and disingenuous. Many who knew her would later describe her as self-consumed and unconcerned with others. Marjorie, however, explained her own behavior as an unwillingness to put up with the average. She freely opened her heart to people, but if they disappointed her, she would toss them away. "I could walk out of any situation. That may sound cold and callous, but the only person I needed to concern myself with was me," Marjorie explained.

At first glance, all of the men in Marjorie's life seemed vastly different from one another. But they all had one thing in common—wealth. "I've always gravitated towards people who were successful, or maybe they've been drawn to me," Marjorie recalled. "I've been fortunate to draw exceptional people to me. They're driven and ambitious."

At the age of nineteen, Marjorie married for the first time. Her relationship with Mitchell Marqui had become serious and he had proposed. On March 28, 1981, they were married in Orlando. At the time, Marjorie was managing the Cheyenne Saloon and working for a man named Porter Freeman. Twenty years later Freeman would go on to become a prominent motivational speaker and write the book *Finally Fit at 50*. Marjorie looked up to Porter and was eager to become a dedicated employee. "I just idolized this man. He was very tough, but he trusted me and gave me responsibilities that I had no business having," Marjorie recalled. "I went out of my way to make sure the responsibility that had been entrusted in me was proven worthy of."

As manager, it was Marjorie's job to oversee the club as well as continue choreographing the dance routines. She put in long hours, often showing up early to make sure business was running smoothly. The more responsibilities Marjorie received at work, the more time she spent apart from Mitchell. After work she and some of the other employees spent late nights partying at various bars and clubs. Meanwhile, Mitchell was busy building his own motorcycle business. Within a year and a half, their marriage fell apart. "I wanted to go out and do things that were a little more age appropriate than would be appropriate for a marriage," Marjorie recalled. "He was understanding. I think he knew that I was too young."

Mitchell filed for divorce, which was finalized on October 11, 1982. Marjorie described their split as amicable. Before she moved out, Mitchell upgraded her car and ensured that she was provided for financially. Although she would marry several more times, Marjorie would often go back to using the last name Marqui, because she said it was "prettier," and a better name for a dancer.

About the same time her marriage with Mitchell was ending, Marjorie began dating a muscular twenty-two-year-old named Larry Tweed, whom she met at the Cheyenne Saloon. Larry couldn't have been more different than Marjorie's first husband. With soft blue eyes and blond shoulder-length hair that formed curly ringlets at the bottom, Larry stood six foot four and weighed about 240. His physical stature belied his gentle, kind, soft-spoken nature. He was a sweet, big-hearted gentleman from South Carolina who played guitar and wrote love songs. Larry's family owned several furniture stores and were very wealthy. Working at the furniture store, Larry earned a sizable income.

With Larry, Marjorie thought she had found someone her age with whom she could party and enjoy her youth. Eight months after her divorce from Mitchell was finalized, Marjorie and Larry married on June 18, 1983, at the First Baptist Church in Longwood, Florida. But as Marjorie continued to work her way up the ranks at the Church Street Station, she became less and less the young party girl and more and more the mature young adult. Her boss sent her to management seminars and promoted her to complex supervisor. Larry, however, was still interested in going to bars and drinking with his friends. Eventually, Marjorie began to see him as too immature. About two years after they married, she left and filed for divorce. "I became too serious for him," Marjorie said, "and kind of outgrew him."

Even before the divorce was finalized on October 9, 1984, Marjorie had already moved on to her next lover. One night a part-time singer named Luke Forest arrived at one of the Church Street Station clubs to perform with the band. When he took the stage, Marjorie couldn't take her eyes off of him. With a deep baritone voice similar to jazz singer Lou Rawls, Luke was mesmerizing. Tall and handsome with strong features, Luke was in his thirties and originally from Ohio. During the day, he worked as a hairdresser at a salon called Regis, which was based in the local mall. Although Regis was a low-cost hair salon, Marjorie said he fancied himself a chic hair designer. "He was so charismatic and so gorgeous," Marjorie recalled. "I was so crazy about this guy."

They began dating and within weeks Marjorie moved

out of Larry's house and into Luke's apartment. Together they made an attractive couple. But theirs was also a destructive relationship. By Marjorie's account, Luke was controlling and manipulative. He insisted on managing their finances and each week required her to hand over her paycheck so he could pay their bills. Then, about a year after they started dating, Marjorie was at work when another employee told her that her car was being towed. She went to stop the tow-truck driver, but was told her Nissan 300ZX was being repossessed due to nonpayment. Marjorie confronted Luke and discovered that he hadn't actually been paying the bills. Instead, he had been gambling away their money.

Luke enjoyed the sport of jai alai, a game that was popular in south Florida at the time. Jai alai was a variation on traditional court and racket sports from northern Spain. It set eight teams equipped with wooden bats and baskets against each other in a fast-speed racquetball-style game. Bettors wagered on the competition, much like horse and dog racing. For Luke, it had become an obsession.

When Marjorie learned her boyfriend had gambled away all of their money, she became enraged. She left him, but after he came crawling back apologetically, they rekindled their relationship. For a while things were good and Marjorie believed that Luke had changed.

Then in 1985 Luke started talking about moving back to his hometown of Cincinnati. Luke's wealthy parents owned an apartment complex there and wanted to sell the building to move to Florida. The Forests offered Luke a cut of the profits and a free apartment if he would come to Ohio and fix up the complex. Marjorie thought it would be a good way to make some quick cash. She quit her job at Church Street Station and Luke sold nearly all their furniture and possessions for about $8,000 and packed the rest in his car. As they drove out of Florida, however, Luke seemed agitated and kept stopping at payphones. After one call, he told Marjorie he had alarming news: The apartment that was supposed to be theirs wouldn't be available for another month.

"What are we going to do?" Marjorie asked.

"How about this," he suggested. "I have some friends who work at a salon in Las Vegas. We could go there and I could get a job for a few weeks."

Marjorie was concerned—Cincinnati was a long way from Las Vegas. But she wanted to believe in Luke. Besides, she didn't really have a choice. She no longer had a job or a place to live.

In the fall of 1985, Luke and Marjorie arrived in Las Vegas, intending to stay only a month. They rented a tiny studio apartment and Marjorie got a job working as a showgirl at the Stardust Hotel and Casino. It was a glamorous job, although not well paying. Soon after, Luke started acting very strange. He claimed he was looking for a job, but at the same time he was pressuring Marjorie to start stripping to earn extra cash. Suggestively, Luke also began dropping hints about bringing another woman into their relationship. It was a toxic situation. "I was blind to a lot of things," Marjorie recalled.

For the next few weeks, Luke claimed he was unable to locate his friends, who had supposedly made the job offer. Once he finally did, he claimed he wasn't able to work in Las Vegas as a hairdresser because his cosmetology license didn't allow him to work outside of Florida.

As one month in Las Vegas stretched into three, Marjorie became suspicious of their plans to move to Cincinnati. To her knowledge, they still had more than $8,000 in savings, but when Marjorie went searching for the money she realized it was gone. Luke had gambled it all away. Marjorie was livid. She packed up her clothes, took their car, and left, intending to return to Florida. But along the way, her vehicle began having mechanical problems. As she was driving through Phoenix, it broke down completely. She stopped at an auto mechanic who told her the car needed an expensive part that would take more than ten days to order.

Marjorie had no idea what she was going to do. None of her friends or family members approved of her relationship with Luke, and she was embarrassed that she had been such a fool. Marjorie had no one in her life from whom she could ask to borrow a thousand dollars. She made her way to a nearby hotel, intending to get a temporary job to earn enough money fix her car and make her way back to Florida. But that plan wasn't to be.

Along the way she passed a strip club called Bourbon Street Circus. Desperate and penniless, Marjorie turned to stripping.

CHAPTER 4

With her flawless figure and natural good looks, Marjorie turned heads at Phoenix's Bourbon Street Circus. One of the club's most popular dancers, Marjorie didn't simply shake her assets, she made stripping into an art form. Gracefully, she strutted onto the stage and shook her hips. Writhing sensually on the pole, she playfully blew kisses and winked at the mesmerized customers. When she danced, Marjorie oozed sex from every pore. For Jay Orbin, it was lust at first sight.

Marjorie had only been working as an exotic dancer for a few days when she met Jay. After accepting a job topless dancing, Marjorie rented a room at an extended-stay motel near the club. Using what little money she had, she put together a few sexy outfits with clothes she bought at a local thrift store. Soon she was making more money than she had ever had in her life. As a club manager, Marjorie's top salary was $850 a week. Dancing at Bourbon Street Circus, Marjorie was making about $500 to $600 a night.

Her stint at Bourbon Street Circus was her first experience as a topless dancer. She would turn out to be a natural seductress. It wasn't just her looks; Marjorie used her charms and powers of persuasion to make the men feel sexy and desired. Highly intelligent, Marjorie had developed an astute understanding of human behavior. Like a chameleon, she seemed to have the ability to analyze people and fashion her behavior to reflect whatever the men desired. Many of the customers would pay her just to sit and talk.

While working at Bourbon Street Circus, Marjorie became familiar with many of the strip club regulars. Those regulars, as Marjorie described them, came to the club to pick up the dancers. They were attracted to girls who typically wouldn't give them the time of day, but they knew how to get them, initially paying for their time and attention. "There were a lot of regulars that knew all the girls by name," Marjorie recalled. "And Jay was one of them."

It was a typical Saturday evening in 1985 when a twenty-six-year-old Jay Orbin first noticed Marjorie. He was alone, sipping a beer, while Marjorie seductively cavorted on stage. That night Jay approached Marjorie, slapped down a hundred dollar bill, and offered to buy her a drink. Marjorie flashed him a sexy smile. She had been standing in her high heels for hours and happily accepted his invitation. Jay was captivated by Marjorie's stunning looks. She was his vision of perfection. The feeling, however, was not mutual. "He was heavy and balding. He had this frizzy, curly hair he wore in an afro and bald on top and thick, thick glasses," Marjorie recalled. "He thought he was pretty suave. He had diamond pinkie rings, cowboy boots, and the tight jeans and the big ol' rodeo belt buckle. He looked like a used car salesman."

While her first impression was less than flattering, when she sat down and started talking with him she genuinely enjoyed their conversation. Marjorie found Jay funny and charming. After first meeting Marjorie, Jay began returning to Bourbon Street Circus six nights a week. Each time he would go, he would pay for Marjorie's time. In between dances on stage, Marjorie would sit beside him and share a drink. Over the next few weeks, Marjorie told Jay all about Luke Forest and her muddled journey to Phoenix.

"That's terrible," Jay told her. "I can't believe any guy would be so stupid to lose you. I would never do that."

Within a few weeks, Jay began asking Marjorie to see her outside the club, but each time she turned him down. Undeterred, he continued to pursue her persistently. After about two months of chatting for five to six nights a week at the club, Marjorie became very fond of Jay. The entire time, Jay continued to pursue her relentlessly.

"Why don't we go out on Sunday?" he asked. "You don't know anyone here. There's so much to do in Phoenix. We could go to the zoo or the park."

Marjorie pondered his invitation for a moment. "Well, a picnic in the park could be nice."

The following Sunday, Marjorie met Jay at the park. At first, it was very romantic. Jay had packed a picnic basket and brought a blanket for them to sit on. Marjorie walked up in a tight pair of jeans and a low-cut blouse. Immediately, Jay commented on how beautiful she looked. As they were eating, Jay pulled out a huge, professional-looking camera and started snapping photos.

"Let me take a picture of you," he said. "I always see you in your clothes from the club. You look so pretty in those jeans."

Throughout the picnic, Jay kept snapping more and more photos. Marjorie felt it was a "turn off." "He's taking pictures and taking pictures and it started feeling creepy," Marjorie recalled. "It was a bit much. The camera was a bit much. So we wrapped up that date."

By the winter of 1985, Marjorie had been working as an exotic dancer in Phoenix for about three months. While she had mixed feelings about Jay, she was enjoying the money she was earning exotic dancing. After paying for her car to be fixed, she was able to put some money away and buy a few other things. "It was just dancing," Marjorie said later. "There was nothing bad going on. I was treated fine."

Although her first date with Jay was a little awkward, she continued to see him at the club. As they grew closer, Marjorie began asking some of the other dancers about him. One dancer told her that Jay was known to find girls who were in trouble or had a problem with an abusive guy and offer to help them out financially. In gratitude, they would usually be his girlfriend for a few days. "He never keeps anybody long," she explained. "But he's quite the ladies' man."

Marjorie thought Jay was quite wealthy. He drove a late-model BMW and was always throwing money around. She agreed to see him again for lunch. This time Jay was a perfect gentleman. For the next few weeks she saw him several more times outside the club. One day he brought up the subject of her living arrangements.

"I've got this house with a spare bedroom," Jay said. "I'm never there. I work all day, I'm out all night. You could stay there for free."

"I don't know," Marjorie said. "I'm not staying long."

"How much are you spending on that hotel room each week?" Jay asked. "You could be putting more money in your savings and setting yourself up."

About a week later, Marjorie took Jay up on the offer, although she told him she only planned to stay in Phoenix for another three weeks. The next day, Jay came by the motel, helped her pack her belongings, and moved her into his house. After showing Marjorie her room, Jay left for work.

"Make yourself comfortable," he said.

When she glanced around Jay's place, Marjorie was disappointed. She was under the impression that he was quite wealthy, but Jay's home was shabby and not up to her standards. There was nothing in the refrigerator and the furniture was scant. On the walls, cheap posters of nude women were professionally framed along with amateur photographs of some of the women in the clubs, wearing skimpy lingerie. *That explains the camera*, she thought.

Marjorie frowned. The place was filthy. She had always been obsessive about cleanliness and began fanatically to dust and mop. For the next few weeks, she worked nights at the club and cleaned Jay's house by the day. Each morning, Jay went to work in his warehouse and each afternoon he came home to take Marjorie out for lunch. Jay had grown to adore Marjorie and wanted to be around her all the time. One night when Marjorie was getting ready to leave for work, Jay urged her to stay at home with him. "Just stay. I'll give you $500," he said. "It's a Sunday. You probably won't make that much."

Marjorie agreed, although she said Jay never actually gave her any cash and she never asked. "I was genuinely very fond of him," Marjorie said. "He was funny. Great personality, down-to-earth, sweetest, funniest thing."

One day at lunch Jay told Marjorie he wanted to take her somewhere special the upcoming weekend. "Buy yourself something nice," Jay said as he handed her a wad of cash. "We'll have a good time."

That weekend Jay took her to an expensive restaurant. After, they went to a club for dancing and drinks. Jay was romantic and Marjorie was impressed. He put his arm around her waist and kissed her passionately. In that moment, the attraction was mutual. That evening, on Jay's couch, they split a bottle of wine. He leaned forward and kissed her again. Kissing turned to heavy petting and eventually they both wound up in Jay's bedroom. But as their clothes came off and they became intimate, Marjorie said the sparks between them faltered. "He's sweating all over me and we're rolling around and then suddenly he's like 'Wow, that was great,'" Marjorie recalled. "I don't know what *he* thought he did, but it wasn't what *I* thought he did. So that was a little traumatizing to me."

Perhaps it was the wine, or performance anxiety, but

whatever the cause, they didn't actually consummate, in the traditional sense that night. Marjorie was less than satisfied. Uncomfortably, she redressed and Jay fell asleep. Marjorie didn't want to hurt Jay's feelings, and she never spoke of the incident.

Sex was something that was important to Marjorie and that night with Jay was quite a turn-off. After that, she lost interest in the wealthy strip-club patron and hastened her return to Florida. On the contrary, Jay was well beyond smitten. The next day, he told Marjorie his feelings.

"I love you," Jay said. "I want you to stay here with me. We can build a life together."

"No. Jay, I have to go." She shook her head. "I have family, I have friends, I have commitments in Florida."

Jay begged her to stay, but she packed up her belongings and left. Marjorie longed for stability, but she still craved excitement and passion. Somehow, in her twenties, she failed to see how contradictory those characteristics can be in a man. To her, Jay Orbin was a nice, sweet guy, but Marjorie was looking for something extraordinary. "At that time, I had things I wanted to do, be, see. I had big dreams," Marjorie recalled. "I had things I wanted to see and that dirty little house in Phoenix was not really anything I could picture being my end of the road."

Although their relationship was short-lived, Jay never forgot about Marjorie. Years later he would still refer to her as "the one who got away."

After her brief stint as a showgirl in Vegas and a stripper in Phoenix, Marjorie returned to Florida and reached out to her old friend Michael J. Peter. He immediately offered her a job topless dancing at Thee DollHouse in Fort Lauderdale.

Marjorie rented an apartment in Fort Lauderdale, a popular tourist destination in south Florida. The city was an urban paradise. Known as the "Venice of America" because of its expansive and intricate canal system, Fort Lauderdale was a major yachting center with more than a hundred marinas and boatyards and forty thousand resident yachts. The city also boasted the finest restaurants and nightclubs. For the next few years, Marjorie would reside in or near Fort Lauderdale.

At Thee DollHouse, Marjorie was pulling in about $1,000 a night, nearly twice what she had made at the Bourbon Street Circus. She bought new furniture and a car and reestablished her life in Florida. A few weeks later, her ex-boyfriend Luke Forest showed up at her doorstep. Once again Luke apologized, and once again their relationship resumed. "He always had a hold on me," Marjorie recalled. "I was still crazy about him and I took him back."

Luke moved into Marjorie's new apartment, but their relationship was still poisoned. About a month later, Luke's parents came to Fort Lauderdale for a visit. Over the course of her relationship with Luke, Marjorie had met the Forests on several occasions and she loved Luke's mother. While his parents were visiting, Luke surprised Marjorie by telling her, "My parents are out here for our wedding."

Marjorie was stunned. Although they had discussed marriage, she hadn't ever formally accepted, and this was the first discussion of a wedding. But Marjorie loved Luke, and she didn't want to hurt his mother. They arranged for a simple ceremony on the beach and were wed on May 9, 1986. This was the third marriage for both of them. Later, Marjorie said that as she walked down the aisle of sand, she knew it was a mistake. A month later, she moved out, leaving Luke with everything she had purchased over the past few months. Their divorce was finalized on August 12, 1986, after just three months of marriage.

Marjorie wasn't alone for long. She began dating a man she met at Thee DollHouse named Joe Cannizzaro. With dark hair, an olive complexion, and a bright smile, Joe was a handsome New York Italian who owned his own tile contracting company. On the surface, Joe was very macho and masculine, but deep down he was sweet and romantic. Joe would often take Marjorie to his job sites and taught her to lay tile. It was a whirlwind romance. "That was a very romantic relationship," Marjorie recalled. "We began seeing each other and got married very quickly."

Less than two months after her divorce from Luke Forest was finalized, Marjorie became Mrs. Joe Cannizzaro on October 10, 1986. Marjorie was twenty-four; he was thirty-three. This was the first marriage for Joe, and although it was Marjorie's fourth, she falsely claimed on the marriage certificate that it was her second.

Marjorie often had a tendency to bend the truth. Her lies were never of much consequence, just details about her family, her educational background, or her mysterious past. To some, Marjorie would claim to speak three languages and have advanced degrees; with others she would have wild stories about the wealthy, famous people she knew. At some point in her life she seemed to develop an excessive need for attention, admiration, and flattery. She would often exaggerate facts about herself or neglect to reveal some of the more tawdry details from her past to impress others.

By 1986, Michael J. Peter was running a veritable empire of skin. He owned eight gentlemen's clubs, including Solid Gold, Thee DollHouse, and Pure Platinum in south Florida, and was grossing more than $10 million a year. Michael monopolized the strip club industry in Florida, often opening three clubs on the same block.

As Michael's strip club kingdom grew, so did the controversy surrounding him. Michael was scathed in the press when an underage stripper, who was working in one of his clubs in Pompano Beach, committed suicide. He was accused of strong-arm tactics against competitors and linked to organized crime. Often the target of legislative restrictions and protests by neighborhood activists, Michael reportedly spent more than $2 million a year in legal fees. In the '80s, when a "family values" committee persuaded Fort Lauderdale commissioners to ban nudity in bars, he flew to Texas to buy body-colored latex in spray cans. The dancers applied a thin coat of latex to their breasts and business resumed.

Throughout the '80s, Michael lived the high life and flaunted his wealth. Known for his taste in luxury cars, he drove a Ferrari, a Rolls-Royce Corniche convertible, a four-door Rolls-Royce, an Excalibur, a Mercedes, and a 1959 Corvette. He slept on a giant bed covered with satin sheets. He owned a home and two yachts in Fort Lauderdale, plus an estate in Orlando, an apartment in New York City, and a mansion in Hollywood. He traveled the world on private jets and enjoyed skeet shooting from an eighty-two-foot yacht he kept docked at his Delmar Place mansion in swanky Lauderdale Isle.

For Michael, image was everything. He was the ultimate playboy and had no plans of ever settling down. When asked about marriage, he often scoffed, "Why take sand to the beach?"

Michael J. Peter literally wrote the book on successful gentlemen's clubs. When he hired a new dancer, she received a "Welcome Kit," complete with a twenty-three-page booklet that taught her how to act. The booklet touched on every facet of a how a stripper should behave, from the preferred heel length of her pumps to the freshness of her breath. Many of his dancers resented Michael's controlling manner. At times, he asked K-9 cops to search the dancers' locker rooms for drugs. His employees took to calling him "Little Hitler." When he stopped by his clubs, the bartenders and managers would fawn all over him and flatter him with excessive praise. "Business is great, Mr. Peter," the club manager would say. Michael was a powerful man and many of the employees were intimidated by him. Marjorie, however, was not.

"How are things *really* going?" Michael asked her one night, when he stopped by Thee DollHouse.

"Well, the bartenders over there have been giving drinks away for the last two hours, the sign out front is not on, there are lights out on the stage, and I think your DJ is drunk," Marjorie bluntly blurted out.

Michael grinned. "Thank you, Marjorie." He loved that she was truthful with him. Soon, Michael started sending Marjorie around to all his clubs to let him know how things operated when he wasn't around. She ended up helping him to do away with a lot of theft and mismanagement. "Michael always wanted to project sophistication and class," Marjorie said years later. "One of the reasons we've always been friends is because I would always tell him the truth. That was our relationship."

One of Michael's business endeavors included a talent agency called Beverly Hills Talent Management, which represented the entertainers who rotated across his clubs. In addition to exotic dancing, his gentlemen's clubs hosted live musicians, comedians, and illusionists who performed with live snakes and tigers. He also employed a dance troupe that at the time was called the Solid Gold Dancers.

A few months after Marjorie began topless dancing at Thee DollHouse, Michael got the notion to transform the Solid Gold dance troupe into a Vegas-style burlesque show. At the time, the dancers toured his Florida clubs performing choreographed hip-hop-style routines. He changed the name of the group to the Platinum Dolls and invited Marjorie to audition. Marjorie not only joined the dance troupe, she ended up assuming the role of the group's producer. It would be the role of her lifetime. Her job involved hiring the dancers, designing the costumes, choreographing performances, and starring in the show. "She single-handedly produced the group from top to bottom," Michael said in court. "She was exceptional."

The gimmick for the Platinum Dolls was for all the dancers to have platinum, bleached blond hair and identical makeup and perform dance routines in matching provocative outfits. While the dancers were meant to look alike,

like dolls, Michael said Marjorie always stood out on stage. "Marjorie was the center of attention, whether she liked it or not," Michael recalled in court.

For the Platinum Dolls, Marjorie went from blond to an almost white shade of platinum blond, a hair color she would keep for most of her life. She got breast implants and hair extensions. She frequented tanning salons, wore sexy clothes, and never left her house without flawless makeup and every hair in place. In promotional photos taken for the Platinum Dolls, Marjorie always posed with her chest protruding and her lips parted seductively. She personified sex appeal.

The Platinum Dolls toured Michael's clubs performing three fifteen-minute shows a night. Marjorie created the concept for each show, which varied each night. Some nights they took the stage to the tune "Big Spender" wearing matching top hats and carrying canes; other nights they would dance in sequined bras and elaborate feather headdresses to an Elvis Presley tune.

Each dancer earned about $300 to $500 a week; Marjorie earned an extra $100 for leading the group. They were also provided a $500 per week costume budget, which Marjorie creatively stretched by designing many of their costumes. For their Vegas-style show, instead of purchasing expensive showgirl outfits from the costume store, she put together the feather headdresses using cheap plastic police helmets she bought from the dollar store and PVC piping, which she used to sprout the feathers. For their rock 'n' roll dance show, she sewed poodle skirts; for other numbers she glued rhinestones or sequins on bras and bikini bottoms.

Marjorie also worked deals through a company called Surf Style near Fort Lauderdale, which sold touristy sweat suits, dresses, and windbreakers. For four years the Platinum Dolls modeled for the Surf Style catalog for free in exchange for twelve of everything in their catalog. They wound up with hundreds of dresses, shorts, and tank tops in every color of the rainbow. Everywhere they went, Marjorie demanded that the dancers dressed identically. The Platinum Dolls would walk through the airport in matching neon pink dresses. This made the troupe very popular and soon they were being booked at venues across the country.

Marjorie saw herself as a mentor for the other dancers. When they went on tour, Marjorie booked only two rooms so she could keep an eye on the girls. "I think that was the most fulfilling job I ever did and the hardest," Marjorie recalled. "I was a mother hen, a confessor, a truant officer."

The other performers Marjorie danced with over the years admired her polished appearance and choreography skills. Charity McLean danced with Marjorie and described her as "an amazing human being." Often taking some of the younger girls under her wing, Marjorie was sweet and thoughtful and went out of her way to help people, Charity said. Marjorie had lots of theories about life and men, and she was constantly passing on that advice to her friends. She showed Charity how to make her own dance costumes and taught her manners and etiquette. "For lack of a better word, Marjorie was my idol," Charity later told police. "She taught me to be a lady and got me where I am today."

In the late '80s, while Marjorie was leading the Platinum Dolls, Michael J. Peter's empire was at the height of its success. His gentlemen's clubs expanded beyond Florida and the Platinum Dolls performed at each club opening. On regular visits to Los Angeles, Michael, Marjorie, and the Platinum Dolls rubbed elbows with celebrities including Don Johnson and Sylvester Stallone. Marjorie remembered riding Harleys down the Sunset Strip in Los Angeles with the rock band Mötley Crüe.

In 1987, Thee DollHouse became an iconic part of pop culture history when Mötley Crüe sang "Girls, Girls, Girls" at Thee DollHouse in Fort Lauderdale. Marjorie even made a brief debut on the small screen when the band filmed the "Girls, Girls, Girls" music video at Thee DollHouse.

Dressed in a fuchsia bikini, Marjorie whipped her blond hair around on stage while the band rocked.

The years Marjorie led the Platinum Dolls were a wild time in her life. In between her brief marriages, she dated many men and attended a lot of parties. In Florida in the '80s, drugs, including a seemingly endless supply of cocaine, were a common component of parties. While Marjorie admitted to occasionally experimenting and sampling a line or two of cocaine at a party, she maintained that she never developed a drug problem.

The Platinum Dolls grew widely popular beyond Florida—performing at the Trump Taj Mahal in Atlantic City, dozens of Las Vegas clubs, Florida cruise ships, and Disney World. Marjorie danced all over the world—Tokyo, Paris, Italy, Honolulu, and Germany. As the Platinum Dolls dominated more and more of Marjorie's attention, her relationship with Joe Cannizzaro fizzled. They divorced on October 19, 1988, about two years after they were married. At the same time Marjorie's relationship with Michael J. Peter had grown sexual.

One late night, days away from the scheduled opening of a new club, Michael and Marjorie were alone in a new city in his hotel room. The other girls were off exploring the local night life. For years, there had always been an intense physical and emotional attraction between Michael and Marjorie. That night, they gave into their desires. For Marjorie it was bittersweet. She had loved Michael since the age of eighteen, but she knew he would never settle down. They would continue brief on-and-off sexual interludes, never becoming serious. Michael truly adored Marjorie. He didn't realize how much until 1989, when she told him she was leaving.

For the previous eight months, Marjorie had been dating Ronald McMann, the wealthy owner of a New Jersey excavating company. Marjorie was twenty-eight; he was fifty-six. With dark hair and a medium build, Ronald was an attractive and extraordinarily wealthy older man. He owned houses in New Jersey and Fort Lauderdale and collected rare cars. Together, he and Marjorie ran in the same circles as Florida's wealthy and elite and over the course of their relationship he aggressively wined and dined her. On two occasions, Ronald flew Marjorie to the Bahamas for lavish vacations and regularly tossed her the keys to his $80,000 Ferrari convertible. For months Marjorie had also been living in his upscale Fort Lauderdale home while Ronald stayed at his primary residence in New Jersey. Marjorie was enamored with Ronald and his wallet. "He treated me wonderful. He was funny, he was nice, he was pretty good-looking," Marjorie recalled. "He was very charming. Very charming."

There was just one problem: He lived in New Jersey. Marjorie told Michael she was leaving and made arrangements for the Platinum Dolls to continue without her. Michael tried to talk her out of it, but she left anyway. She moved to New Jersey and she and Ronald were married.

Unfortunately, husband number five would not be the happily ever after Marjorie was looking for.

CHAPTER 5

With Ronald McMann, Marjorie thought she had found someone who could provide her the lifestyle she deserved. Although he was twice her age, Ronald swept her off her feet. He bought her expensive gowns, furs, and jewelry. Together they ate at the best restaurants, and every weekend they would go into Manhattan for Broadway shows including *Cats* and *Phantom of the Opera*.

Marjorie moved into Ronald's sprawling estate in South Orange, an affluent town in New Jersey just outside of Newark. Parked in his barn-sized garage, Ronald stored his rare car collection, which included a Ferrari Testarossa, a Ferrari 308, a vintage Jaguar XK120, a vintage Jaguar XKE, and a vintage Corvette. He collected cars, fine art, and antiques.

Soon after they married, Ronald did something Marjorie considered incredibly romantic. He brought her to his attorney's office and had his excavating company signed into her name. Ronald even changed the company name to Marco Contracting, as in "Marjorie's Company," and had all the excavating equipment repainted her favorite color—hunter green. "It was the sweetest thing I ever saw," she said. "I thought, 'he really trusts me.'"

Later, in retrospect, Marjorie would find the whole thing very suspicious.

For the next year Marjorie became very active in Ronald's business, learning to do bookkeeping and payroll. He took her to job sites and taught her how to operate the equipment, from backhoes to bulldozers. Marjorie recalled one Easter morning, when there was no traffic on the highway, riding in the equipment as they drove down the freeway. "I was in hard hats at five a.m. in the morning on job sites. It was fun. Everything was great between us," Marjorie recalled. "We did this dirty construction business and then we'd take the Ferraris into Manhattan for a Broadway show."

At one point, however, Marjorie said, she became aware of some shady aspects of his business dealing. After he'd been married to Marjorie for just short of a year, Ronald had paperwork drawn up to have the business state certified as a Women's Business Enterprise. In New Jersey there were government construction jobs in which state rules required a certain percentage of contracts to be fulfilled by minority businesses. As a certified women's business, Marco Construction had the ability to overbid other contractors and still get jobs because the companies were required to fulfill a certain minority quota.

In 1989, Ronald hired a new bookkeeper, Gilda Bloomenthal, to work in the McManns' basement office. In her late thirties, with short, curly red hair, Gilda was fond of big earrings and spandex pants. Over time, Marjorie and Gilda became very friendly. Each morning Marjorie would get up and have coffee with Gilda in the basement office. One morning, Gilda asked her some pointed questions.

"So this company is completely in your name. His name is not on anything?" Gilda asked. "Did he tell you why he did this?"

"No," Marjorie said. "He never really explained."

Over the next few weeks, Gilda brought documents to Marjorie's attention that showed there were taxes that weren't being paid. Marjorie asked Ronald about it a few times, but he brushed off her concerns. Gilda, however, continued to push. She was concerned that Marjorie would be held personally accountable for the company's mounting debts. "It got up to almost $50,000, which is a lot of money, but to him and what we were running through that company and all the equipment that he owned, it really wasn't," Marjorie recalled. "I didn't know why he was doing this."

When Marjorie confronted Ronald, he wouldn't give her a straight answer. Their disagreements became more and more heated. Eventually it escalated into an ugly blowup. Ronald left for a few days to stay at his Fort Lauderdale home. Meanwhile, a furious Marjorie called several of their contractors and the IRS to alert them of the situation. She copied every document in their basement office and sent them to the IRS.

On the phone with her mother, a normally collected Marjorie was in a panic. Concerned, Marjorie's mom called Michael J. Peter and told him, "I think Marjorie's in over her head." Together they drove out to New Jersey and moved Marjorie out of Ronald's house and back to Fort Lauderdale. During her marriage to Ronald, Marjorie had purchased a 1988 green-and-tan Eddie Bauer Ford Bronco, which she took with her when she left. Marjorie filed for divorce and in the papers wrote, "All assets and debts of Marco Contracting revert back to Ronald McMann." She thought the debt was taken care of with the divorce papers. Unbeknownst to her, a tax lien would be placed in her name.

With all her worldly possessions loaded in the back of her Ford Bronco, Marjorie pulled into the driveway of Michael's Fort Lauderdale mansion. Michael offered her a place to stay and gave her back her job choreographing and dancing with the Platinum Dolls. But this time things between them were different. Marjorie was no longer a naïve teenager, and Michael had become less interested in having a different woman in his bed every night. Also, for the first time in their relationship, they were both single. They began a serious, committed relationship.

For the next few years, Marjorie lived with Michael in his mansion and shared in his extravagant lifestyle. Together, Michael and Marjorie lived a life of luxury and indulgence. They vacationed in the Caribbean on yachts and traveled to the south of France, home of the Cannes Film Festival. He bought her jewelry, diamonds, furs—anything she wanted.

In the late '80s, Michael J. Peter's life of opulence was profiled on an episode of *Lifestyles of the Rich and Famous,* a popular show in the '80s and '90s featuring the extravagant lifestyles of wealthy entertainers, athletes, and business moguls. Swabbed in furs and dripping diamonds, Marjorie draped herself on Michael's arm as he showed off his estate. In the episode, Michael, dressed in a suit and flashy necktie, stepped out of a private helicopter carrying a briefcase and talking on a hefty brick of a cell phone. He explained how his lifestyle mirrored his business. "Gentlemen's clubs are a world of fantasy and flash," he explained. "To live in it, you have to lead a life of fantasy."

By 1990, Michael's empire of strip joints had gone international. He owned upward of fifty clubs worldwide in Athens, Barcelona, London, Paris, and Mexico, and employed five thousand employees. His business had gone from grossing ten million dollars a year to a hundred million dollars a year. Branching out beyond strip joints, Michael launched a men's magazine, similar to *Esquire*, titled *Platinum.* He also produced a line of pin-up calendars and was active in the movie, recording, and music video industries.

Marjorie was often involved in his projects—modeling in his magazine, posters, and calendars and appearing as a dancer in a few music videos. She also had a feature role in a few small movies, produced by Michael's companies, appearing most prominently in a low-budget, soft-core porn flick called *No More Dirty Deals.* In one scene, Marjorie danced on the stage in a short black patent leather trench coat and sunglasses. She tore open the coat to reveal a binding black leather bustier with heavy metal buckles. In another scene she was wearing a skin-tight royal blue body suit that hugged her curves and amplified her cleavage. Her platinum hair was long and straight with thick bangs. Marjorie opened the bedroom door and flashed a sensual look to a man lying on the bed. She climbed on top of the bed, straddled the man, and tossed her hair from side to side.

There was undeniable chemistry between Marjorie and Michael. Beyond their intense sexual connection, they formed an emotional bond. Throughout her relationships, Marjorie had difficulty getting close to people, but Michael probably knew her better than anyone. There were, of course, some things Marjorie kept secret. For instance, Michael never knew how many times Marjorie had actually been married or that she was infertile.

Marjorie was about two inches taller than Michael, and in heels she towered over him. In most pictures, they posed together sitting down. In one photo, they were holding hands seated on the bow of a yacht at sunset. She was dressed in a blue striped dress with high shoulder pads. He was wearing a matching blue and white pullover. In another they were on the couch with their legs tangled together. Marjorie was dressed in ripped acid-washed jeans and cowboy boots. Her wavy blond hair swept down past her waist. But for Michael, Marjorie was more than just a beautiful woman who looked great on his arm; he loved her. The millionaire bachelor playboy who scoffed at the thought of settling down had fallen for Marjorie in a way he never expected.

In 1991, Michael took Marjorie to New York to spend the holidays with his parents. After dinner, in front of the tree, he gave Marjorie her gift—a four-carat diamond engagement ring. She enthusiastically said yes. Michael's dad was astonished—he never thought his son would settle down. But Michael told him she was "the one."

But when Michael and Marjorie returned to Florida things were different. To Michael, a switch seemed to flip in her. Before she seemed to understand that his business required him to be around beautiful women. Now that they were engaged, she was jealous, insecure, and possessive. It became clear to Michael that if they got married, Marjorie expected him to become a different person. To Marjorie, however, Michael was suddenly acting like a "caged tiger." He appeared to be intentionally flaunting other women in her face. In her view he regretted proposing and was intentionally flirting with other women in an act of defiance.

Michael's wandering eye caused frequent arguments. A few weeks after proposing, Michael broke off their relationship. He told Marjorie that he had made a mistake and he wasn't the marrying kind. But deep down Michael knew he couldn't provide her what she really needed. "Marjorie wanted to settle down, stay in one place, have children," Michael said in court. "That was always her main goal—to have a family."

After their break-up, Marjorie continued to work for Michael and lead the Platinum Dolls. They still loved each other but there were too many other factors that doomed their relationship. Michael offered to buy Marjorie a condo, but she stubbornly refused. Instead, she rented a place near Fort Lauderdale for $600 a month. Her one-bedroom, one-bathroom 900-square-foot cottage was quite a contrast from Michael's lavish mansion. Painted yellow with white shutters and flower boxes on the window sills, the cottage had hardwood floors throughout and a quaint kitchen. By her early thirties, Marjorie owned scads of clothes, but the home had just one small closet, so Marjorie went into the attic crawl space, bought a roll of carpet, and put dowels on the attic walls. Up in the attic she stored her ironing board, sewing machine, and all of her clothes. It seemed to infuriate Michael that she lived in this tiny place and refused to let him buy her a condo. He would regularly stop by for drinks, look around the house, and snidely say, "Well, this is nice."

In the beginning there was some tension in their relationship, but eventually they went back to being good friends. Michael never stopped loving Marjorie. He vowed he would always be there for her when she needed him. Years later, he would keep his promise.

In 1992, after her break-up with Michael, Marjorie married for the sixth time at the age of thirty-one. Milan Radesits was a handsome, dark-haired dancer and Marjorie's longtime friend and partner in the pas de deux, a sexy type of partners' ballet. Milan was Danish, and spoke with a thick accent. They married in April 1992, just a few months after her break-up with Michael.

But their marriage was destined to fail. Milan was openly gay, with a visa which was set to expire. Marjorie agreed to the sham marriage to prevent her friend from being deported to Denmark. "He's a great guy, good friend," Marjorie recalled. "I just wanted to help him get his green card."

They went down to the local courthouse in Fort Lauderdale and had a quickie marriage ceremony, which was soon followed by a quickie divorce. Again, Marjorie went back to using the last name Marqui.

Nearly a year following her break-up with Michael, Marjorie was still living in Florida dancing with the Platinum Dolls. But she felt trapped. To her it seemed as if there was an unwritten rule that she still belonged to Michael. On Fridays she would go out dancing with her girlfriends and occasionally a guy would flirt with her. But when they found out who she was, they would back off. "Nobody would have anything to do with me because of Michael," Marjorie recalled. "I couldn't do anything or go anywhere because I had 'property of Michael J. Peter' stamped on my butt. I had to leave."

In early 1993, Marjorie left Florida for good. She packed her possessions in her green-and-tan Ford Bronco and moved to Nevada. For the next several years she worked as a full-fledged Vegas showgirl. At first she danced in a show called Crazy Girls at the Rio. Later she landed a job running a small dance troupe at Club Paradise called the Club Paradise Dancers, doing the same choreography and dancing she had been doing for the Platinum Dolls. For two years, five nights a week, Marjorie danced on stage wearing elaborate feather headdresses and tiny rhinestone bikinis.

While working in Las Vegas, she ran with a fast-paced, hard-partying group, who club-hopped until the sun came up. On the weekends, they took trips out to California and Catalina Island to go water skiing. Marjorie had a few more intense relationships—one with a Saudi prince and another with a performer in the Pirates of the Caribbean show at the Treasure Island Hotel. She was also briefly involved in a tumultuous relationship with a well-known celebrity.

When Marjorie was younger, she enjoyed the wild party life—dancing all night and partying until dawn. But by thirty-three, she was burnt out on the lifestyle. More than ever, she felt unfulfilled. She longed for true companionship. In her mind she pictured a parallel world where she cooked, cleaned, and cared for a loving family. More than anything, she wanted to have a baby.

Then, one day in 1994, Marjorie received a call from a forgotten fling. It was Jay Orbin. By the mid '90s, Jayhawk International was a booming business and Jay spent half of the year on business trips across the country. Jay was thirty-five and seemed destined to remain a lifelong bachelor. He had never been married, and although he had dated dozens of beautiful women, none were too serious. After all this time, he was still in love with Marjorie.

For ten years, in every city he traveled to, Jay thumbed through the phone book looking for Marjorie's phone number—calling dozens of women across the country with names similar to Marjorie Marqui. Then on a trip to Las Vegas, he saw a familiar face on a billboard advertising the Club Paradise Dancers. It was Marjorie. Jay's heart skipped a beat. He was awestruck. Suddenly, images of the woman he had been searching for for a decade were all around him—on billboards, on top of taxi cabs, and on flyers across the city.

Breathlessly, he stopped at a payphone and flipped through the phone book as he had done so many times before. He found Marjorie's number and ripped out the page. Jay would keep that yellow piece of phone book paper in his wallet for the next ten years. Immediately he dialed the number and, to his surprise, she answered.

"Remember me?" he asked.

"Jay? Jay Orbin?" Marjorie said, stunned to hear from him. "How did you get this number?" She wasn't aware it was listed.

"I have been looking for you for ten years," he said.

Jay explained his long quest to find her and how he saw her face on a billboard. Jay told her he was in town and asked if she'd like to get together. That evening they met for a drink at the Rio bar. When Marjorie arrived, Jay was floored. She was even more beautiful than he remembered. To Marjorie, however, Jay looked very similar. Although, she said he was even more of a caricature of a salesman than she remembered—cowboy boots, pinkie rings, and a huge rodeo belt buckle. Only now she said he was "heavier and balder."

As she sat down at the bar, Jay seemed to be holding his breath. After a few moments he exhaled, "Do you mind if I smoke?"

"What do you mean?" Marjorie asked.

"I've been brushing my teeth, eating mints," he said. "I don't want to ruin my breath."

"It's okay. I smoke, too."

"Oh, thank God," he sighed.

They sat in the bar drinking, smoking and catching up on the past ten years. As they talked, Marjorie found herself laughing and having a genuinely good time. A nice, down-to-earth, normal guy like Jay was such a welcome change from the self-consumed playboys she had been dating. They ended up talking until the sun came up. Jay returned to Phoenix the next day, but their relationship continued long distance. For the next several months they spoke for hours each night by phone.

When Jay visited Vegas, their relationship again became sexual, although Marjorie said she still didn't find it satisfying. At that point in her life, however, she was looking for something else. Jay showed her the stack of torn phone book pages with Marjorie's name. It was incredibly touching. Obviously he loved her very much. Maybe Jay was exactly what she needed.

Eventually, Marjorie came out to Phoenix for a visit. By then Jay was living in a much nicer home. Pictures of scantily clad women were still hung on the walls, but the place was spotless and a week's worth of food was prepared in the refrigerator. Clearly, Jay was trying hard to impress her. She stayed for a week. The day she was scheduled to return, Jay got down on one knee and proposed.

"I've loved you my whole life," he told her. "I want to marry you."

Marjorie face looked pained. "No, Jay."

She enjoyed his company but she wasn't in love with him and she couldn't imagine a life with him. If she came to Phoenix she knew she wouldn't be happy.

"I can't marry you," she said. "I'm sorry."

Jay was disappointed, but he didn't give up. In early 1995, Jay came to Las Vegas for a visit. In Marjorie's apartment, they had an emotional talk. Marjorie confessed the one lingering regret she had for her life.

"I have everything I ever wanted," Marjorie cried. "The only thing I want that I can't have is children."

Jay told her that if she would consider marrying him, he would do anything in his power to give her a child, including actively pursuing fertility treatments.

"I want you to come to Phoenix," he said. "I'll do anything that you want."

Jay thought of it as a chance to start a family with the woman of his dreams. Marjorie felt Jay could give her the stable family life she secretly longed for so desperately. "Being the salesman that he was, he made me an offer I couldn't refuse," Marjorie recalled.

On July 22, 1995, Marjorie Ann Kroh-Marqui-Tweed-Forest-Cannizzaro-McMann-Radesits became Marjorie Ann Orbin.

They eloped at the Little White Wedding Chapel on Las Vegas Boulevard. There were no guests; Jay's friends and family didn't even know he got married until after the fact.

For her seventh wedding, the bride wore white. Her sequined dress had billowing sleeves and a low-cut neckline that accentuated her ample, fake breasts. Marjorie's platinum blond hair looked almost white in contrast to her well-tended tan. She wore it curly, with bangs teased high. Metallic pink lipstick glossed her pouty lips; her almond-shaped eyes were painted with heavy black shadow.

In one of the wedding pictures, she posed with her arm around her new husband, holding a cheap bouquet of red and white carnations between them. Her gaze had drifted from the camera lens with seeming disinterest; her smile appeared feigned.

By contrast, Jay appeared to be beaming with pride for his new trophy wife. He was dressed in a black suit with a blue bowtie. His thin, dark hair was slicked back with his neatly trimmed beard encircling an unabashed grin.

He looked, simply, like a man in love.

There would be no way for him to know at the time how quickly their picture-perfect union would come unraveled, or how tragically it would ultimately end.

CHAPTER 6

In the summer of 1995, Marjorie traded feather boas and fishnet stockings for rubber gloves and floral-print aprons. Leaving the spotlight behind for good, she uprooted her life in Vegas, moved to Phoenix, and took on her new role as suburban housewife. Although her new quiet life with Jay would be quite a change for the former showgirl, Marjorie seemed destined to play the part.

At first glance, Jay and Marjorie made for quite the mismatched couple. He was casual, down-to-earth, and easygoing; she was glamorous, flashy, and high-maintenance. Marjorie had traveled the world on yachts and private jets; Jay had never lived more than fifty miles from where he had been born and raised. She was impetuous, marrying six times by the age of thirty; he was a workaholic who seemed like he would never settle down.

Of all the men in Marjorie's past, Jay Orbin seemed like the least likely for her to end up with. By her own account, she never found him attractive, and although he was relatively wealthy, compared to many of her past relationships he was a pauper. Marjorie had been with millionaire playboys, exceptionally wealthy business owners, celebrities, and Saudi royalty. None of them had come close to fulfilling her needs.

Over the years Marjorie had developed a theory about men. She believed that like a pendulum swinging from one extreme to the other, guys who are exceptionally successful, charismatic, and wealthy also have exceptionally bad character traits. She called this her "pendulum theory." Marjorie said, "Guys in the bottom of the pendulum swing are easier to deal with." When she met Jay again, it was at a time in her life where she was looking for someone who was ordinary, unexceptional, and easy to control. In her eyes, that was Jay. He was "in the middle of the pendulum swing," Marjorie recalled. Jay was just a nice guy who could provide stability and security.

For his part, Jay was desperately in love with Marjorie. He adored and doted on her, showering her with gifts and attention. In Jay's eyes, Marjorie was perfect. He would do anything to make her happy. That included giving her the one thing no one else could, the one thing she desired more than anything—a baby.

Jay and Marjorie had a tenuous bond. When he made the offer to actively pursue fertility treatments, Marjorie made a "counter offer." She agreed to come to Phoenix and proceed with fertility treatments for two years. If after that time she was not pregnant, she would leave, "no hard feelings, no harm, no foul." According to Marjorie, Jay agreed to those terms.

It was a reckless and potentially perilous relationship. Marjorie had difficulty staying interested in relationships with guys she was crazy about. Now she had married a man to whom she wasn't even attracted. She hadn't married Jay for love or even money, but she had still married to fulfill her own selfish desire.

A few months before their Las Vegas wedding, Marjorie quit her job dancing at the Paradise Club and moved in with Jay. Immediately, Jay kept his promise to her to spare no expense and exhaust every avenue possible to give her a child. He hired a pricey fertility specialist to explore their options and they decided to try in vitro fertilization, a process by which egg cells are fertilized in a laboratory dish and implanted in the womb. The procedure requires four to five daily ovary-stimulating hormone injections which cause a woman to produce multiple eggs.

The injections were painful and left large bruises all over Marjorie's body. The hormones caused her ovaries to swell and left her nauseous. Marjorie became consumed by constant hot flashes and woke up drenched in sweat. Over the next few months, she underwent seven surgeries as doctors attempted to cultivate and retrieve her eggs. Every day she went back to the clinic for blood draws and ultrasounds. Several times Marjorie hyperstimulated, which caused her abdomen to fill with fluid. With her stomach inflated, she couldn't breathe or sleep. Twice Jay had to rush her to the emergency room for doctors to drain the fluid. "It was like going through hell and back," Marjorie recalled. "It was very difficult, it makes you crazy, it makes you depressed."

For months they tried to conceive, but each failure left Marjorie consumed by bitter disappointment. The procedure was expensive and Jay spent more than $60,000. As they went through the treatments, Marjorie started to see Jay differently. An extraordinarily patient and caring man, Jay was sensitive to her needs and genuinely concerned about her health. He rubbed her back when she was in pain and bought her a recliner so Marjorie could sleep upright. He rearranged his travel plans and attended every single doctor's appointment and surgical procedure.

Marjorie was not passionate about Jay when they first married, but during this time she began to develop genuine feelings of love toward him. One night they were up late talking and the conversation became very emotional.

"I'm sure we're going to get pregnant," Marjorie told him. "And if we don't, it doesn't matter. I'll stay."

Understandably, Jay's parents were shocked when their son suddenly returned from Las Vegas with his new bride.

They had only met Marjorie a few times and weren't exactly impressed. Marjorie was just so different from their family. The Orbins lived on a budget, had simple tastes and a close circle of friends. Joann was a wife of the '50s, a conservative June Cleaver–type.

In her short skirts and high heels, Marjorie looked like she had just stepped off the Vegas stage. Joann's first impression was that Marjorie seemed self-consumed and materialistic. Also, she seemed entirely uninterested in developing a close mother-daughter type of relationship.

Marjorie could tell Jay's parents didn't approve of her, but she had never expected they would. In Marjorie's eyes, Joann was just jealous of the way Jay adored her and catered to her every whim. The tension between Jay's parents and Marjorie was obvious. Oddly, Jay didn't seem to notice.

As Marjorie sometimes had a tendency to do, she bent the truth about her past with the Orbins—sharing stories that cast her in only the most flattering light. Jake and Joann never knew about Marjorie's former profession as a stripper or that she had originally met Jay at a topless club. Marjorie only said that she used to work as a showgirl and choreographer. Marjorie also told Jay's parents she had been married only once before and that she was a widow. She said her only previous husband was Mitchell Marqui.

"Mitchell and I were newlyweds, and very much in love, when he died," Marjorie said.

They were driving through a part of Florida known as Alligator Alley when their car was clipped by another vehicle and spun out of control, she said.

"Mitchell was killed instantly," Marjorie said somberly. "I was in a coma for six weeks. When I regained consciousness, the doctors told me he was dead."

"Oh my god," Joann said, her eyes welling with tears.

Marjorie said she had barely survived and had to undergo several corrective surgeries to repair scars on her face. It was a heartbreaking tale. After hearing that story, the Orbins felt sympathetic toward Marjorie. They couldn't imagine anything worse than losing a loved one in such a violent way.

Of course, it was a lie. Marjorie was not a widow. She and Mitchell had divorced in 1982 and he was alive and well, living in Longwood, Florida. Perhaps Marjorie was embarrassed by her past and didn't want Jay's parents to judge by her by her failures. Whatever the motive for the lie, years later when the Orbins learned the truth, they were perplexed. It was such a bizarre thing to lie about.

There was something about Marjorie that filled Joann with concern, but she kept her reservations to herself. Joann believed Jay's choice of spouse was none of her business and she wasn't about to drive a wedge in their relationship. Besides, Jay seemed so happy. Joann saw the way he looked at Marjorie with such love in his eyes. Begrudgingly, the Orbins dismissed their initial misgivings and welcomed Marjorie into their family.

While Jay's parents seemed troubled about Marjorie in the beginning, Jay's brother, Jake Jr., was thrilled to hear his brother had settled down. At the time, Jake Jr. was living in San Diego and working for the Parks and Recreation department. Excitedly, Jay called to tell him he had married "the love of his life." A few months later, Jake Jr. came to Phoenix for a visit. To him, she seemed like the perfect housewife—she cooked, cleaned, and took care of the house. They seemed happy. "I would come over three or four times a year. A couple times I would stay at their house in Jay's back bedroom. She'd be cooking the meals like everything's normal," Jake Jr. recalled. "She was a homebody person that just kept remodeling. She did decoupage, sponge painting, everything."

Jay's close circle of friends were surprised by the impetuous marriage. Jay wasn't exactly the brash, spontaneous type. But when they met Marjorie, it was easy to see what Jay saw in her—she was beautiful, sexy, and glamorous.

Marshall Roosin could tell his best friend was smitten.

To him, Marjorie seemed wonderful. Very few of Jay's friends knew that Jay had first met Marjorie at a strip club. Jay was intentionally vague, saying just that "they had dated when they were younger." Marshall was under the impression that he and Marjorie were once high school sweethearts.

The first time Jay's friend Mario Olivarez was introduced to Marjorie he was put off. Mario and his wife met Jay and Marjorie at an Arizona State University football game. They were all dressed casually in sweatshirts and jeans; Marjorie showed up wearing a mink stole and high heels. "I was embarrassed to be with her," Mario recalled. "I was like, 'Oh, my god. Here we are at a college game and she's dressed like she's ready to go to the ball or something.'"

Mario looked at Jay, expecting him to be embarrassed as well, but he didn't seem bothered. Jay was just too infatuated. On multiple occasions, Mario tried to be friendly with Marjorie, but she seemed uninterested. After awhile, he stopped going over to Jay's house and they only hung out when Marjorie wasn't around.

The truth was that Marjorie wasn't particularly interested in Jay's friends. She didn't like him spending time with anyone but her. Occasionally, she would go on a double date with Marshall and his wife or attend a social gathering. But Marjorie complained about his friends, calling them an inconvenience and claiming they "glommed" onto his life.

Jay, who was very social and outgoing, gradually started spending less and less time with his buddies. For a time, Jay didn't find this bothersome. He accepted that his friends and his marriage would remain separate aspects of his life. He was willing to do whatever it took to make his marriage work.

Marjorie's transition from Vegas showgirl to housewife appeared seamless. She cooked and cleaned, and when Jay was out of town she helped with the business. When he came home, Marjorie always had a platter of food prepared. He never did a load of laundry and each time he stepped out of the shower, she handed him a hot, fluffy towel straight from the dryer. "We had very traditional roles. In ten years I never put gas in my vehicle. I never worried about the bills or anything. And he couldn't tell you where a spoon was in the kitchen," Marjorie recalled. "We both catered to each other completely."

Attending do-it-yourself classes at the Home Depot, Marjorie learned how to lay tile, construct shelving, and sponge paint. She did the plumbing and landscaping and even single-handedly constructed an addition to the house. In a few months, Marjorie had transformed Jay's bachelor pad to suit her own discerning tastes. Their house was like a showroom—never a dish in the sink or a towel on the floor. Jay was proud of Marjorie's handiwork, happily funding each of her projects. Jay rarely spent a dime on himself. But when it came to Marjorie, he was generous, paying for her to get hair extensions and permanent makeup procedures.

Over the years, Marjorie had developed an impressive collection of clothes and jewelry. She had a black fur coat and a white fur coat, a mink stole and a mink ball jacket, as well as diamond, ruby and emerald necklaces, rings, and earrings. She also had a collection of over fifty pieces of the classic brown and tan Louis Vuitton purses, backpacks, shoes, wallets, luggage, gym bags, scarves, and an umbrella. Marjorie loved designer clothes and accessories and Jay often surprised her with a new handbag or piece of jewelry.

Meanwhile, they continued the in vitro fertilization treatments. Then in late 1995, after months of trying, Marjorie found out she was pregnant. Jay and Marjorie were both overjoyed. Marjorie was thirty-four and had all but given up on the chance of having a baby. Now her greatest dream was coming true—she was going to be a mom. Marjorie reveled in pregnancy. She would look down at her tummy and envision her baby growing inside her. Her child would be perfect.

Months passed and her pregnancy progressed. One afternoon, while Jay was away on a sale in Quartzsite, a town about 130 miles away from Phoenix, Marjorie went to the pharmacist to fill a prescription. It was still early in the pregnancy, and she was on medication. Marjorie handed the cashier her credit card, but it was declined. She asked them to try again and again, but each time it came back declined. Marjorie called the bank and discovered the account had been seized. She was mortified. "I want this money into this account right this second," she demanded. Eventually they returned the funds and she was able to fill her prescription.

When Jay came home they learned that Marjorie was $50,000 in debt to the IRS—the result of her marriage with Ronald McMann five years prior. Jay found a creative solution and quickly sorted through the legal tangle. All of the couple's assets were signed over to Jay's name, including the green-and-tan Ford Bronco Marjorie had driven for nearly a decade.

Because of the tax lien, Marjorie couldn't even be a signer on Jay's bank credit cards. To provide her with spending money, Jay set up a separate bank account in which he would deposit $500 a week. All of the bills were paid by Jay and the allowance was for anything else she needed or wanted. Marjorie used the money for groceries, cosmetics, cleaning supplies, tile, curtains, and things for the house. Like clockwork, each Monday Jay deposited money into the account. If Marjorie wanted to make a larger purchase, she just had to ask and Jay would either buy it for her or give her the cash. She became completely financially dependent on Jay. At the time it seemed like a wise solution. Marjorie would come to bitterly regret that decision.

* * *

Noah Jacob Orbin was born on August 26, 1996. He was an adorable, healthy baby boy who had his mom's dark eyes and his dad's crooked smile. Jay was ecstatic to be a father. Excitedly, he called all of his friends to tell them he had a son. They had never heard him so happy. In a photo taken the day of Noah's birth, Jay has a wide smile plastered across his face. "When they brought him home from the hospital, he was beaming, as happy as can be, just smiling away," Jake Jr. recalled.

When Marjorie held her son for the first time, tears streamed down her face. She was overwhelmed with emotion. This was what she had been waiting for her entire life. Noah became her everything. Both parents loved their son fiercely. It is common for parents of children born through in vitro fertilization to idolize their children and Jay and Marjorie were no different. Noah became the center of their world. They called him their "miracle baby."

By the time Noah was born, Jayhawk International was thriving and Jay still traveled two weeks out of every month. Jay loved his business and enjoyed his time on the road, but now things were different. Now he had a family. He wanted to stay close to home to be there for his son's first words and other significant moments in his life.

Jay decided to make a career change from wholesale to retail sales. He leased space at a strip mall in west Phoenix and opened a store selling the same Native American art and jewelry he sold wholesale. Jay was optimistic and signed a three-year lease on the space. But business was slow. Some days he'd sit at the shop all day long without a customer. It was frustrating for Jay. The Orbins were hemorrhaging money. He tried not to worry Marjorie with the finances, but it weighed heavily on his shoulders. Jay's mother started to help him run the shop so Jay could go back on the road to supplement their income. According to Marjorie, she also helped run the store, while breast feeding and caring for Noah. Increasingly Jay spent more time on the road just to make up for what the shop was losing.

Despite the money issues, Marjorie and Jay seemed like a happy family. With Noah, their lives were complete. He was an adorable child. When he was first born he had a little fuzz of dark hair like his father, but when he was a few months old his hair lightened to blond. He was sweet, affectionate, and playful. When Noah was ten months old, Jay and Marjorie bought a puppy—a small white Maltese they named Sasha. Noah thought the puppy was his little teddy bear. He would carry Sasha everywhere, holding her around the neck. At night, the dog slept in his bed.

The Orbins were already a tight-knit family and after Noah was born, Jay became even closer to his parents. For years, there was a family tradition that every Sunday Jay had dinner at his parent's house. With Noah, he created a new tradition. Every Sunday morning he was in town, Jay would take Noah to McDonald's to play in their indoor jungle gym. Afterward, they would go to his parent's house so Noah could spend time with his grandparents. Joann would make brunch and they would talk and play games for hours. Rarely, Marjorie would stop by, but she never stayed more than an hour.

It was always slightly uncomfortable when Marjorie was around. There were never any disagreements or arguments; there was just no connection. Something was a little off about her manner. It was like she was acting the part of Jay's loving, devoted wife.

For each birthday, the entire family got together for dinner, cake, and presents and Marjorie always attended. She planned the annual Super Bowl party at Jay's house, bought presents, and baked cookies. Each Thanksgiving was spent at Jay's parents' house, while Christmas was held at Jay and Marjorie's. But there was always tension between Marjorie and the Orbins.

Joann's birthday was around Easter and each year she begged Jay and Marjorie to bring Noah over for an Easter egg hunt. Marjorie, however, refused. She didn't believe in Easter and didn't want her child celebrating the religious holiday. It caused constant turmoil between Joann and Marjorie. After several years of contention, Jay simply rearranged his travel plans to be out of town for the Easter holiday. Marjorie didn't quit when she became fixated on what she wanted. Whatever the argument, she usually prevailed because Jay just wanted peace in the household.

Noticeably absent from any family gatherings was anyone from Marjorie's family. When the Orbins asked about Marjorie's family, she told strange and sometimes contradictory stories. Marjorie said she came from a large, estranged family. Her father was dead and she hadn't seen her mother in more than a decade. She spoke poorly about her mother, saying she only called when she wanted something. Marjorie claimed she was mostly raised by her grandparents in the Orbin's home state of Pennsylvania.

Marjorie also told her in-laws that she was one of nine children, but her siblings were spread across the world. She said that her twin brother, a male model turned gigolo, was living in South Africa with a wealthy widow. Marjorie even showed Joann a magazine, pointed to a handsome blond male model, and told her that was her twin. Two of Marjorie's siblings were also twin sisters, she said. They worked as dancers performing with Siegfried and Roy in Las Vegas and at the Moulin Rouge in Paris.

Of course, the Orbins never met any of these relatives. For years they didn't meet anyone in Marjorie's family. Eventually Marjorie's sister, Colleen, came for a visit. But she wasn't a glamorous model who traveled the world; she was a heavy-set truck driver who lived in Texas. Marjorie told the Orbins that Colleen had been previously married and had children but her husband died in a car accident. According to Marjorie, Colleen had remarried but had only a platonic relationship with her husband and was involved in a lesbian relationship with a woman who lived with them.

These stories about Marjorie's family were all untrue. Marjorie was not a twin. Her grandparents did not raise her in Pennsylvania. And Colleen was her only sibling. At the time, the Orbins believed all of Marjorie's stories; they had no reason not to. In hindsight, Jake Jr. said it's impossible to know if anything she ever told them was true. "It turns out they were all lies, once you start looking into them," Jake Jr. recalled. "They all sound so ridiculous now."

In truth, after high school Marjorie drifted apart from her family. Embarrassed by her background, she had scant contact with her mother and never spoke to her stepfather. Her closest relationship was with her sister, Colleen, but even they only spoke a few times a year.

In 1998 Marjorie got a call from the fertility clinic she and by had used to conceive Noah. Additional frozen eggs were being stored and they wanted to know if they would be willing to donate them to other couples. Jay and Marjorie always wanted more children, but after the difficulties they underwent conceiving Noah, Marjorie was wary. But she couldn't stand the thought of seeing another baby and wondering if it was hers. She was unwilling to donate her eggs. They decided, once again, to try a frozen embryo transfer.

In 1997, Marjorie learned she was pregnant again. She and Jay were both thrilled at the thought of adding a new baby to their family. Again, the pregnancy was delicate and each week Marjorie went back to the clinic for an ultrasound. Weeks passed and Marjorie began picking out baby names and fantasizing about decorating the new baby's room. But during one ultrasound, the doctors told her some devastating news: The baby had no heart beat. Jay was out of town and Marjorie called sobbing.

"We're going to lose the baby," she cried.

Jay got on the first plane to Phoenix to be by her side.

Instead of waiting for Marjorie miscarry, the doctors

performed an emergency procedure to remove the fetus. Marjorie was distraught. After the procedure the obstetrician told her it would be too risky to try again. Noah would be the Orbins' only child. He became the center of their world.

For several years, Jay and Marjorie had a good relationship. It wasn't passionate or sexual, but they had a solid bond based around Noah. Jayhawk International had become very successful and Marjorie wanted for nothing. "We were living our dream life," Marjorie recalled. "We had our child, his business, our business, was growing and growing."

The extent of Marjorie's role in Jay's business would later come into question. According to Marjorie, when she first came to Phoenix, Jay's Rolodex consisted of six boxes of business cards on the passenger seat of his truck. Marjorie claimed to have computerized his business, revamped his catalog, and run the sales while Jay was away. "We were ensconced," Marjorie said. "We were a team."

Contradictorily, Jay's family and friends claimed Marjorie exaggerated her role in Jay's business. While she did answer the phone while Jay was away, most of the calls went straight to his cell phone. Jay handled all the sales and inventory and met with all the clients. Marjorie's involvement in Jayhawk International consisted of little more than filling a few orders and occasionally answering the phone, according to the Orbins.

In addition to helping out with the business, in whatever capacity, Marjorie found other ways to earn extra money. While working as a dancer over the years, Marjorie had learned to do her own nails and hair extensions. In Phoenix, she started doing hair extension procedures for a few of the women she met at the gym. A complete hair extension procedure takes twelve to thirteen hours of individually weaving strands of synthetic hair and attaching it to the natural hair. Out of her house, Marjorie did the processes for less than half of what a professional salon would charge. Her clients stopped by, drank coffee, and watched movies while Marjorie infused each small section of hair. One of her clients, a female body builder, would stop by every two months for the thirteen-hour sessions. Over time, they became close friends. "Marjorie was a great friend to me. She helped many in need and she was the most dedicated mother I ever knew," the friend recalled. "She was totally remarkable."

Twice a year Marjorie spoke to Michael J. Peter by phone. Each time they communicated, Marjorie told him that things between her and Jay were going well. Michael was happy to hear she had found the stability she had been searching for, but each time he spoke with her he felt a twinge of sadness. Michael had never married and although he had dated a slew of women, all his relationships eventually fell apart. Out of all the women in his life, Marjorie was the best. Each time he heard her voice, he lamented losing her.

"I miss you," Michael told her. "Why don't you come back to Florida?"

"I can't do that, Michael," Marjorie said. "I have a child now. Everything is different."

"You can bring your son," he pleaded.

"I would never do that," Marjorie said. "I would never take my son away from his father."

Marjorie's focus was entirely with Noah and being the perfect mom. She wanted him to have the best of everything. Appearances were always very important to Marjorie. She was equally consumed with how Noah looked as she was with herself. She dressed Noah in baby sailor suits and collared designer polo shirts with matching shoes. Noah was like her little fashion accessory.

An extraordinarily protective mother, Marjorie seemed unwilling to relinquish control of Noah, even for a moment. She barely allowed him out of her sight and did not trust anyone enough to even babysit. A strong bond formed between mother and son that went beyond that of a normal mother-son relationship. It was obsessive and unnaturally possessive.

For the most part, Marjorie was a loner who kept to herself and focused entirely on Noah. But as her son got older, she did make a few friends with whom she became very close. In 1999, Marjorie reconnected with Charity McLean, a career stripper she used to dance with a decade earlier. They first met while Marjorie was choreographing the Platinum Dolls but over the years they had lost contact.

Charity had since relocated to Scottsdale and coincidentally become a member at the same gym Marjorie belonged to. One day they ran into each other. At first, Charity didn't recognize Marjorie, but once they started talking they quickly reconnected. Marjorie longed for a friend and a connection to her previous life. Charity became one of her closest companions.

Charity was thirteen years younger than Marjorie, and at five foot zero, about eight inches shorter. Aside from the age and height, they looked quite similar. Like Marjorie, Charity was pretty and thin with large breasts, brown eyes, and bleach-blond hair. Charity became like Marjorie's little sister. Charity thought Marjorie had everything and said she was a "super mom" when it came to Noah. At the time, Charity was close friends with an openly gay gentleman named Bryan Todd Christy, who went by Todd, and his boyfriend, Oscar Moreno.

Todd worked as a cashier at the local Fry's grocery store where Marjorie shopped. When he first saw Marjorie at the grocery store, he immediately noticed her resemblance to Charity. "I mean hair, style, everything," Todd later told police. "She had the boobs, the body, you know, this and that. I go, 'Oh my god! That looks like Charity's sister or . . . Charity's mother.' " Although Todd never told Marjorie that he first thought Marjorie could be Charity's mother, because "Marjorie would be pissed . . . because age is everything to her."

After Charity and Marjorie became friends, Todd started hanging out with her all the time. Todd, who was in his forties, was slender with brown eyes and hair. He dressed in flamboyant attire and spent all of his money on designer clothes, jewelry, and watches. Todd came from a large, well-to-do family; he had four brothers and five sisters. One of his brothers, Tom Christy, was a retired FBI agent.

In his early twenties, Todd had married and had two children. When his children were very young, Todd realized he was homosexual and left his wife. She took sole custody of their children and later remarried. Todd's children didn't learn he was their real father until nearly a decade later. Todd had a lot of female friends and immediately took a liking to Marjorie.

Over the course of their friendship, Todd met Jay on a half dozen occasions when he had lunch or dinner at the Orbins' house. Todd thought Jay was a nice person. From Todd's experience, his sexuality sometimes posed a problem with straight men. He called it a "testosterone thing." But Jay wasn't like that. He was always very nice, polite, and respectful toward Todd.

Throughout their friendship, Marjorie would often confide in Todd. She told him that her relationship with Jay was more of an arrangement and they didn't have much of a sex life. "It was a relationship that worked for both. They both got out of it whatever they needed," Todd later told police. "Her, maybe financial support and a wonderful child. Him—would be a trophy wife."

Years later, Todd Christy would come to play an important role in Marjorie's life.

In 1999, after the lease expired on the Jayhawk International store front, Jay went back to selling wholesale merchandise full time. He purchased a warehouse in Phoenix and resumed traveling two weeks out of every month. It pained him to be away from Noah. He idolized his son and cherished the time he spent with him. Pictures of Noah were pasted on the dashboard of his work truck and he carried extra copies in his wallet and handed out copies to all his clients in every city he visited. "Have you seen how big Noah is getting?" Jay would ask, beaming with pride.

Jay had always been security conscious, but after Noah was born he became fanatical about safety. He developed a phobia of dying in a car accident. It wasn't an irrational fear. On every trip he seemed to see at least one terrible collision. These drivers were on their way to work or headed to church when suddenly, out of nowhere, a vehicle ran off the road and tore their worlds apart. No one ever seemed to see it coming. It could happen to him, Jay believed. He was driving more than three hundred thousand miles a year, and twice a year he drove clear across the country back east to Florida. It used to not worry him, but now he had a family. He was plagued by the thought of what would happen to Marjorie and Noah if he died. Much more than the average person, Jay worried about dying.

Because the assets were all in his name, Jay wanted to be sure Marjorie and Noah would be well provided for in the event of his death. He purchased two insurance policies that totaled nearly one million dollars. The sole beneficiary: Marjorie Orbin. In his will, Jay also bequeathed all of his assets to Marjorie and Noah.

One day he sat down and penned a letter that began, "Marjorie, if you are reading this, then something has happened to me." The letter went on to outline what Marjorie should do to maintain Jayhawk International if he were to die. Jay told Marjorie his "in case of" plan. All of the documents, Jay said, were secured inside the warehouse safe.

One day, Jay also pulled his friend Gary Dodge aside. "Gary, you know, if I die . . ."

"Get out of here." Gary rolled his eyes. "I don't want to talk about this."

"No!" Jay said. "This is serious."

By the expression on his face, Gary could tell Jay was upset. "Okay. What is it?"

"If I die," Jay repeated, "I want to make sure Marjorie and Noah are taken care of."

Jay told Gary he had purchased several life insurance policies and written letters instructing Marjorie what to do in the event of his death. Jay said he had placed these letters in different envelopes and labeled them with what should be done in the first few weeks and months with the business. The instructions were meticulous, covering everything from organizing the merchandise to mailing out a final farewell letter to his clients.

"In one of these letters," Jay said, "I told her that you would take my biggest buyers and that in exchange you would give them ten percent of those sales. Would you do that?"

"You're nuts, Jay!" Gary smirked. Gary knew Jay was a diligent planner but he thought the idea of a detailed death plan was crazy.

"No, Gary!" Jay grabbed his shoulder. "This is really important. This is to take care of my family!"

"Okay. Okay," he said. "Of course I will."

They didn't speak about it again. It was a seemingly innocuous conversation. But after Jay's death, the story would seem much more significant.

Although Jay was gone a lot for work, he remained actively involved in Noah's life. When he was out of town, Jay spoke to Noah every day by phone. At home, his focus was completely on his son. Each time Jay returned home was like Christmas. Noah had many different sports memorabilia collections and Jay added to them each time he came home, surprising him with baseball cards, gloves, figurines, and other collectables. Noah idolized his father. Like most young boys, he wanted to grow up to be just like his dad. "He was such a proud father. He loved that kid," Jake Jr. recalled. "When he was in town he'd be spending time with Noah, teaching him baseball, whiffle ball, reading stories to him all the time. That was all he did."

Occasionally, when Jay watched the news or listened to Rush Limbaugh, a curious Noah would sit on his lap and ask questions. Jay would tell him simple facts about politics and current events. One time while Jay was in Tucson for business, his son called.

"Dad, there's two great things happening tomorrow," Noah exclaimed.

"What's that?" Jay asked.

"President Bush is coming home, and so are you!" Noah said excitedly.

Jay thought his heart would burst with pride. He told several of his friends that story.

Jay and Marjorie's mutual adoration for their son was perhaps the only thing they ever really had in common. As Noah grew older, the couple began living increasingly separate lives. While their relationship had grown closer during the fertility treatments, the passion never really ignited between them. Before the pregnancy, they had a sparse sexual relationship, but after Noah was born, what little sex life they had completely dissolved. Marjorie showed practically no affection toward Jay. They hardly ever touched. "For the first few years, it didn't bother me. It was actually better that there wasn't anyone making sexual demands on me anyway," Marjorie recalled. "In many ways, it made our relationship easier. There are two of the main things in relationships that cause fights—money and sex. That one was just eliminated from our relationship."

But Marjorie was a very sexual person and over the years she began to long for a physical connection.

Despite their obvious differences, Jay's friends and family believed Jay and Marjorie's relationship "worked." Flipping through their family album, the Orbins appear to be a perfectly normal family. The family swam in their backyard pool, played games, took their dog to the park, and even posed for annual Christmas card pictures.

In one photo, Jay, Marjorie, and Noah were huddled together for the camera. Noah was wearing a blue striped shirt and an adorable grin. Jay was dressed in a Hawaiian button-down shirt with his arm around his son. Marjorie, wearing a black dress, leaned with her head towards Noah. Both parents had wide smiles on their faces. They look like an ordinary happy family.

Sadly, it was all a façade.

CHAPTER 7

There was a dark side to Marjorie that went beyond her troubles with the truth. To many, Marjorie appeared to be a devoted wife and mother. Others say that underneath that guise, she was a manipulative, conniving woman who would do anything to get what she wanted. Marjorie could be a loving, compassionate friend and a cold, deceitful enemy. She was capable of great kindness as well as behavior that can only be described as disturbed.

By 2000, Jay and Marjorie had been together for five years—nearly longer than her many previous marriages combined. While they led mostly separate lives, the arrangement seemed amicable. Jay paid the bills; Marjorie took care of Noah and kept up the house. But over the years, with Jay away more than half the year, Marjorie grew lonely. It was difficult and Marjorie often felt abandoned.

Noah was four. He was a sweet, precocious child, but also quite a handful. Impulsive and often irritable, Noah had difficulty paying attention, was easily distracted, and never listened. When Marjorie and Jay took him places, he would fidget and squirm in his seat, barely able to sit still. At home he spent hours running and spinning around the house. Jay and Marjorie were concerned. They took Noah to a doctor and he was diagnosed with Attention-Deficit

Hyperactivity Disorder, commonly known as ADHD. The doctor prescribed Ritalin, which helped him to calm down.

Still, Jay and Marjorie were anxious to find an activity that would help focus Noah's energy, so they enrolled him in karate classes at GilBride's Black Belt Academy, a karate studio located in a strip mall in north Phoenix. Inside the small building, floor to ceiling mirrors covered the walls and shiny gold trophies lined bookshelves around the studio. At the edge of the red and blue floor mats was a seating area for parents to watch as their children trained. From those seats, Marjorie watched every single practice.

At first Noah would not pay attention to his instructor. He would spin and do cartwheels on the mat, bumping into the other students. But after months of classes it seemed to click and Noah began to master the techniques and progress through the various belt levels. Noah excelled at martial arts and soon started competing in karate tournaments across the state.

Both parents were proud of his accomplishments, but Marjorie was fervent about his tournaments. She pressed and bleached his uniform until it was the brightest possible shade of white. Noah had to look his best; he had to be the best. Marjorie helped him practice his karate routine and traveled with him to each tournament. Because of Marjorie's training, Noah mastered fast, controlled routines. Soon karate trophies covered his bedroom dresser. "He just loved it," Marjorie recalled. "It changed who he was."

Several of the parents who took their children to the karate studio were friends. They chatted while they watched their children practice from the seating area and arranged group outings. Marjorie became a fixture at the GilBride's and the unofficial studio seamstress. All of the other parents brought their children's uniforms for her to alter and sew patches on. The studio owner was Mark GilBride, a muscular, well-built man in his forties, with thinning dark hair he wore slicked back. Marjorie was flirtatious with him and there were rumors of an affair between the two.

Mark, however, was happily married and later maintained that nothing developed.

At one tournament, Marjorie met a mother named Sharon Franco whose son was around Noah's age. Tall, thin, and beautiful with long brown hair streaked with blond highlights, Sharon was a divorced mother of two in her forties who had full custody of her daughter and son. Sharon wore skin-tight jeans and low-cut tank tops that showed off her perfect figure and sun-kissed tan. Marjorie always gravitated towards attractive people, and Sharon became a good friend.

They went out to lunches, and Sharon often came by the house to gossip. Marjorie bragged to Sharon about her exciting life as a former Las Vegas showgirl and her relationship with millionaire Michael J. Peter, whom she described as her ex-husband. She told Sharon about all of the strip clubs he owned and showed her the video of the episode of *Lifestyles of the Rich and Famous*. Sharon was impressed. "She had a great body, a great house, and she got to stay home," Sharon later told police. "I decided to hang out with her all the time."

Marjorie also seemed to go out of her way to be helpful—taking care of Sharon's children when she was in a jam and giving her advice about relationships. Sharon was grateful.

"I'm a good friend because all my girlfriends are strippers," Marjorie told her. "We look out for each other."

Sharon also thought Marjorie was highly educated and extremely intelligent. Marjorie told her she had advanced degrees in law and psychology and that she spoke several different languages, including Italian. Of course, those were lies. Marjorie had never attended a day of college; her education had ended with high school. She also told Sharon that her family was spread all over the country and that she did not have any brothers, but she did have a few sisters. Her family would not approve of her current lifestyle, Marjorie said, especially Jay.

By the way Marjorie interacted with Noah, Sharon believed she was a dedicated mother, albeit a tad strict. She noticed that Marjorie would hardly allow anyone to touch her son or get him food. Noah wasn't allowed to spend the night anywhere and if he had to go to the bathroom, Marjorie went inside the men's room or stood outside the door. She was obsessive about Noah. He hung around her neck and she would carry him everywhere.

At the karate studio, Sharon met Jay. She thought he seemed like a nice guy—he was funny and was easy to get along with. So Sharon was surprised when one day Marjorie pulled her aside and told her their entire relationship was a sham. Marjorie said she only came to Phoenix because she realized she could make some money. She wanted a baby, but said Jay was sterile. He was the reason they needed fertility treatments, and his genes "had to be washed," so that there was very little of Jay in Noah. Marjorie described her relationship with Jay as an "arrangement."

"Jay likes the arrangement because he has a beautiful wife and child to show off," Marjorie told Sharon.

"So there's nothing between you, sexually?" Sharon asked.

"We have no relationship at all." Marjorie sighed. "He's not there for me."

Marjorie's list of grievances was staggering. She complained that Jay had a "small penis," and "did not satisfy her sexually." Jay was a "controlling pain in the ass," Marjorie said, and if she did not follow his rules she would have no recourse for Noah. Jay would kick her out onto the street, with nothing, no money, and leave her to fend for herself. The only reason she put up with Jay was because he took care of her and Noah financially. "He's just a paycheck," Marjorie told Sharon. Marjorie also said she was sure Jay had a girlfriend in Tucson, but she had to stay faithful to him. "If I ever cheated on him," Marjorie said, "I would be out on the streets and be without Noah." Sha ron felt sad for Marjorie. She thought she was a nice woman trapped in a loveless marriage.

In 2002, around the time Noah started kindergarten, Jay and Marjorie bought a 2,600-square-foot house at 17445 N. 55th Street in an upscale suburb of northeast Phoenix. The house was a single-story, four-bedroom, four-bathroom home with a three-car garage, originally built in 1996. It was stucco, painted light red, and the front yard was landscaped with gravel and desert plants. A walkway cut through the yard, leading up to a covered arched entryway. In the backyard were an expansive built-in pool and a small grassy area.

Marjorie loved the house and was eager to make it her dream home. She focused her energy on remodeling and decorating—tiling the floors and sponge painting the walls. She bought all new furniture, curtains, and appliances, repositioned the kitchen island twice and even replaced the kitchen sink. With Noah so young, they needed to install a fence around the pool. Jay got several quotes from different fencing companies. Instead, Marjorie purchased the concrete and single-handedly installed a white wrought-iron fence for a fraction of the cost.

The improvement projects seemed to be for more than just the home. They gave Marjorie goals, and occupied her frantic mind. She spent months remodeling, crossing project after project off her to-do list, until everything was perfect.

That fall Noah started school at Copper Canyon Elementary, one of the top-ranked public schools in the Paradise Valley School District. With his ADHD, Noah struggled at first but over time he became a good student.

Marjorie, however, did not make many friends in her new neighborhood. She was known as a loner who kept to herself, neighbors recalled. One neighbor described her as "the most unfriendly person I have ever met." A mother at Noah's new school said she was known as a "Barbie" among the parents.

Jan Beeso, a neighbor of Jay and Marjorie, came to know the couple through her son. The boys attended the same school and became friends. The few times she met Marjorie, however, she thought she seemed aloof and distant. One Halloween Jan ran into Marjorie and Noah while they were out trick-or-treating.

"Where's Jay?" Jan asked.

"He can't walk this far," she said snidely. "He is obese."

Jan was taken aback. She had met Jay a few times and didn't find him to be obese. Jan took her son by the hand and they kept walking.

Over the years Jay had put on some extra weight. On the road he would eat at McDonald's and Burger King and order pizzas at his hotel room. At his heaviest, Jay weighed close to 280 pounds. Marjorie often talked about Jay's weight. At social gatherings, when someone asked about her husband, Marjorie would point Jay out as "the fat guy over there."

Admittedly, Marjorie was bothered by Jay's weight gain. At home when Jay reached for a soda or bag of chips, Marjorie would make comments like, "do you really need that?" Often, she encouraged him to take better care of his health. "If I ever mentioned that he should exercise or eat healthier, it made him mad," Marjorie recalled. "He didn't want to talk about it."

Consumed with her own physical appearance, Marjorie spent hours each day at the gym. When Noah was born, she gained some extra weight, which made her uncomfortable. She even went to a plastic surgeon and got a $7,800 quote for liposuction, but decided to first try to get it off by diet and exercise. Marjorie became disciplined, working out every day for hours and eating the same prepared meals each day for seven months.

The local L.A. Fitness became like her second home. Friends at the gym say she was obsessive about her workout routine. Men took notice of Marjorie at the gym when she flaunted her body in skimpy workout outfits. She loved the attention. Physically, Marjorie became remarkably strong for a woman. Lifting free weights with the men, she could bench press upward of a hundred pounds. She took pride in her body and enjoyed showing off her strength.

By 2003, Jay was attending more and more of Noah's karate tournaments. He was well liked among the other parents. "Jay was a good, likeable person," one father said. "He worshiped Noah and was very supportive of his karate." But a few of the parents started to notice a change in Marjorie. While she had always been competitive, Marjorie became obsessive, almost vicious, about Noah winning. At his tournaments, Marjorie would turn to Sharon Franco and make nasty comments about the other boy Noah was competing against.

Sharon would later tell police she believed Marjorie had gone so far as to sabotage the children Noah competed against. On several occasions, Sharon claimed, Marjorie sprinkled itching powder in the other boy's uniforms so they couldn't compete and Noah would win by default.

Janice Matthews's son took classes at the same karate studio. He was very talented at martial arts, and Marjorie seemed jealous the boy was better than Noah. One day an instructor praised Janice's son as one of the best students in the class. Marjorie was furious and seemed to direct her anger at Janice. Marjorie started asking the other parents questions about her: "What is she wearing?" "What is she doing?" "Where is she going?"

Marjorie wanted to know anything she could about Janice. She started spreading cruel rumors about her to the other parents. Suddenly, Janice started receiving bizarre phone calls. Marjorie's number would show up on the caller ID, but when she answered the phone no one spoke. One day when Janice took her son to school, she noticed graffiti on the walls mocking her son. Janice was shocked and embarrassed.

A few days later, Janice and her son went to the karate studio and noticed a letter plastered around the studio and placed under the windshield wipers of the cars in the parking lot. The lengthy, typewritten letter libeled Janice and her son. When she read the letter, Janice burst into tears. Hysterically, she went around the studio collecting more than two hundred copies. The letter was anonymous, but Janice was sure Marjorie was the sender. Many of the other parents believed Marjorie was behind it. "Everyone was sure Marjorie sent the letter," recalled one father. "But she never admitted to it."

Studio owner Mark GilBride confronted Marjorie about the letter, but she denied it. Marjorie said she believed Janice was behind the letter. "They're just looking for attention," Marjorie said. "That's why they're blaming me."

Janice was terrified. She believed Marjorie was stalking her.

"She's trying to ruin my life," Janice told the other parents. "She's terrorizing me, calling me at all hours and hanging up. I'm afraid!"

For the next year, Janice lived in constant fear. She switched her son's karate classes to another day and notified their school about the problems with Marjorie. But Janice never stopped looking over her shoulder. When she was driving, Janice would nervously glance in the rearview mirror, constantly watching for Marjorie's car. At home, she would peer through the blinds, expecting to see Marjorie looming outside the front door. For months, Janice wouldn't even allow her children to play outside without supervision. She felt terrorized.

After the letter incident, rumors swirled about Marjorie. There was talk of a lesbian relationship and an affair she had with the owner of the karate studio. To some, it seemed like Marjorie had multiple personalities. Many who got a glimpse of Marjorie's sinister side would often question whether she may have been bipolar or had some other mental disorder. Marjorie had never been diagnosed or treated for any mental condition. "She would do anything for anyone," one father said. "But she was also a very cold woman."

When Sharon Franco heard about the letter, she confronted Marjorie, who again claimed Janice was lying. At the time, Sharon believed her friend. She knew Marjorie was jealous of Janice, but she didn't want to believe her friend was capable of doing something so despicable. Soon, Sharon would have reason to believe it was all true.

By late 2003, Marjorie seemed dissatisfied with Jay and her mundane life as a housewife. With Noah in school and Jay gone half of the month, Marjorie spent most of her days alone. For years Noah had been the center of her world. Now he was older and Marjorie had grown lonely and discontent. She filled her days shopping, creating home improvement projects, and working out at the gym. But the quiet life she once craved now seemed dreary.

Marjorie had once loved Jay for what he did for her and for giving her Noah. Gradually, however, that love appeared to develop into disdain. She had become resentful. She thought that he didn't deserve her. In her eyes Jay developed more and more flaws. He was overweight, sloppy, and disgusting. The more time Jay spent on the road, the more Marjorie realized she was happier when he wasn't around.

Marjorie wanted an attractive, passionate lover who would make her feel desired. She was ready to move on with her life and she began looking for something more. But there was a problem—Noah. Marjorie told Sharon Franco she was ready to leave Jay. Because Sharon had full custody of both of her children, Marjorie began asking a lot of legal questions. Losing even partial custody of Noah to Jay was not an option, Marjorie said.

"He'll never take custody of Noah," Marjorie told Sharon. "If Jay ever tries, I'll take care of him."

If anything happened to Jay, Marjorie said, she would be provided for with his huge life insurance policies. She had a lot of money and merchandise stashed and she knew how to pawn items and get money quickly when she needed it. Sharon laughed it off. She thought Marjorie was just being facetious.

Gradually, Marjorie's threats became increasingly overt and disconcerting.

A year earlier, Marjorie's friend Charity McLean had left Scottsdale and moved to Las Vegas to take a job stripping at the Spearmint Rhino. Despite the distance, Marjorie and Charity remained close friends. Sometimes they spoke two or three times a day. Marjorie told Charity that both she and Jay had what they wanted from the relationship—he was a good father and he did a lot for her. But now Marjorie seemed ready to separate from her husband. She talked about Jay moving out of the house and finding someone new. One day, Marjorie said, both she and Jay would each find the love they deserved.

For Marjorie; it appeared the marriage was over. Jay, however, hadn't seemed to notice. While Marjorie spoke openly about leaving her husband, Jay never mentioned anything to anyone about splitting from Marjorie. Jay's family and friends never perceived a change in his behavior. Everything appeared perfectly normal. Jay continued to grow his business. He made wise investments through his E Trade stock account and donated money to the George W. Bush re-election campaign. When he was at home he spent time with Noah and taught him how to hit a softball. Occasionally he went to the strip club with his friends, although not nearly as often as he did before he was married. If Jay believed his relationship was in trouble, he told no one. If he was aware of the way Marjorie felt about him, he didn't seem bothered.

In early 2004, Jay purchased a massive warehouse to base Jayhawk International at 2629 S. 21st Street in Phoenix. The 4,000-square-foot building was located in a small strip mall in a commercial district of south Phoenix. The warehouse consisted of four small offices in the front and a large open warehouse in the back. South of the entryway was a carpeted receptionist area, which consisted of a desk and file cabinets on the back wall. Two separate doorways led from the front office to the rear warehouse. In the lobby was a receptionist area and restroom. The east wall consisted of floor-to-ceiling metal, cage-like bars. On the rear wall was a large overhead garage door where Jay parked his white cargo truck.

The main warehouse was a large open room with a cement floor, which Jay filled with shelf units placed in rows to create aisles. Kachina dolls, pottery, Native Amercian artifacts, bow and arrow sets, baskets, and opaque storage boxes filled with jewelry lined the shelves. The logo on the storefront was of a hawk, its wings spread broadly; on top of the image were the words JAYHAWK INTERNATIONAL.

Jay was regimented. Each weekday he was in town he was at the warehouse by eight a.m. He took orders, packed boxes, arranged merchandise, moved hundred-pound crates, and sent dozens of shipments each week.

By 2004, Jay's business was bigger than ever—he had upward of two million dollars worth of merchandise on hand and was earning about $200,000 to $300,000 a year. Jay had single-handedly built a thriving, successful business. Next to his son, it was his proudest accomplishment.

Meanwhile, with her home perfectly remodeled and decorated, Marjorie turned her attention on herself. Her new goal was to lose weight and get in better shape. She ramped up her exercise routine and began spending three or four hours a day at the gym. Marjorie became fanatical about working out and went on extreme crash diets. Soon she dropped down to about 120 pounds. At five foot eight, she was stick thin. Sharon Franco admired her dedication and the results she was getting at the gym. She started working out with her.

Marjorie was hardcore about losing weight and was willing to go to extremes. Marjorie boasted to Sharon about one of her extreme weight-loss techniques—crushing up her son's Ritalin and snorting it. For children diagnosed with ADHD, Ritalin has a calming effect. But on people not afflicted with the disorder it has the opposite effect. Similar to cocaine, Ritalin will cause energy and weight loss in drug abusers. Once, Sharon said, Marjorie asked her to find cocaine for her.

"Whatever," Sharon said, rolling her eyes. "I don't know where to get that stuff."

Around this time, Sharon became alarmed by some strange behavior on Marjorie's part. Sharon knew Marjorie was overprotective—she wouldn't even allow Sharon's teenage daughter, a certified babysitter, to watch Noah. But what Sharon once viewed as a tad overprotective, she now saw as obsessive. Marjorie always had to have complete control over Noah. When Jay was out of town, Sharon said Marjorie would give Noah an "overdose" of Ritalin so he would fall asleep and no one would have to watch him.

It wasn't just Noah that Marjorie controlled. Marjorie often bragged about her ability to control men. When she and Jay first got married, Marjorie told Sharon that each time he went to see his friends she would put medication in his drink that would make him vomit and get diarrhea. This was so he would get sick and come home early. Marjorie said this would cause Jay to associate seeing his friends with getting sick. Marjorie believed that over time Jay would forget about seeing them—like training a dog. Sharon found this outrageous. But she was also confused— Marjorie claimed Jay was the controlling one.

* * *

Sexually, Marjorie was insatiable. She often complained that Jay showed her no affection and didn't fulfill her needs. Marjorie told numerous people that Jay was not well endowed and was unable to satisfy her. Their relationship had become platonic, she claimed. But Marjorie still longed for passion and companionship. "Jay and my relationship was very personally respectful, but we didn't even touch for years," Marjorie recalled. "Not even a hand on the shoulder. For years the only physical contact I had was with my son."

Only Marjorie knows how many lovers she had while married to Jay. But in 2004, the year of Jay's murder, there were at least two. Both former lovers would later testify in court about the explicit sexual details of their relationships. Those two men were at complete opposite ends of the spectrum—one was a sixty-year-old man, the other a teenage boy.

Jessiah Rueckert was a nineteen-year-old karate instructor at GilBride's karate studio. With short dark hair and a goatee, Jessiah was tall and fit, with bright blue eyes and a long slender face. On his bicep was a tribal-style tattoo and he typically wore a silver chain around his neck. A black belt who had trained in karate since he was a child, Jessiah dreamed of one day becoming a cop and had plans to apply to the police academy. Jessiah was the son of Noah's karate instructor, Steve Rueckert.

Jessiah was also Sharon Franco's boyfriend.

Sharon had met Jessiah at GilBride's and they began dating months prior to his and Marjorie's affair. Although Jessiah was half her age, Sharon was infatuated.

"He's so hot!" Marjorie told Sharon. "I'm jealous."

To Sharon, Marjorie would make comments about how she wished she was with such a virile younger man. Marjorie had known Jessiah since the age of fourteen, but over the last several years she had watched him grow into an attractive young man. One day Marjorie offered to alter Jessiah's uniform. When he stopped by Marjorie's house, she was very flirtatious. As he handed her the uniform, she leaned forward and whispered in his ear a sexually explicit remark. Soon she had seduced Jessiah.

They began a steamy, secret affair. When Jay was out of town, Jessiah would come to her house and they would make love in the Orbins' bed. After sex, Marjorie would tell Jessiah how unhappy she was with Jay.

"I deserve more," Marjorie said. "This is not what I wanted."

Marjorie told Jessiah she was leaving Jay and wanted to be with him.

Throughout the course of their relationship, Sharon Franco had no idea about the affair or her friend's betrayal.

Marjorie's affair with Jessiah lasted for months. But the closer Jessiah became with Sharon, the further he withdrew from Marjorie. She seemed to sense Jessiah was moving on because she became more intense and sexually experimental. Marjorie started talking about how she wanted to have a threesome with Sharon and Jessiah.

It was all getting too strange for Jessiah. Their affair had been going on for too long. He felt guilty and worried that Sharon was going to find out. Jessiah loved Sharon; Marjorie was just a fling. In March 2004, Jessiah told Marjorie he wanted to stop seeing her. She was livid. She started yelling at Jessiah, pleading with him not to leave her. Marjorie even threatened to call Sharon and tell her of their affair.

"Jay and I are getting divorced," Marjorie screamed. "I need someone to be with!"

That same day Marjorie and Sharon's friendship came to an abrupt end. Earlier in the morning Sharon had gone to the courthouse in downtown Phoenix to dispute a traffic ticket. While she was waiting, Sharon called Marjorie from her cell phone. They chatted as usual, gossiping about the parents at the karate class. A few hours later, Jessiah called. He seemed distressed and anxious. Jessiah said Marjorie called him out of nowhere claiming Sharon was having sex with another man. Jessiah said he knew Marjorie was lying but it was very strange.

"She just went off," Jessiah said. "She was freaking out."

Sharon was stunned. She thought Marjorie was trying to break them up so she could be with Jessiah. Sharon began to see Marjorie in a new light. She began to believe her friend was emotionally disturbed and she decided to cut her out of her life. She stopped taking her phone calls.

That was when things got scary.

Marjorie called Mark GilBride and Jessiah's father Steve Rueckert and admitted her affair with Jessiah. Then, Sharon claimed, Marjorie started to stalk her. She started calling her cell and work phones compulsively, ten to twenty times a day. Sometimes she would leave messages about having sex with Jessiah; other times she wouldn't say anything at all. This went on for weeks. Sharon became terrified.

She thought back to what Janice Matthews had told her about being terrorized by Marjorie. Suddenly, Sharon realized it was all true. Sharon moved, installed an alarm on her new house, and changed her last name. She was terrified that Marjorie would find out where she lived or where her kids went to school. She told her children that if they ever saw Marjorie to call the police. "If you see her, run and get an adult," Sharon told them.

Sharon felt hurt and deceived by her former close friend. She wouldn't learn the extent of Marjorie's betrayal until much later.

CHAPTER 8

The summer of 2004 brought scorching temperatures to the Valley of the Sun. Seeking solace from the blistering heat, Marjorie took Noah to the movie theater at the Desert Ridge Marketplace, an outdoor shopping plaza in northeast Phoenix. For the next two hours she and Noah munched on stale theater popcorn and candy in air-conditioned comfort. The movie ended around seven p.m.; the sun was still hanging low in the sky. As they exited the theater, warm air filled their lungs. They strolled across the outdoor plaza toward a large plateau fountain where children were laughing, dancing, and splashing in the water. Behind the fountain a band was playing.

Marjorie stopped, momentarily mesmerized by the sight. The music and laughter seemed to spin around her. "It was all so magical and beautiful, I could hardly believe it," Marjorie wrote in a flowery love letter detailing the memorable night. She grabbed Noah by the hand. They walked to a café and sat down at a table on the patio. Suddenly Marjorie was overcome by an overwhelming sense of emptiness. She had Noah by her side, but she still felt incomplete. She looked up at the sky. Puffy white clouds stood out against the dimming sun. She lowered her head; her eyes filled with tears. "I became overwhelmed with feelings of loneliness and longing for someone to truly love and share such beautiful nights with," she wrote. "Something happened that night. Someone heard my prayers."

The next day she would meet a man who would play a large part in her life during the summer of 2004. His name was Larry Weisberg.

The following morning Marjorie dressed in draw-string yoga pants and a sports bra and swept her hair into a high ponytail on the top of her head. Around nine a.m., she headed to L.A. Fitness for her morning workout routine. Noah came along to play in the gym's child-care room. Toward the end of her workout Marjorie noticed an attractive older man watching her as he jogged on the treadmill. They locked eyes for a moment but he looked away. He was muscular and tan with soft blue eyes and strong, masculine features. His feathered blond hair was graying at the sides.

The man was Larry Weisberg, a sixty-year-old divorced father of two who worked as a production manager for Tri Star Visual Communications, a full-service graphic design and production company in Phoenix. Marjorie was drawn to Larry. As he got off the treadmill, she approached him and introduced herself.

"Do you have any children?" she asked.

Larry grinned. "I actually have two grown children and two grandsons."

He told her he was very close with his grandsons and cherished the time he spent with them. Marjorie smiled. It meant a lot to her that he liked children. "I have a little boy named Noah," she said.

In a letter, Marjorie wrote that the moment she met Larry was like a "slow motion scene in a movie . . . I remember nodding and responding, but I don't remember hearing anything but the sounds of the music and children's laughter from the night before as I looked into your eyes. My head was spinning. I had to struggle to keep my composure. I could not get you out of my mind after that."

For the next week, Marjorie fantasized about Larry. Each time she went back to the gym, she glanced around, hoping to run into him again. The following Saturday, she noticed Larry lifting weights. Her heart fluttered. She wrote about how she was drawn to him by "some kind of gravitational pull."

"I was hoping to run into you," she said coyly as she approached him. She handed him a piece of paper with her phone number on it. "Call me."

Larry looked down at the piece of paper in his hand and then at the large diamond ring on her left ring finger.

He smiled sheepishly. "You're married."

"No. I'm not." Marjorie shook her head.

"Well, that ring, to me, indicates that you're married," Larry said.

"I'm divorced," Marjorie insisted. "I just wear this to keep other men away."

Marjorie told Larry that she had been divorced for nearly seven years and that her ex-husband was a traveling salesman. Larry was flattered that a younger, attractive woman seemed so interested in him. He had seen her at the gym before and found her striking.

"Given that you aren't married," Larry said, "what are you doing tomorrow?"

The next night, over dinner, Marjorie spoke at length about Jay and her living arrangement. Marjorie explained how for his business her "ex" traveled the majority of the year. When he was in town, he lived at his warehouse and slept in a bunk bed. Occasionally, he would come by the house and sleep on the couch. The $500 Jay gave her every week—Marjorie said that was alimony and child support. She and her ex had never had a relationship to speak of, even from the beginning. Noah's not even his child because his sperm wasn't strong enough, Marjorie claimed. "He has no idea."

For the next few weeks, Larry and Marjorie got to know each other over drinks, lunches, dinner, and run-ins at the gym. After a few dates, Marjorie went back to Larry's house and they made love for the first time in his bed.

Marjorie was impetuous. Very quickly the affair went from a casual fling to a serious relationship. Marjorie seemed to see in Larry the solution to all of her woes. In her writing, she described Larry as her "one true love." She said he was "her soul," and told him, "I love you in so many ways I have never known."

She had only known Larry for a few weeks and didn't know much about his background, personality, or character. Somehow, that didn't seem too terribly important to Marjorie. She simply pasted the qualities she was looking for in an ideal man over the top of who Larry actually was. Marjorie wanted a new man in her life. That summer that man was Larry.

Marjorie envisioned starting a new life with Larry. Over the course of their relationship, she wrote dozens of notes, letters, and cards to Larry. In those letters she described how she stopped letting people into her life, but the moment she saw Larry, she dropped all of her barriers. "I have been alone for so long. I created my own little isolated environment. Men often ask me out or attempt to pursue me. I don't seem to be able to even pretend to show interest in people that are average," she wrote. "When you spoke to me with such tenderness and emotion about how much you adore your children and how special your grandchildren are to you, it melted me. It is clear to me that your huge heart, your devotion to those you love, and your big arms around me are what I need and why I have spent so long unwilling to settle for anything less."

Marjorie also described their intense sexual connection. "You are sexy and dangerous and hot. When you hold me I respond like nothing I've known. You touch me and I'm on fire."

Larry was a practical man, a sensible realist, but he was

taken with Marjorie. He had been alone for years and had forgotten how nice it was to have a partner. Marjorie was beautiful, passionate, exciting, and intense. She told him he was sexy and made him feel wanted in a way he hadn't felt in years.

Like so many men before him, Larry was seduced by Marjorie's charms.

But when he first came to her house, he quickly realized that her ex-husband was more than just occasionally sleeping on the couch. It was obvious a man was living there. Jay's clothes were hanging in the closet and his possessions were scattered across the house. Marjorie made excuses about how Jay traveled so often, he just left his stuff at her place.

To Larry, it seemed like Marjorie was still deeply entangled with her ex. He had reservations about starting a relationship with a woman who hadn't moved on from her past. If he and Marjorie were going to be together, Larry wasn't willing to share her.

"You know you're going to have to do something about the living arrangements," he told her matter-of-factly.

"I know," Marjorie said. "I spoke with Jay. I told him it's time for him to move out."

"And he was okay with that?" Larry asked.

"He asked if there was somebody else," Marjorie said quietly. "I didn't answer him."

Marjorie said that Jay understood it was over and was looking for a place of his own, near Noah's school, to stay close to his son. Jay had even consulted a realtor named Tom Ellis, Marjorie said, who was showing him houses. According to Marjorie, Jay agreed to give her the house and pay it off in full so Noah's life would not be disrupted. A week or so later, Marjorie told Larry that Jay had found a house and was making an offer. Larry appeared to believe that Marjorie's "ex-husband" was moving out. With Jay out of the way, he grew closer to her.

One Saturday afternoon, he took Marjorie and Noah to

meet his daughter, Jodi, and his two grandsons. Jodi Weisberg was in her mid-thirties, with a sturdy frame, shoulder-length brown hair and hazel eyes. She and her husband, Brad Fritz, lived in a nice neighborhood across from a park.

Initially, Jodi thought Marjorie seemed like a nice woman and a devoted mother. Over the next couple of months, she spent a lot of time with Marjorie. Noah was close in age with Larry's eldest grandson, Devon, and they brought the boys to the park to play. During one get-together, Marjorie pulled Jodi aside to complain about Jay. She called him a "Disneyland Dad" who was gone all the time and made it up to Noah with gifts and outings. She said Noah needed a good father figure; she wanted that man to be Larry.

"Noah thinks Larry *is* his dad," Marjorie said.

Jodi flinched; she gave Marjorie a surprised look. "Really?"

On several occasions, the normally over-protective Marjorie allowed Jodi to watch her son overnight while she and Larry went on dates. One night, after dropping off Noah at Jodi's house, they went back to Marjorie's place. They were chatting on the couch when, as she did during many of their conversations, she brought up their future. Marjorie wanted them to live together. Larry was entranced by this mysterious, impetuous woman who came into his life and stirred up his world. Increasingly, he was beginning to picture their future together.

By the end of July, Marjorie and Larry spoke every day. Larry was sleeping at the house every Friday and Saturday night, when Jay was out of town, and a couple of nights during the week. Each morning when Jay left for the office, Marjorie's first call was to Larry. By August, they were in a committed relationship. She continued to press him about living together. With her words, Marjorie painted an enticing picture of their future. "I cannot wait to be able to see you every day and wrap my arms around you when you come home." When Jay moved out, Larry would be free to move in, she said. They even discussed the possibility of selling both their houses, merging their funds, and buying a new house together.

Sadly, Jay was completely in the dark about Marjorie's plans with her new lover. Contrary to what Marjorie had told Larry, Jay was not considering moving out and he hadn't made an offer on any house. Even by Marjorie's own account, Jay had no idea she was having an affair.

As the sweltering summer was winding down, Marjorie and Larry's romance was growing hotter. Marjorie had ignited a passion in Larry. He was bewitched by Marjorie and how she made him feel.

Throughout her life, Marjorie's relationships often ran congruently. This situation, however, was exceptionally messy. She was living two lives: one as Jay's doting wife, another as Larry's girlfriend. It was a dangerous game. Both men believed they had a relationship and a future with Marjorie.

The volatile situation was about to explode.

CHAPTER 9

A concert of frenzied arcade melodies resonated throughout Jillian's game room at the Desert Ridge Marketplace. Animated spacecraft, motorcycles, monsters, and zombies flickered across the large video screens as tickets spilled from the games. Children wiggled joysticks, tossed skee balls, and fished stuffed animals from crane machines.

Near the rear of the arcade, gazing mesmerized at the screen, Noah was seated behind the steering wheel of Dale Earnhardt's No. 3 car, racing around the digital NASCAR track. Beside him in the adjacent game, his father was following closely in his virtual car. As they approached the final lap, Jay eased up on the gas pedal, allowing the No. 3 car to increase its lead. Noah's car burst past the checked tape, causing the red light on the top of his machine to glow brightly. He turned to his father, a toothy grin plastered across his face.

"I won, Dad!" Noah exclaimed.

"Alright, buddy!" Jay replied.

A slight boy with a shaggy blond bowl cut, Noah was dressed in a tiny designer striped polo shirt and jean shorts. He looked at his dad with adoration as Jay helped him down from the game's driver seat.

It was August 26, 2004, Noah's eighth birthday. And it

would be the last day he would ever see his father alive. Jay Orbin had just thirteen days left to live.

Noah ran over toward his mother, who was seated at a barstool with Jay's parents. Marjorie glanced down at her son. "Are you ready for cake and presents?"

Noah nodded his head. "Yep."

It was a family tradition that each birthday Jay's family celebrated together by going out to dinner. This year, Noah wanted to spend it at Jillian's, a massive entertainment complex that featured video games, a billiards lounge, a bowling area, and two restaurants.

That afternoon, the arcade hosted a birthday party for Noah and several of his friends. Jay's parents and some of his friends, including Marshall Roosin and his wife, attended as well. Everyone dined on burgers and chicken wings, and Noah spent hours playing games with his father and friends. Afterward, they bowled and everyone crowded around the high-top tables to sing "Happy Birthday" as Jay carried out a carrot cake glowing with candles.

"Make a wish," he said as Noah blew out the candles. When Noah saw his large pile of presents, his eyes went wide with excitement. One by one he tore off wrapping paper, uncovering sport's memorabilia, collectables, toys, games, and clothes. His favorite gift: a Nintendo Game Boy Advance.

Marjorie chatted pleasantly with Jay's parents and smiled normally in all the pictures. That night, Jay tucked his son into bed and gave him a hug. Noah wrapped his arms around his dad's wide neck and squeezed tightly. "I love you, Dad."

"I love you, too, son," Jay said as he kissed Noah on the cheek.

Early the next morning, Jay packed a duffle bag with clothes and dressed in his typical short-sleeve button-down shirt, shorts, and tennis shoes. Marjorie made him coffee and Jay grabbed his bag, keys, and briefcase and left the house, headed for his warehouse.

"I'll call you when I get to Tucson," Jay said. "I love you."

"You too," she responded evasively.

Jay would spend his last two weeks on earth conducting business as usual. If he sensed something was wrong with his marriage, he didn't mention it to anyone. He never complained about his wife or seemed the slightest bit dissatisfied with their relationship. On the contrary, Jay seemed happy in his final days. He didn't seem to notice any signs that Marjorie had been engaging in a sordid affair. It was possible he was truly unaware. But if he had even the slightest inkling that Marjorie was being unfaithful, perhaps there was a reason he told no one. Jay was an intensely private man who didn't believe his personal problems were anyone else's concern. His entire life, in every business endeavor he tackled, Jay was a success. Failure was not something he was accustomed to and admitting his marriage was failing would have caused him tremendous embarrassment.

For the last year of his life, Jay had buried himself in his work. When he was at home he doted on his son, while Marjorie helped with the business, attended occasional family functions, and kept the house. Maybe Jay was unaware Marjorie was leading a secret second life. Maybe he ignored that gnawing feeling in his gut that something was terribly wrong. Or, maybe he knew but bore the burden in silence. The only person who knows for sure wouldn't live to talk about it.

What is known is that Jay was harboring his own secret from his family and friends. After his death, the truth would be exposed.

On the morning of Friday, August 27, Jay arrived at his business warehouse, driving the beat-up green-and-tan Ford Bronco that had once belonged to Marjorie. He parked in the garage and transferred his bags to the cab of his twenty-four-foot white cargo truck. For the next few hours he loaded the back of the truck with clear storage boxes filled with hundreds of thousands of dollars worth of Kachina dolls, turquoise jewelry, Native American artifacts, and Southwestern art.

Before leaving the warehouse, Jay opened the wall safe, removed a .38 pistol, and slid it in the well-worn tan Louis Vuitton briefcase he carried with him wherever he went. Wholesale jewelry sales were a high-risk business and Jay was fanatical about security. He traveled with multiple weapons, one in his briefcase and one in the driver's side console of the truck, and was secretive about which routes he took.

Around noon, Jay left Phoenix and headed east for a planned business trip to Florida to sell a large amount of turquoise jewelry. Jay's usual trips were two weeks, but four times a year Jay traveled all the way across the southern United States and into Florida. For this trip, Jay was scheduled to be away for three weeks.

Unexpected circumstances, however, would cut that trip short.

As soon as Jay left the house that morning, Marjorie called Larry Weisberg. "I miss you."

After work, Larry came by the house with an overnight bag. It had been days since Marjorie had been with Larry and she longed to see him again. Larry wrapped his arm around her waist and slid his hand up her thigh as they shared a long, passionate kiss.

She pulled back from his lips and smiled seductively. "I want you."

As Noah played games in the other room, she and Larry went to the master bedroom. Fervently they ripped off each other's clothes and made love in the Orbins' bed.

In early September 2004, a ferocious storm was brewing over the Atlantic Ocean, miles off the coast of Florida. As the storm approached the Florida panhandle, fierce 145-mile-per-hour winds tore through suburbs, ripping roofs off houses, closing schools, and canceling football games. The entire state, for 435 miles from Tallahassee to Key West, was enveloped by rain and wind. The storm, dubbed Hurricane Frances, was a Category 4 and the third major hurricane of the deadly season, which caused roughly $50 billion in damages and 3,132 deaths. As Jay headed toward the East Coast, he heard the news on the radio that the storm was approaching Florida. Hoping that it would soon pass, Jay continued en route.

Jay's first stop was in Tucson, Arizona. He checked into the La Quinta Inn, a cheap motel he frequented, and spent the day selling merchandise to a few of his regular retailers. That night he went to TD's Showclub, an upscale strip joint. Later, from his room, he made nine calls to Nora Bess, a dancer at the club. She never answered the phone.

The following morning Jay left for Las Cruces, New Mexico. For the next few days he conducted business and made sales. From August 29 through August 31, he stopped in San Antonio and Houston, Texas, and then headed towards New Orleans, Louisiana. The road was lonely but Jay made the most of it. Each weekday at noon he filled three hours listening to Rush Limbaugh's radio program. A staunch Republican, Jay hung on Rush's every word.

Along the 1,700-mile trek from Phoenix to Florida, Jay kept in close contact with his family by phone, calling his mother nearly every day. Joann was a Democrat and sometimes he called just to discuss politics. Every couple of days he would also speak to his friends Marshall Roosin, Mario Olivarez, and Gary Dodge. If they called and he was busy, or out of cell phone range, Jay would usually return the calls within an hour. He also spoke with Marjorie and Noah sometimes two or three times a day.

In early September, Jay arrived in Pensacola, Florida. Hurricane Frances was massive and sluggish, crawling across the state at a snail's pace. As it neared east central

Florida it appeared to weaken and stall, but by September 3, it became clear to Jay that the vast storm would make business nearly impossible. Frustrated, he turned his truck around and headed home.

On the drive back toward Arizona, Jay called Marjorie. He told her about the storm damage and flooding he had seen across Louisiana and into Florida. Irritated that the trip had been a bust, Jay complained that several of his customers had closed their businesses. On top of that, many of his biggest clients had not bought as much merchandise as he expected because of a drop in tourism due to the hurricane. For the next four days Jay wearily made his way through Birmingham, Alabama; Jackson, Mississippi; and back across Louisiana and Texas, staying at motels along the way.

Marjorie, meanwhile, continued to see Larry almost every day. By late August, Larry was staying at Marjorie's house several nights a week. They went out to dinners and to the movies, while Jodi babysat.

At around 11:30 a.m. on September 7, Jay arrived in Tucson, a mere 120 miles from home. He checked back into the La Quinta Inn, room 112, and ordered dinner from Pizza Hut.

On Wednesday, September 8, Jay woke up early to make business calls and take orders. He planned on being home that afternoon, by the time Noah got home from school. It was Jay's forty-fifth birthday, and although he didn't usually make a big deal about it, he was happy he'd be spending this year's with his son.

At around eight a.m., he called Marjorie. He was on his way home.

"I need to make up for the lost sales," Jay told Marjorie. "I was thinking I may come home for a couple of days and go back on the road, if you don't mind."

"Actually, Noah and I are sick with strep throat," Marjorie said.

A few days prior, Marjorie told Jay, Noah's school sent

home a note stating that someone in his class had been diagnosed with strep throat and that Noah may have been exposed. Marjorie had begun to have a sore throat and she was worried that she was ill. Jay was concerned. Because he personally handled so many aspects of his business, it would be devastating if he were out of commission due to illness. Marjorie encouraged Jay to continue working to avoid getting sick. According to Marjorie, Jay told her that he planned to come into Phoenix and stop at the warehouse to make some calls and check his e-mail to see if any of his clients would be able to see him. Maybe, Jay said, he could do a quick run to Utah or take some posters to El Paso.

Despite Marjorie's claims that Noah was ill with strep throat, Noah went to school that day.

On the drive back to Phoenix, Jay received a call from his brother, Jake Jr., wishing him happy birthday. At about 8:30 a.m., he also spoke to his mom. Joann exuberantly wished Jay a happy birthday and asked where he was.

"I'm just outside Tucson," he said.

"That's great!" Joann exclaimed. "You'll be home to celebrate your birthday with your son!"

"No," Jay said. "Marjorie and Noah are sick."

"That's a shame."

Joann told him she was looking forward to seeing him. Jay sent her his love and said, "I'll talk to you later."

But he never would. It was the last time Joann would ever hear her son's voice.

CHAPTER 10

The events that transpired the evening of Jay Orbin's forty-fifth birthday would be shrouded in mystery for years to come. Evidence would provide scant clues. Secrets and lies would cast clouds of suspicion. Theories would be conceived, dissected, and debated in court.

What was known was that on the afternoon of September 8, Jay arrived in Phoenix. He went to his warehouse, checked his e-mail, browsed the Web, and made a few phone calls. Late that afternoon, he stopped at a gas station a few miles from his house. Jay was headed home.

Sometime after five p.m., Jay Orbin was murdered.

In an instant, everything changed. For a time, however, things seemed quite normal at Jay and Marjorie's house. The day after Jay's birthday, Thursday, September 9, Marjorie called Noah out sick from school. That morning she prepared her son's breakfast and cleaned the house, as Noah lounged around and played computer games. By late afternoon, however, he started to feel better and Marjorie said she realized he was not that ill.

At around five p.m., Marjorie took Noah to a nearby Target Greatland and went shopping. Along with a large amount of cleaning supplies, Marjorie bought men's boxer briefs size 32-36 for Larry, a few cosmetics for herself, and a Nintendo Game Boy Advance game for Noah. The total bill: $482.31. Marjorie charged the purchases on one of Jay's credit cards.

Afterward, she returned home and shampooed her carpet. The next day a healthy Noah returned to school. Around noon, Marjorie stopped by a Scottsdale Lowe's Home Improvement store and purchased $175 in hardware supplies.

That weekend she stayed busy cleaning and organizing the garage. Marjorie was constantly taking on new home improvement projects, redecorating and remodeling the house. Her latest venture: epoxy coating the garage floor. She spent the next several days painting the garage floor with a speckled beige-colored sealant. She also patched a hole in the garage door and installed a video security monitoring system outside the front porch. Larry came over and helped her move boxes.

The following week, Marjorie did more shopping. On September 13, she spent more than $1,000 on sheets, décor, and home improvement supplies at Home Depot, Walmart, and the Great Indoors. The next day she bought an elaborate water fountain for the front entryway at a cost of $1,133 and another $1,263 worth of clothes, lingerie, and more items for the house. On September 15, she returned to Walmart for a car battery jumper, a small ramp, paint, caulk, and drywall tools at the cost of $194, and more home improvement supplies from Home Depot for $293. Two days later, she purchased a front-load dryer for $940 and spent another $652 at Cost Plus and Pier 1. That week she also returned to Lowe's four times, charging $919.

Her six-day shopping total was nearly $6,500. All purchases were charged to Jay's American Express and Capitol One credit cards or paid for with his Bank of America debit card.

That week Larry came by frequently and slept over several nights. He started leaving his underwear, socks, shirts, jeans, and shoes at the house. Marjorie even cleared out a drawer for Larry to keep his clothes in. For the next few days, Marjorie filled a few orders from Jay's clients, went to the gym, and took her son to school and karate classes. A few of Marjorie's friends also came by to swim or watch movies.

Meanwhile, no one had heard from Jay. A few of his friends and business associates called the house looking for him. Marjorie told them all that he never came home on his birthday and instead took a detour business trip. Jay wouldn't be home for another week or so, depending on his sales, Marjorie said.

Around noon on September 14, Marjorie left a message on Jay's cell phone. "I have a couple messages that need to get to you, a couple of people need you to call back. I couldn't answer their questions. Give me a call when you get a chance."

That night she left another message: "Hey, it's me. I still have some messages for you, and trying to call you back."

That Saturday, Larry and Marjorie met at Jodi Weisberg's house. When Marjorie pulled into the driveway with Noah, Jodi came outside.

"Hey, where's my dad?" Jodi asked.

"I just saw him out back in the alley," Marjorie replied.

Jodi went out back and saw her father dumping several large black trash bags into the large alley dumpsters. It seemed strange to her. Her father lived alone and it seemed unusual that he would have so much trash. At the time, however, Jodi didn't give it much thought.

That weekend, Noah asked about his father constantly. Every morning before school, Jay called his son to speak with him. Suddenly, those calls stopped. Noah wanted to talk to his dad. Marjorie assured him he would call soon.

Meanwhile, Marjorie was behaving like Jay would never return. She appeared to be inserting Larry into her husband's place, like they were interchangeable pieces in a puzzle. Throughout September, Larry practically lived in the Orbins' house. Marjorie had packed up Jay's clothes in boxes and stored them in the top of the closet to make room for Larry's stuff. Soon, Larry's clothes were hung up in the master closet and his toothbrush was near the sink. Larry, Marjorie, and Noah were living together like a family. Larry took on the role of Noah's surrogate dad with ease. After school, he played basketball with Noah in the Orbins' driveway.

One morning, after spending the night at Marjorie's, Noah walked out of his room and instead of saying, "Hey, Larry," said, "Hey, Dad."

The remark caught Larry off guard. He gave Marjorie a surprised look. He pulled Marjorie aside. "What's this?" But she just smiled, turned around, and walked out of the room.

Meanwhile, the calls from people looking for Jay became more frequent. Jay's friends and family had been calling Jay's cell phone but the calls went straight to voicemail. Dozens of messages went unreturned and the Orbins were becoming increasingly concerned.

Joann called several times. Each missed call made her more anxious. It was not like Jay not to call her back. After speaking to Jake Jr., she really began to worry. Jake Jr. said he hadn't heard from Jay on his birthday, September 10, and Jay hadn't even sent a card, something he did every year.

Where could he be? Joann wondered.

Joann called Marjorie.

"He's not home yet." Marjorie sighed. "It will be a couple more days."

"Oh, I haven't been able to reach him," Joann said anxiously. "How are you doing?"

"I'm fine. Busy. I'm trying to get the garage floor epoxy painted before he gets home."

Marjorie seemed aggravated so Joann let her go. Jay would call soon, Joann reasoned. He was probably just busy with customers.

By mid-September, Marjorie was receiving dozens of

calls from Jay's friends and business associates, all looking for Jay. Orders were piling up at Jayhawk International and shipments weren't being sent. Customers called wanting merchandise and placing orders that Marjorie couldn't handle. Her home and cell phone rang incessantly. She told everyone she had spoken to Jay a few days prior and he'd be home on the 20th.

"He'll be back on Monday," Marjorie said. "Try him then."

Finally, September 20 arrived. It had been twelve days since anyone had heard from Jay and his family and friends were anxious to speak with him. That morning Marjorie left a message. "Just checking to see if you are in yet. It's 11:20, talk to you later."

An hour later, Jay's mom called. "It's your mother. Give me a call."

Two hours passed and no one heard from Jay.

Then at 1:27 p.m. Jay's friend Bob Macy glanced at his cell phone and saw Jay was calling. Relief washed over him. *Finally*, he thought.

"Jay. Where've you been, man!" he said.

There was no reply.

"Jay? Jay? Are you there?"

He pressed the phone close to his ear—Rush Limbaugh's program was blaring in the background; he could hear it distinctly. But no one spoke. Confused, he hung up.

At 1:31 p.m., Mario Olivarez noticed he had missed a call from Jay. He called back but there was no answer. A few minutes later Kenny Smith, one of Jay's clients from New Mexico, also received a call from Jay's cell phone. When he answered he, too, heard nothing.

He called back and left a voicemail. "Why don't you get a better phone and give me a call? Talk to you later, bye."

Five other business associates and friends received calls from Jay that day but no one heard his voice, although a few heard Rush Limbaugh's. The last call made from his cell phone was at 1:44 p.m.

That night, Noah was very upset. He was asking about his dad, crying constantly. Marjorie called Jay's phone, so he could hear his father's voice. "Hi, Dad," Noah said, bawling. A second later Marjorie took the phone, "Hello, hello. Noah's trying to talk to you and your mother's been calling." Abruptly, the phone call ended.

Eventually, Marjorie sat Noah down and told him that she didn't know where his father was, but he might not be coming home.

"Something horrible must've happened to your dad," Marjorie said tenderly. "He could've been hurt by some very bad people."

Noah burst into tears. He seemed confused.

"When I'm all grown up," he said through tears, "I'm going to go be a doctor so I can fix Daddy."

Marjorie wrapped her arms around her son.

"It's going to be okay," she said, rocking him. "We have Larry. We have Larry to take care of us."

That night, Joann called Jay's phone again. "Call me. I am really worried." Throughout the evening she kept looking at her cell phone, anticipating that Jay would call her back. He never did. She was overcome by a feeling of uneasiness. Early the next morning, she called Jake Jr. at his home in San Diego.

"Jay's missing," Joann sobbed.

When his mother explained how long it had been since she had last spoken to Jay, Jake Jr. became very worried. It was so unlike Jay to not call. For the next two days, Jay's family hounded Marjorie, urging her to call the police and report Jay missing. Meanwhile, she continued to shop, spending another $1,659 on clothes, arts and crafts, and home improvement supplies.

On September 22, Jake Jr. called Marjorie to ask if there had been any news.

"No," she said. "I've been calling and calling."

Jake Jr. tried to offer a way to find Jay, but Marjorie was abrupt, upset, and seemed tired of suggestions. Marjorie said she had been talking to everyone, looking for Jay.

"How's Noah handing everything?" Jake Jr. asked.

"Noah knows that his dad is missing and might not come home anymore," she said. "He knows that there are terrible people out there and his dad would want him to be strong."

That comment took Jake Jr. aback. Jay had only been missing for two days. It seemed premature to be telling him this. That afternoon, Marjorie called the Phoenix Police Missing Persons Detail. "I need to report my husband missing."

CHAPTER 11

Marjorie, if you are reading this, then something has happened to me. Out of the corner of his eye, Jake Jr. saw those words scribbled across a piece of paper in his brother's handwriting. As he picked up the letter his stomach lurched. It was dated six months before Jay vanished.

Tentatively, Jake Jr. continued reading the letter addressed to Marjorie. *I'm sorry dear, just remember you were the love of my life and Noah and you are the best thing I have ever done. I will love you both always and I thank you both for all you've given my life.* The letter went on to list all of Jay's life insurance policies, which totaled nearly one million dollars. The last line read, *No open casket for me.* In Jake Jr.'s hands the letter seemed to weigh ten pounds. It was a sinking realization that he might never again see his brother alive.

It was September 24, and Jake Jr. was standing in the kitchen of his brother's home, his world turned upside down. Just yesterday everything had been so different. He had gone to his job at the San Diego Parks and Recreation department and had dinner with his girlfriend, Shelly. Although Jake Jr. knew his brother was missing, he expected to hear anytime that Jay was home safe, having lost his cell phone or something of the sort. Instead, that night he got a call from his father. "Your mother's crying all the time," he said. "We need you."

When he heard the agony in his father's voice, Jake Jr. knew the situation was dire. Without hesitation, he told his parents he would be there the next day. He informed work about the family emergency and packed his bags. Early the next morning he and Shelly made the six-hour drive from San Diego to Phoenix.

Jake Jr. was a balding, heavy-set man with sparse white hair and his brother's bright blue eyes. He was a divorcee with no children of his own, and his parents, brother, and nephew were practically his only family. His girlfriend, Shelly, was full-figured with an alabaster complexion and short, wind-blown blond hair. On the drive to Phoenix, Jake Jr. called Marjorie to arrange a time to meet to discuss Jay's disappearance.

"Do you have Jay's vendor list?" he asked. "I thought I could start calling his clients to see if anyone has seen him."

"It would be at the warehouse," Marjorie said, "on the computer."

"You haven't been to the warehouse?" he asked, confused.

"No. I've been really busy."

"You need to check it out! Maybe Jay's there. Maybe the truck is there. Maybe something has been disturbed."

"Do you think there is a chance he could be there?" Marjorie asked.

"You never know," Jake Jr. replied. "If you want, I will look for you."

"No. No. I'll do it."

"Can I come by the house tonight?" Jake Jr. asked.

"I'm really busy," Marjorie said abruptly. "I have to pick up Noah from school and its Friday so he'll probably have a friend and then I'll have to feed them. I guess you could come over around six or so."

*   *   *

Detective Jan Butcher was assigned as the lead investigator on the Jay Orbin disappearance. At the time, the Phoenix Police Department had been receiving nearly one hundred missing person's reports each month, and cases were distributed by alphabetical order. Because Jay's last name began with an O, Butcher got the case. Like with any typical missing persons case, she began by doing a routine background check and running license plate numbers. Soon she would discover that there was nothing routine about this case.

Jan Butcher was a five-year veteran of the Phoenix Police Department's Missing Persons Detail who had aspirations of one day becoming a homicide investigator. She had wanted to be a cop ever since she was a little girl. After receiving a bachelor's degree in Justice Studies and a master's in Public Administration from Arizona State University, she joined the Phoenix Police Department in 1995. Her identical twin sister, Lynn, also became a sergeant in the department. Butcher was slender and unassuming, with soft blue eyes that stood out against her bronze complexion. While she had a soft-spoken manner, she was intensely serious about her investigations.

On most missing persons cases, the person in question typically is found alive. At first, Butcher had no reason to believe Jay would be any different. About ninety percent of cases involve people who vanish to avoid their responsibilities, or because they are addicted to drugs or having a secret affair. Roughly ten percent of cases end in tragedy. Butcher discovered nothing unusual in Jay's initial background check. He had never previously gone missing and there were no apparent financial problems.

To find Jay, Butcher had to learn as much as possible about his life—his job, habits, routines, and relationships. She began by contacting the people closest to him, starting with Marjorie. The morning of September 24, two days after Marjorie reported her husband missing, Butcher called Marjorie. On the phone, Marjorie calmly explained that she had last spoken to Jay about a week before his disappear-

ance and that it was unusual for him to be gone so long
without calling. According to Marjorie, Jay normally traveled in his white cargo truck loaded with $700,000 in
wholesale Southwestern merchandise and $30,000 in cash.
Marjorie said that she thought Jay was driving that truck
when he went missing. Marjorie explained that Jay returned
from Florida on September 8, but continued onto another
business trip because she and Noah were sick. He was
scheduled to return on September 20. When Butcher asked
when she had last spoken to Jay, Marjorie said September
17. However, Marjorie couldn't tell Butcher where Jay was.

"That's not that unusual," Marjorie insisted. "Jay was often secretive about his routes because his business is so high
risk." Jay would often tell customers he was in route to one
location when actually headed in the opposite direction.

But as Marjorie spoke, Butcher got an unusual impression. Most wives who report their husbands missing are
frantic, hysterical, and beside themselves with worry. On
the contrary, Marjorie appeared calm and collected. Almost immediately, there was just something about her that
didn't sit well with Butcher. When Butcher asked about the
Orbins' marriage, Marjorie described it as "more of a
friendship," and claimed her husband had "no sex drive."

"Do you think it's possible he had a girlfriend?" Butcher
asked.

"No!" Marjorie said, without hesitation. "I wished he
would find someone who would show him affection and
tenderness. But, no, I don't think so. I mean, it was physically unlikely."

"Are you referring to Jay being unable to perform, sexually?" Butcher asked.

"Pretty much, yes."

In a subsequent conversation, Marjorie implied that Jay's
business was dangerous and that it might have played a part
in his death. "Just for your information, most of the people in
this business are dirt bags," Marjorie said. "And, um, gam-
blers and thieves. They're all con men in this business."

"Was Jay's business in any way, as far as you know, involved in anything illegal?" Butcher asked.

"No! Jay's a Boy Scout," she said. "He's a pretty simple guy. A normal guy. Nice, funny, sweet."

Marjorie listed a number of people she said were jealous of Jay's success and others who owed him tens of thousands of dollars. The list included nearly everyone in his life, from his former business partner to his closest friends.

From what Marjorie was saying, it seemed reasonable that Jay had been robbed and murdered on his business trip. Butcher had seen that kind of thing before. It seemed like a plausible scenario.

That afternoon, after speaking with Butcher, Marjorie drove to the Jayhawk International warehouse. Parked in the back was Jay's white work truck, which she had told police Jay had last been seen driving. The Orbins' green Ford Bronco, however, was gone. Marjorie gathered Jay's checkbook and briefcase. She then went to the wall safe, opened it, and removed a handwritten letter, wrapped around several envelopes. Marjorie unfolded the letter and read the fist line: *Marjorie, if you are reading this, then something has happened to me.*

She tucked it into her purse and left. At home, she sat at her kitchen table and carefully opened each envelope, reading Jay's instructions about what she was supposed to do in the event of his death. In the envelope marked "first week" were instructions to remove some of the valuables from the warehouse.

Marjorie returned to the warehouse, but this time Larry went with her. Inside the safe were coins, baseball cards, and other valuables of Jay's and Noah's. Marjorie cleaned it out. She also located Jay's computers, which she knew contained his client list; Larry helped dismantle Jay's wooden, L-shaped work desk, load it in the cargo truck, and bring it back to the house. In accordance with

Jay's wishes, Marjorie was preparing to manage Jay's business from home.

Jake Jr. and Shelly arrived in Phoenix that afternoon and stopped by his parents' home. Joann was a wreck, crying all the time; Jake was doing his best to stay strong. "We'll find him, Mom," Jake Jr. said, hugging her tightly.

Around four p.m., Jake Jr. drove to the Phoenix library to use the Internet to track down contact information for police, sheriff's offices, and Native American reservations in the outlying areas of Phoenix. He spent the afternoon calling agencies across the state to see if there were any reports on Jay's work truck. Frustratingly, there were none.

At around six p.m., Jake Jr. and Shelly went to see Marjorie. As he pulled his car into his brother's driveway, the car's headlights reflected off a white plaster patch on the aluminum roll-up garage door. He got out of the car, approached the door, and examined it closely. The patch was about ten to twelve inches wide and eight inches tall. He took out his cell phone and snapped a photo with the camera. There was something about it that left him with an eerie feeling.

Suddenly, Marjorie appeared on the front porch with a scowl on her face.

"What happened?" he asked, as he tucked his phone back in his pocket.

"Oh, that. I backed into the garage door," she said.

Seeing the irritated look on her face, Jake Jr. chose not to push the issue. When Noah saw his uncle, he rushed over and gave him a warm hug. Locked in an embrace, Jake Jr. whispered to him, "Do you know why I'm in Phoenix?"

"Yeah, 'cause Dad's missing," Noah sulked. "He might never come home."

Shelly took Noah by his hand and took him to another room to play, so Jake Jr. could speak with Marjorie alone in the kitchen. Marjorie told him that she had gone to the warehouse and discovered the cargo truck. Jay's merchandise was still in the back, Marjorie said. The two rear doors were opened and there were two handguns in the front, as there always were.

"So he's driving the old Bronco?" Jake Jr. asked, bewildered. "Does he normally take it on business trips?"

"On short trips, if he's selling out of a suitcase."

Slowly, Jake Jr. shook his head. Nothing was adding up. "Do you have his vendor list?"

Marjorie left the room to retrieve the office computer. While Jake Jr. was alone, he glanced around the kitchen. It was clean and spotless, except for piles of papers on the table. The handwritten letter from his brother got his attention. While he was calling hospitals and police stations, Marjorie had been sorting through life insurance documents. She was acting like Jay was already dead and buried.

An overwhelming sense of dread was plaguing him, and being around Marjorie wasn't putting him at ease. Marjorie emerged from the other room with a milk crate full of computer parts. Jake Jr. reassembled the computer and searched for the client list, which contained over 2,800 names on eighty-five pages. While Jake Jr. was printing the document, Noah came into the kitchen. "I'm hungry. When's dinner?"

Jake Jr. gave Marjorie a quick look, but she turned her focus on Noah. Earlier, Marjorie had claimed she would be busy feeding Noah and his playmate. Noah hadn't eaten and there was no playmate. Marjorie dug through the kitchen drawer and produced a Chinese take-out menu for a restaurant called Jasmine Palace. They called to place an order and around 7:30 p.m. Jake Jr. took Noah with him to pick up the food, while Shelly stayed with Marjorie. On their way back to the house, Jake Jr. glanced at Noah and forced a smile. He was having difficulty sorting through Jay's disappearance and he couldn't imagine what was going through the mind of an eight-year-old. They were almost back to the house when Noah brought up his father.

"Uncle Jake, this is really weird," he said.

Noah told his uncle that his dad had called a couple of times, but he kept repeating himself. Each time his dad would ask how he was, then pause and say, "Good, well you take care, I'll talk to you later." Then he hung up. "It was like a tape being played or something," Noah said.

Back at the house they all ate dinner. Afterward, Jake Jr. grabbed the client list and he and Shelly left to go back to his parents' house for the night. The drive back was quiet. Jake Jr. was deep in thought, processing everything he had learned. Shelly broke the silence. "Marjorie showed me the letter."

Shelly said that when she read it she was overcome with emotion. "I burst into tears the second I read that first line," she said. "I looked at her and it didn't even faze her. I don't know how anyone could not be emotionally touched reading a farewell letter from their husband."

With a pained look, Jake Jr. continued to stare at the road. Shelly didn't want to say what she was thinking; she didn't have to. He was thinking it, too, but wasn't ready to face it. Marjorie was his sister in-law; she had been part of their family for nearly a decade. And she was the mother of his only nephew. He shook the idea from his mind. *It wasn't possible for her to hurt Jay,* he thought. *It simply wasn't possible.*

On Monday, September 25, Marjorie surprised Larry with tickets to a Sting concert at the Cricket Pavilion, a Phoenix concert venue. That night, Jodi watched Noah while Marjorie and Larry enjoyed a romantic evening. The next day was Larry's grandson's sixth birthday, and Jodi had arranged a small party with some of his friends from the neighborhood. That afternoon, Marjorie surprised the birthday boy by renting a pony for the day. Jodi was stunned. That night, Jodi pulled her father aside. "What does she do?"

"Well, umm, she gets child support," Larry said. "And she also does hair weaves."

"And she makes money that way?" Jodi asked, perplexed. "What else does she do? I mean, does she work? How could she afford that?"

"I don't know," Larry said nonchalantly.

On the morning of Monday, September 27, Joann called Marjorie. She and Jake wanted to go down to the warehouse and look around.

"I've been there," Marjorie said. "There's nothing there."

"What are you afraid we'll see?" Joann pressed.

"Nothing," Marjorie scoffed. "Fine. We'll go."

That afternoon, Marjorie picked up Jay's parents and brought them to the warehouse. On the drive there, Marjorie's cell phone rang. It was Detective Jan Butcher, wanting to know if she could check out the warehouse.

"As a matter of fact, I'm on my way there right now," Marjorie said. "You are welcome to access anything."

At about 1:20 p.m., Butcher and Sergeant Mary Roberts, of the Missing Persons Detail, drove to the warehouse at 2629 S. 21st Street to search for clues. The building was a plain, nondescript beige stucco. The detectives tried the front door and found it unlocked. As the detectives entered, they were immediately approached by Jay's parents and a tall blonde who identified herself as Marjorie Orbin. She was wearing a black sports bra and spandex athletic shorts with her hair in a ponytail.

After speaking briefly with the family about when they each had last heard from Jay, the detectives scoured the warehouse for clues. There were no telephones or computers in the offices and the file cabinets were empty. On the floor, under a table in the main office, Detective Butcher noticed a worn light brown Louis Vuitton briefcase. She examined it and found it empty. When Butcher pointed the briefcase out to the Orbins, Joann grew very concerned.

This was the same briefcase Jay took with him everywhere.

As Butcher approached the back warehouse, she noticed the large white cargo truck. It was the same truck Marjorie had reported missing. Marjorie explained that while she had originally thought Jay was driving the truck, she later realized that he had left in the green and tan Ford Bronco, which he liked to take on shorter trips. She didn't explain why she hadn't told Butcher which vehicle Jay had been driving.

"Are there any mechanical problems with the Bronco?" Butcher asked.

"It feels like it's shaking all over the place and it stalls at times and if you push on the gas, there's no air conditioning," Marjorie said. "It's horrible."

Marjorie continued to insist she had no idea what happened to Jay. She spoke with conviction and seemed believable, but she didn't seem particularly bothered about her husband's disappearance. On the contrary, she seemed quite at ease. "She was very convincing," Butcher recalled. "But she wasn't concerned; she would answer questions but never really volunteer anything."

Butcher examined the truck. The back doors were open and rows of merchandise lined the shelves. The cab of the vehicle was littered with fast food wrappers and garbage. An empty gun holster lay on the floor. In the driver's side door was a loaded Ruger P85; another loaded gun was found resting in the center console.

About a half an hour after the detectives arrived, Marjorie said she needed to leave to pick up Noah from school.

"After we're done here, can we come by and look through some of Jay's belongings at the house?" Butcher asked. "It may help find information which could locate your husband."

"Uh, no. I won't be home," Marjorie stammered. "I will be at Noah's school helping out this evening."

They agreed to meet two days later, September 29, at ten a.m., at Marjorie's house. Marjorie tossed Butcher the warehouse key. "Can you set the alarm and lock up when you're finished?"

After Marjorie left, Butcher spoke with Jake and Joann Orbin. Unlike Marjorie, who appeared unaffected, the Orbins were highly concerned and totally distraught. Both were in their seventies. Jake was plump and nearly completely bald, with small blue eyes and a wide engaging smile; Joann had a warm, round face framed by short, curly graying hair.

"Joann is thinking the worst," Jake said. "She's crying all the time. She thinks he's dead. I just can't think that way about Jay. I will remain positive that he is alive until I'm given absolute proof to contradict this feeling."

When Butcher asked about Jay's marriage, Joann said, "It worked. They both seemed happy."

There weren't any financial problems or anything else to explain Jay's disappearance. He took great care of both Marjorie and Noah and when he was out of town Marjorie helped out by filling incoming orders, although she was not familiar with the way the business ran or operated, Joann said.

Jake said that his son would likely not tell him if he had a personal problem. "We're very close," he said. "But he probably wouldn't come to me for help. We don't really share that type of personal information with each other."

"Do you think Jay could be living a second life with another woman?" Butcher asked.

"No. No." Jake shook his head. "He's too busy for anything like that."

Right away Butcher could tell the Orbins were normal, genuinely nice people, and she felt sympathetic toward them. She assured them she would keep them informed on all the developments. "I promise you I will do anything and everything I can to find out what happened to Jay."

CHAPTER 12

After several weeks with no contact from Jay, his family and friends all believed something terrible had happened. The prevailing theory was that he was involved in a car accident on his way back to Phoenix. His friends all assisted in the search, calling hospitals across the country. But as word spread about Marjorie's callous demeanor, the whispers started. Marjorie was distant and often unavailable. Some of Jay's friends were calling her three or four times a day for updates. When she did speak to them, she sounded irritated and inconvenienced. Most of the time, she didn't bother to return their calls.

A few days after Jay's disappearance, Marjorie changed her outgoing answering machine message: "If you have any information regarding the situation with Jay, please leave that information. It is very important. Any other calls regarding the status of the situation will be called back when there's something to tell. I can't possibly answer every phone call, okay? So if you have any information, please leave a message. Thank you, bye."

As part of her missing persons investigation, Detective Butcher spoke with many of Jay's friends and associates. No one had a bad word to say about Jay, but they had mixed opinions about Marjorie. Jay's best friend, Marshall Roosin, was communicating regularly with Marjorie, and believed she was genuinely worried about Jay.

"One thing you need to know, and it's a problem, everybody has different personalities, okay?" Marshall explained to Butcher. "Marjorie comes across as very cold. Now I've known her for ten years, okay? Marjorie was the love of Jay's life."

According to Marshall, Jay and Marjorie had a happy marriage. "He told me that their marriage was perfect, because he would be on the road two weeks a month. They couldn't get on each other's nerves because it was nice when they were actually together."

Marshall confirmed Marjorie's claims about Jay's seedy business competitors. "The Indian jewelry business is like used car sales," he said. "The lowest denominator of people. They'll do anything to undercut you, so Jay was always very secretive of what he did."

"What's your gut feeling on this, Marshall?" Butcher asked.

"My gut feeling is the worst possible scenario," Marshall said instantly.

"Which is . . . ?"

"That he's dead."

"Okay," Butcher said, "due to like an accident, or?"

"No." Marshall paused. "To foul play."

Gary Dodge, Jay's friend and jewelry supplier, agreed that there were "some shady characters in the jewelry business who will stab you in the back every time they can." He also relayed to detectives the conversation he had had with Jay a few years prior about outlining what to do in the event of his death. To him, it seemed Marjorie was following her husband's wishes.

"Gary, how does Marjorie appear during this, the fact that you know Jay's missing and things like that?" Butcher asked.

"Well, you know from the beginning she was basically trying to follow what Jay told her," he said. "And she was real tight on information because a lot of it's got to do with the business."

According to Gary, Marjorie seemed distraught and "burst into tears" when they talked about Jay. "She would tell me things like I hope Jay doesn't get mad at me for this," he said. "It seemed like she was doing what he would have wanted her to do or what she was instructed to do."

Still, while Gary and Marshall defended Marjorie, they both admitted they didn't really know her. In fact, no one in Jay's life appeared to know much about Marjorie. Jim Rogers, who had been friends with Jay for twenty years, told Butcher he couldn't offer an opinion on Marjorie. "I always saw her at the Christmas parties and I've talked to her on the phone a few times, when Jay was out of town, but I just didn't know her all that well," he said. "It's kind of weird, too, because Jay and I were pretty close."

Bob Macy, Jay's friend of eight years who also worked in the Native American jewelry business, said Jay and Marjorie were not like a typical couple. "It was a really strange kind of relationship with Jay and her," he said, adding that it was unusual that Marjorie didn't seem more concerned. "When I talked to her two times there was no emotion," he said. "I know there are many other things that just don't sound right."

"Does that seem kind of odd?" Butcher asked.

"My wife, I'm telling you, if I was missing, she would have called at least ten times, and Jay was the last one that got a phone call," Bob exclaimed. "She didn't even know where he went!"

Out of all of Jay's friends, Mario Olivarez was the most suspicious of Marjorie. From the beginning, he was adamant that she knew more than she was saying. Mario explained that he had been calling every hospital from here to Florida asking about their "John Does," while Marjorie would not even return his messages. "It's like everything here is an inconvenience to her," she said. "It's altering her gym days and her *this* day and her *that* day."

Mario never really got along with Marjorie, he explained, because she was more of a "loner." He described her as "snooty," "hardcore," and "controlling." During the interview with Butcher, Mario kept going back to Marjorie's bizarre behavior. "A lot of this doesn't add up," he said. "It's like a piece of the puzzle is missing that somebody's not saying."

The interviews with Jay's friends shed tremendous insight on his life and marriage. Through all of the information Butcher gathered, there was nothing to indicate that Jay was the type to skip town without telling anyone. The more Butcher learned about Jay, the more she was beginning to believe that she was searching for a dead man.

As Butcher continued to speak to Marjorie, her suspicions grew. Marjorie insisted that she and Jay had a unique relationship. They hadn't been intimate in years but they had a very strong bond, based on their mutual adoration of their son. "I mean we have a very, very good relationship," Marjorie said, "and I do not want anything, anyone making anything ugly out of anything we have."

Still, even if their relationship was a friendship, it was unusual that Marjorie didn't appear more concerned. Although, Butcher noted, Marjorie did seem troubled about one thing—money. As they were discussing Marjorie's last conversation with Jay, she interrupted to explain that she was having a "minor problem" that she didn't know what to do about concerning Jay's client list.

"I have Jay's will and I have Jay's power of attorney and I have a big package of instructions on what to do," Marjorie said. "And over and over and over and over again in these packages it says release that mailing list to no one!"

"Okay," Butcher said slowly.

"I know his mother is, you know, her main concern, she wants to find him. We all want to find him," she said. "My main concern and what Jay would want me to be doing would be following his instructions and protecting his livelihood for the boy!"

Marjorie continued to rant about Jay's mom. "She has his mailing list and she is calling customers all over the country. Well, she is calling every single customer and there are over $300,000 in receivables and no one will pay if she continues doing this!"

Butcher was stunned. *What kind of wife cares more about a client list than her missing husband?* she thought.

"Okay, I can . . . I'll certainly talk to her," Butcher said haltingly.

"I don't want to fight with her. We have sort of a contentious relationship at times and most of the time everybody plays nice, but I don't want to stick my hand out and say give it to me," Marjorie said. "But that would really help me out financially, because I'm afraid everyone that she tells that Jay is missing, if he ends up being gone, they're not going to pay their bill . . . which is going to hurt me!"

Reluctantly, Butcher told her she would investigate the client list. "Alright, well, Marjorie, hang in there."

"Well, I mean . . . I'm past being emotional about Jay," Marjorie said matter-of-factly. "I mean I, I still refuse to believe he's not gonna come, you know, bustin' in the door any minute, complaining about getting screwed over by some shyster mechanic, you know?"

That last statement stuck with Butcher, more than anything else. "I don't know how you report somebody, your husband, missing and a few days later you can say you're past being emotional," Butcher recalled. "I don't see it. It was a very odd comment. Very, very strange."

Meanwhile, Jake and Joann Orbin had gone from desperate to hysterical. Page by page, they had gone through Jay's client list, calling every customer across the country. They couldn't locate anyone who had actually spoken to Jay since his birthday. No one, of course, except for Marjorie.

When they were with Marjorie, she seemed to have explanations for everything. On the surface, she appeared worried. Everything they asked of her, she did, although sometimes begrudgingly. But the more they learned, the more questions arose: Where had Jay gone? Why hadn't he called anyone? Who used his phone on the 20th?

Jake Jr. was beside himself with worry. He was doing everything he could think of to help find Jay, but he felt entirely powerless. "He's your little brother, you want to protect him," Jake Jr. recalled. "When we were looking for him, I just couldn't get over just not being able to find him. We were thinking he was on a trip, on the side of a cliff, where do you start, we were calling sheriff's offices, Native American reservations, hospitals, everybody."

Jake and Joann's long-time family friend Dave Lane was a policeman who had worked in the Phoenix Police Department for more than three decades. After Jay went missing, they called him for advice and he recommended a private investigator named Steve Kopp.

Jake Jr. called Kopp and explained everything he knew up until that point. He told him that they didn't know much about Marjorie's background before she married Jay and were concerned by her strange behavior. During the conversation, Kopp asked if he would mind if he contacted a psychic whom he had used for twenty years and had had good luck with.

"I don't believe in that stuff," Jake Jr. said. "But try any avenue that would help."

A few days later Kopp called. "I heard from the psychic and I don't have good news. She said the crime scene is the warehouse. There were two guys that have been watching the area for a long time." The psychic said Jay would be found next to a truck in a wooded area, between Flagstaff and Phoenix, Kopp explained.

"Well, I hope you're wrong," Jake Jr. said.

Kopp also said he had learned some very unusual things about Marjorie's background. In the '80s and '90s, Marjorie had lived all over Florida and she had a brief criminal record for indecent exposure in the '90s. But most extraordinary was what he discovered in her marital records. "From what I found, Marjorie had been married six times before she married your brother."

"Six times!" Jake Jr. said, shocked.

The room was spinning. Jake Jr. was astonished. He knew that Marjorie had been married before, once, maybe twice, but six times? She had been lying to his family for years. His sister-in-law, the woman he had thought he knew for ten years, didn't even seem to exist.

Continuing her investigation into Jay Orbin's disappearance, Detective Butcher obtained Jay's cell phone and financial records to trace his movements in the days leading up to his disappearance. Credit card receipts showed Jay stopped at a gas station in Phoenix on September 8, his birthday, at 9:16 a.m. Surveillance video showed he was driving the large white cargo truck. At around 4:35 p.m., he stopped again at a gas station a few miles from the Orbins' house. This time, he was driving the green Ford Bronco.

Butcher also contacted Jay's banks to review activity on his accounts. Each account only had a single signer: Jay Michael Orbin. After he disappeared, the bank activity became highly unusual. Thousands of dollars in cash had been withdrawn from the accounts. Each day after September 13, someone had been withdrawing $500, the maximum amount allowed each day through the ATM, as well as making tens of thousands of dollars in phone transfers. Butcher subpoenaed the ATM video and noticed that the person who had been withdrawing the money was a woman in her forties, with bright platinum blond hair—Marjorie Orbin. When Butcher confronted Marjorie about this, she admitted she had been withdrawing the money and storing it in an envelope.

"What is the reason for this?" Butcher asked.

"In case the accounts get closed, I need to make sure I have money for groceries and whatever," she said. "I need to make sure that a roof stays over the child's head. That is what Jay would want me to do."

Marjorie explained how the bank accounts were in Jay's name and that his farewell letter left her instructions on what to do in the event of his death. "This is what he told me to do and left in writing. Some of it in writing, but I need to do what he told me to do," Marjorie said. "The will gives me everything . . . everything is to go to me and to Noah to take care of that child. I mean I live for that child."

"And if Jay shows up?" Butcher asked.

"Then we'll handle it!"

When they spoke at the warehouse, Marjorie told Butcher she would be unavailable because she was helping out at her son's school. At this point, Butcher had become highly suspicious of Marjorie. She called the principal of Copper Canyon Elementary School, which Noah attended. As Butcher suspected, Marjorie hadn't been at the school. She had lied.

Butcher next contacted the Arizona Department of Public Safety to conduct a search for the Bronco's license plate. As it turned out, the Bronco had been reported numerous times between September 19 and 25, at two separate locations, both of which were a few miles from the Orbins' home. After it had been parked on one block for days, neighbors had reported it and an abandoned vehicle sticker had been placed on the windshield. A few days later, the vehicle had been moved.

The afternoon of September 27, Butcher drove to that neighborhood to speak with residents and found two separate people who reported seeing the driver of the vehicle. Both witnesses described a thin woman in her forties, with long, platinum blond hair. It was a description that fit Marjorie to a T. Right then, Butcher knew this was more than just a missing persons case. Marjorie's behavior, the Bronco, the unusual bank activity—to Butcher, it all pointed to murder.

"Things just weren't adding up," Butcher recalled. "It just wasn't making sense. At this point, foul play was suspected in Jay's disappearance."

CHAPTER 13

Detective Jan Butcher had only been working the missing persons investigation for four days, but already she was convinced police would not be finding Jay alive. Everything about this case stunk to high hell of foul play, especially Marjorie's growing list of lies.

On September 28, a Tuesday, the case took another peculiar turn. At 12:40 p.m., Butcher called Marjorie at home to discuss witness reports about a woman matching her description being spotted near the abandoned Bronco. There was no answer. A few hours later Butcher called again. And again. And again. She left four messages on her home and cell phone.

At 5:50 p.m., Marjorie finally returned her call. Normally soft spoken and nonconfrontational, Butcher was pressed to take a harsh stance with Marjorie. "I kind of get the feeling that you're really not available and willing to help us in finding Jay."

"You get that feeling, huh?" Marjorie snapped. "Umm, I, they're, his family is calling everybody all over the world and, you know, just doing just about, you know, everything that I can see that can be done, while I have been taking care of a child."

"I had called you earlier this afternoon," Butcher said.

"I just got home!" Marjorie said, indignant. "Well, you know what? I'm already feeling like I'm having to defend myself here. Jay's parents, you know, who will run around like chickens with their heads cut off, and yes, I suppose, that absolutely does look like they're more concerned than me. But it seems to me that they're running in circles and stirring up unnecessary emotion and effort that's not being productive."

"So you think being concerned and showing emotion is . . ."

"No! That's not what I said!" Marjorie interrupted. "His mom's going down there wringing her hands and playing the martyr saint, you know, and I feel bad for her. I'm very concerned about Jay. I speak more matter-of-factly."

"Well, what do you think about this?" Butcher pressed. "I mean where do you explain Jay would be for the last week and a half or so?"

"I can't explain it!" Marjorie said.

Butcher had asked her that question a dozen different ways, but each time Marjorie maintained she "had no idea" where her husband was. Butcher brought up the two witnesses' descriptions of a woman with long blond hair driving the Bronco. Marjorie dismissed it. "I wouldn't know anything about that. . . . How do they suppose I've taken care of the situation and what is the crime?"

"This is a missing persons investigation!" Butcher exclaimed.

Marjorie said that she had no way of telling if Jay was alive and that she wasn't afraid of police finding his body. "I don't think he's dead."

"Have you spoken to Noah about Jay being missing?" Butcher asked.

"I've discussed the possibilities, yes."

Those possibilities, Marjorie said, included Jay's truck breaking down, a car accident, or "worst case scenario:

that he could be dead . . . I told Noah that would be terrible, but you know what he would want us to do? Jay would want us to be brave and take care of each other."

Butcher shifted the conversation back to how Marjorie said she was too busy to meet the night before because she was busy helping at Noah's school.

"Well I checked up on the school," Butcher said.

"I was there," Marjorie replied, indignant, "doing things for a number of other things, other places."

"Okay, and see, now you're kind of changing your . . ."

"Now I'm getting angry!" Marjorie shrieked. "You contacted, you contacted my son's school? A police officer called my son's school!"

Butcher then asked Marjorie if she would be willing to take a polygraph test. Marjorie repeated the question to someone in the background: "She wants me to take a polygraph!"

Suddenly a male voice piped up, "Tell her to go fuck herself!"

"Who's that?" Butcher asked.

"None of your fuckin' business!" Marjorie yelled. "A friend of mine."

Butcher was taken aback. Directly, she told Marjorie what she thought. "All of the investigations in missing persons cases I've been involved in, it's kind of unusual that you're not as cooperative as most of the other . . ."

"In what way am I not being cooperative?" Marjorie interrupted.

"I'm just trying to conduct an investigation in order to locate your husband!"

Suddenly, without preamble, Marjorie blurted out something stunning. As she revealed this unexpected bit of information, Butcher's jaw gaped. Throughout the interview, she had been taking notes, but she dropped her pen. This was an issue that needed to be addressed in person.

"Well, how come you didn't tell me that when I . . ." Butcher asked, dumbfounded.

"How do I know what I need to tell you? There's never been instances like this! I haven't done anything wrong!" Marjorie said, her voice shaking with fury. "Do I need to tell you the color of my toenail polish?"

"Ma'am," Butcher moaned, "I don't care what color your toenail polish is."

"You know what I mean! How much of my personal life should I divulge?"

"Well, I would love for you to be completely honest with me. . . ."

"Completely honest," Marjorie said, "about everything in the entire world?"

"The investigation!" Butcher exclaimed. "As it relates to the investigation!"

"Oh! This relates to the investigation?"

"Yes, ma'am, it does!"

At about 8:45 p.m., Marjorie was in the front living room of her home on the phone with Jay's brother.

"I figured out the code to get into Jay's voice mail," Jake Jr. said slowly, trying to gauge Marjorie's reaction. "I listened to all the messages."

"Uh-huh," Marjorie said, half-listening.

She glanced at Larry Weisberg, who was sprawled across the couch staring at the television. Earlier, while Butcher repeatedly tried to contact her, Marjorie had been busy shopping. That morning, after dropping off Noah at school, she ran errands. She went to the AT&T store to replace Jay's cell phone and stopped by the bank to withdraw $500, as she had been doing every day for a week. At Circuit City, she bought a new DVD player and stereo equipment. That afternoon Marjorie stopped by the Arizona Piano Gallery in Scottsdale and purchased a new grand player piano. Ever since Marjorie was a little girl she had dreamed of owning her own piano. The instant Marjorie glided her fingers across the keys, she knew she had to have it. On a whim, she charged the $10,000 piano on one of Jay's credit cards and had it delivered to the house.

All the while, Butcher and Jay's friends were leaving messages on Marjorie's cell, desperate to learn if there had been any developments. At around three p.m., Marjorie picked up Noah from school. When she returned, Larry was sitting in her living room. Marjorie turned to Noah. "Go play in your room and we'll figure out dinner in a bit."

Around 5:50 p.m., Marjorie sat down at her kitchen table to check her voice mail. Message after message was from Detective Butcher. Marjorie called her back. Following their heated phone conversation, Marjorie ordered a pizza. After dinner, at about 8:45 p.m., the phone rang again. It was Jake Jr. As he was telling Marjorie about Jay's voice mail messages, suddenly she was startled by a loud bang on the front door, followed by a muffled shout. The fierce pounding reverberated through the walls and shook the paintings.

Marjorie shot Larry a terrified look. With the palm of her hand, she covered the phone and mouthed, "Oh my god! What is that?"

There was another thud. And another. And another. Larry rose from the couch. "What the hell?"

Abruptly, the front door blew off the hinges. Eight police officers wearing black boots, tactical body armor, and helmets rammed through the foyer, shouting and leveling automatic weapons at Larry and Marjorie. Marjorie let out a bloodcurdling scream and dropped the phone to the ground. A truculent Larry rushed at the men, flailing his arms and shouting, "Get the fuck out of here!"

"Get on the ground," one of the men shouted. "Get on the ground."

Brazenly, Larry continued to yell. Again they ordered him to the floor. When he didn't comply, one of the SWAT officers shot him with a Taser gun. Larry immediately froze, let out a pained yelp, and fell onto his back. Two officers grabbed his arms, forced him onto his stomach, and cuffed his hands behind his back.

A few feet away, Marjorie slowly put her hands in the air. All the color had drained from her face. She dropped to her knees and in a distressed voice screeched, "Jake, if you're still on the phone, come get Noah!" One of the SWAT team members pushed past Larry toward Marjorie, and with the tip of his gun, directed her to the floor. In the prone position, Marjorie was placed in handcuffs.

Meanwhile, Larry continued to resist. Hands cuffed behind his back, Larry rolled back and forth, kicking at the officers. He was tased a second time. One of the officers grabbed his head and slammed it into the tile floor. Larry's face split open and blood splattered across the tile foyer. Again Larry was tased; only this time he stopped resisting.

As officers headed down the hallway, Marjorie shouted, "There's a little boy in the house! There's a little boy in the house! Don't hurt him. Don't scare him." Inside a bathroom, Noah was found curled up in a corner, trembling. One of the officers scooped him up and carried him outside. In just minutes, the SWAT team had secured the Orbin home. They notified Detective Butcher who was a few miles away in her vehicle.

After the disturbing conversation with Marjorie earlier that evening, Butcher secured a search warrant and assembled officers from the Special Assignments Unit to clear the house. Although she and Marjorie had an appointment to meet at ten a.m. the following morning, she thought it best not to wait. From the way Marjorie was behaving, she didn't know what to expect.

Half an hour later, Butcher and Detective Amy Dillon of the Missing Persons Detail, arrived at the house, along with three detectives and two evidence technicians. The front door was wide open and detectives were already buzzing in and out carrying clear evidence bags, searching for evidence and photographing the scene. Patrol cars and a fire truck lined the sidewalk. Revolving red and blue lights flashed across the neighborhood.

As Butcher entered the house, she noticed a large man

sulking on a stool, with his arms cuffed behind his back. Clearly this was the same person who was cursing in the background over the phone. *Who was this man?* Butcher wondered. His aggressive behavior with the SWAT officers was certainly suspect. *Could he have been involved in Jay Orbin's disappearance?*

The house was lavish and upscale, exquisitely decorated. The front door opened on a tiled entryway and a spacious front living room elegantly furnished with a plush sofa and glass tables facing a top-of-the-line entertainment center. In the corner of the room was a freshly polished grand player piano. Through the sliding glass back doors, Butcher could see an intricate white wrought-iron fence blocking off an expansive swimming pool. A gas barbecue grill and outdoor sofa were situated on the covered patio.

On the couch in the living room, Marjorie was fuming. Her handcuffs had been removed and she was hugging herself around the waist. As Butcher spoke to Marjorie, she appeared frazzled, muttering to herself about the SWAT team "busting down the door."

"I know you're still looking into the case," Marjorie exclaimed. "But when you asked if you could look at the house and said how about tomorrow? I said well, I'm busy tomorrow. How about the next day? But it comes to this?"

Clearly, Marjorie was livid.

"Well, let me explain things to you, Marjorie," Butcher said.

"I thought we agreed upon a time!" Marjorie slapped her hands on her knees.

Ignoring her remark, Butcher read Marjorie her Miranda warnings. A few yards away, paramedics were treating Larry for a large gash above his eye and a bloody nose. His face was smeared with dried blood.

"Okay, who's that gentleman?" Butcher began. "Your friend here?"

"His name is Larry," Marjorie said. "He's a friend of mine that I met at the gym."

"How long have you known him?" Butcher asked.

"Like two or three months and, yes, we are involved."

"Did Jay know about Larry?" Butcher asked.

"He knew that I knew him. I had mentioned that I was, had worked out with him a couple of times, but no, he did not know that we were becoming involved."

Butcher jotted down information about Marjorie's lover. It was a salacious confession. But Butcher was more interested in the revelation Marjorie had made earlier on the phone. This was a twist that could have interesting repercussions for the investigation. On the drive to the Orbins' house, Butcher repeated Marjorie's words in her head: "Jay and I are not married."

In the summer of 1996, Jay and Marjorie were newlyweds and she was in the third trimester of her much-anticipated pregnancy with a boy she planned to name Noah. But that day she went to the pharmacy to refill her prescription, everything changed. Her bank account had been seized because the IRS had levied a $50,000 tax lien against her for a debt stemming from five years earlier, when Marjorie was married to her fifth husband, Ronald McMann. Marjorie told Jay all about the tumultuous end to her marriage with Ronald and how, in the divorce, she had signed the company back into his name.

"I thought this was done years ago," Marjorie told Jay. "That was not my debt; that was his debt."

Jay assured her it would be fine.

"Don't worry." Jake rubbed his wife's pregnant belly and smiled. "It will be all right. We'll figure it out."

Jay told Marjorie that if it came down to it, he would pay off the debt in installments.

The next day, Jay and Marjorie went to see his attorney and learned how serious her situation truly was. As Marjorie's husband, the lawyer said, Jay would be held responsible for the debt. Installment payments were not an option.

Jay's business would be audited, his property seized. Jay began to panic.

"It's a shame you didn't know this was still ongoing when you got married," the lawyer said. "You could have done a prenuptial agreement."

They discussed various ways to protect Jay's finances, and eventually Jay made the suggestion. "What if we undo the paperwork?" Jay didn't want to call it a divorce. That's not what it would be, he told Marjorie. They would still live together as man and wife; the only difference would be on paper. Marjorie agreed that it was the best option and they had their lawyer draw up divorce papers.

Before they signed the papers, Jay spoke with Marjorie. "If we do this, I don't want to tell anyone about it. It'll be between you and me."

"Yeah. Of course," Marjorie said. "Our little secret."

Their divorce was finalized on January 2, 1998.

For years, Jay and Marjorie talked about going back to Las Vegas and getting remarried with a prenuptial agreement in place. They would do it on the same day as their first marriage, so their anniversary would stay the same. But as more time passed, they decided that this arrangement worked for them. Nobody in Jay's life knew of the divorce—not his parents, his brother, or his closest friends. It was a secret Jay had kept for nearly seven years. Marjorie, however, had told someone—Larry Weisberg.

By signing the divorce papers, Marjorie had unwisely entrapped herself. With the divorce, if she left Jay she would be entitled to little more than child support. All of the assets, all of the accounts, were in his name. Marjorie did, however, remain the primary beneficiary of Jay's life insurance.

"We are living together as a family," Marjorie told Butcher as police continued to search her home. "As far as I'm concerned that's all that."

Marjorie explained that she and Jay were working toward living "separate lives." Jay was planning to purchase a house a few blocks away; Marjorie would continue to live at the house and maintain primary custody of Noah. It would be an amicable split.

"Okay, now the extended family, Jay's parents, they don't know that you guys aren't married?"

"They don't know that, no!" Marjorie exclaimed. "And I promised him I would tell no one or humiliate him, because his family and friends think he has been living a normal, perfect life with a pretty wife and beautiful child and everything's happy and rosy, and it's all a big farce!"

A moment later, Marjorie tempered the statement. "You know, not a farce, but it has been a façade that the two of us agreed upon, you know, to have a family and, you know, this would give Jay the opportunity to have an appearance of something that he really didn't have."

Just then, Jake Orbin Jr. arrived at the house. When he had heard the commotion on the phone, he'd dropped everything and rushed over. For the past week he had been staying at his parents' house. As he drove up to the house and saw the fire truck, police cars, and investigators, the knot in the pit of his stomach grew. His first thought was that his brother had been found dead. But when he arrived, an officer informed him that this was just part of the missing persons investigation. Outside the house, Jake Jr. saw a muscular, older man being questioned by police. The man looked out of place among the detectives and paramedics. As one of the detectives led him through the house toward Noah's room, he only caught a little of what Marjorie was saying to Butcher.

"Thank you for coming, Jake," Marjorie said. "Did you hear that? Were you on the phone?"

"Yes, I was," he said solemnly.

"It is the most terrifying thing in the world!" Marjorie exclaimed.

Jake Jr. grew very quiet. He didn't know what to believe. After the SWAT team cleared the premises, Noah was allowed back into his bedroom. When Jake Jr. spoke to him he was lying in bed, hugging his dog, Sasha. Noah seemed more confused than upset. He didn't want to leave the house; he wanted to stay with his mom.

While Detective Butcher was interviewing Marjorie, Detective Amy Dillon spoke with Larry Weisberg on the front driveway. Following his aggressive confrontation, Larry was subdued. He held a bandage to the gash on his head as they spoke. Larry told the detective he had only known Marjorie a few months and had never met Jay. "All I know is that he *was*, I mean *is*, a businessman."

Marjorie and Jay had been divorced for several years, Larry explained, and they had an arrangement where Marjorie would take care of the home and Noah, while Jay supported the family financially. He thought the relationship was strange, but it was "none of his affair." When pressed further, he said, "It's not my place to disclose information about Jay and Marjorie's relationship."

Larry flatly refused to go into any detail regarding his relations with Marjorie or his feelings toward her. He said he lived on his own and made a good living. "I can understand where you're coming from, you know, am I gonna knock off this guy?" Larry laughed. "I don't even know what he looks like."

Larry was adamant in his defense of Marjorie. He described her as a good woman and highly intelligent. "She," Larry said pointing Marjorie's direction, "does not know one thing. She is worried sick because of that little guy in there. Jay Orbin idolized that little guy and vice versa."

While Detective Dillon was jotting down notes Larry asked, "What has happened? Can you tell me? Did you find him?"

"Sir," Dillon said, "we're trying to find out what happened."

"Well, we don't know what happened. We have no idea.

We've been speculating. Ask your partner!" Larry said. "What you expect to find here is beyond my imagination. We're totally innocent, and I'm looking you straight in the eye and telling you that."

After completing her interview with Marjorie, Detective Butcher joined the other officers searching the house. It was still unclear what had happened to Jay, and detectives weren't quite sure what they were looking for. The house was clean but the kitchen was cluttered. Paint rollers, caulking guns, wood filler, air fresheners, and piles of paperwork littered the table and kitchen island.

Off the laundry room was the door to the garage. Inside, several detectives were sorting through neatly labeled storage boxes and cataloging evidence. As Butcher entered the garage, she noticed that it was spotless. The floor was coated with a fresh speckled epoxy coating and new pieces of cardboard covered the glass windows. On the garage door was a large patch, which covered both the interior and the exterior of the door.

Butcher left the garage and headed down the hallway toward the master bedroom. She noticed several picture frames hanging on the walls in the hallway. Some of the full frames contained pictures of Marjorie and Noah; not a single one contained a photograph of Jay. *Had she taken Jay's photos down because she couldn't stand to look at him?* Butcher wondered.

The house had four bedrooms off of the hallway. The office contained a desk with a hutch and a computer. A tanning bed was situated in the center room; on the floor were piles of papers and some blond hair extensions. The bedroom farthest west was Noah's room.

Clothes and underwear were strewn across the floor in the master bedroom. Near the king-sized bed Butcher noticed several unopened boxes of electronic stereo equipment. Along the back wall there was a wood dresser. Butcher opened one of the drawers and found several pairs of brightly colored men's bikini briefs. Butcher picked up a pair and noticed they were very small, much too small to fit a 280-pound man. Most of the other drawers were empty, save for a new pair of men's shorts. A black purse in the bedroom contained an envelope with $3,332.00 in cash. It was the money Marjorie had admitted to withdrawing from the ATM each day. Several receipts for stereo equipment and the piano were also in the purse.

At about 10:30 p.m., Butcher was walking through the hallway when Noah emerged from his bedroom, groggily rubbing his eyes. "Where's my mommy?"

Butcher crouched down and said sweetly, "She's inside, having a seat on the couch. Did you want to sleep in your mom's bed tonight?"

"Yes! Yes!" Noah said enthusiastically.

"Why don't we step into your room and then when we're all done, we'll have you transferred to your mom's room, okay?"

Noah's room was painted blue and had an entertainment unit along the wall, with a Nintendo video game console and a computer. It was lit up by a nightlight. A dog was curled up on the floor. As Butcher entered the room, the dog barked.

"Sasha!" Noah said as he pointed his finger at the dog. "Naughty, naughty. Do not bark or our head aches!"

Sasha dropped her head. Butcher patted the dog on the head and ran her fingers through her fur. "How long have you had her?"

"I don't know." Noah shrugged. "Ever since I was born."

"You've had a lot of people here, talking to you and stuff," Butcher said gently. "I just need to ask you a few questions about your dad."

Noah nodded.

"Do you know where he's at right now?"

"No! We don't know!" Noah emphatically shook his head. "We don't know if he's still in his truck or if he got hurt or got in a car accident. My mom called every hospital. She called the police. They said there was no car accidents."

"That's why we're here. You know that right? To try to find him. Do you remember when you last talked with your dad?"

"I think last Monday or something."

Noah said he never saw his father after he left for Florida. Butcher quickly realized that he was unaware of what had happened to his father. Butcher left the room and closed the door softly behind her. As she walked toward the living room, she winced. If her gut was correct, Noah had lost his father. It was heartbreaking.

After leaving Noah's room, Butcher saw Marjorie still sitting on the couch. "Marjorie, if you can just scoop him up when we're done here, he wanted to make sure he sleeps with you tonight."

At about 1:30 a.m., detectives concluded their search. Room by room they had rummaged through the house, seizing paperwork, letters, receipts, checks, bank statements, life insurance policies, cell phones, computers, and items Marjorie had taken from the warehouse. The evidence was secured in Detective Dillon's vehicle and taken back to the police station.

That night Marjorie barely slept. Larry had left. His blood was still smeared across the foyer, covered by paper towels. Police had torn the house up from top to bottom. Marjorie spent most of the night trying to put the house back together. As the sun was coming up, Marjorie curled up on the couch and drifted off to sleep. The next morning, a Friday, she awoke to the sound of the telephone ringing. It was Larry.

"Get ready," he said. "I'm taking you to an attorney."

When Larry arrived, Marjorie was stunned. His face was beaten and bruised, and there was a large scab over his eye. Larry drove Marjorie to meet his friend, Warren Levenbaum, a senior partner at the firm Levenbaum & Cohen. He was a fast-talking gray-haired attorney from Boston with a square face and tight, thin lips. He established his practice in Arizona in 1972, specializing in accident and injury cases. His firm primarily handled auto accidents, wrongful death, dog bite, personal injury, and medical malpractice suits.

At the attorney's office, Marjorie told Levenbaum the same story she had been telling Jay's family.

"I have no idea what happened to Jay," she insisted. "His business was very high risk."

"Was he involved in drugs?" Levenbaum asked. "Did anyone he knew have any kind of mob ties?"

They discussed the possibilities that it could have been "a hit."

"I just want you to deal with the police for me," Marjorie said, "so they don't break into my home, terrorizing me and my son again."

Levenbaum assigned Marjorie to one of the firm's new associates, Rob Webb, a young, dark-haired attorney from New Orleans.

Over the next few days, Marjorie tried to continue on as everything were normal. Noah was terrified. He didn't want to go to school. Anytime anything made a sound, he would be wrapped around his mother's leg. Meanwhile the phone rang constantly, with calls from Jay's friends and family searching for him. With each day that passed, Jay's loved ones became more suspicious. Every call caused Marjorie to become more irritated and defensive. Through it all, Marjorie clung to Larry.

For the next few weeks, Detective Butcher sorted through evidence collected during the search and continued speaking with Jay's family and business associates to determine his movements in the days leading up to his disappearance.

To Butcher there was no doubt Marjorie had something

to hide. Her husband, or ex-husband, was missing, and she was already moving her new boyfriend into the house. Butcher confirmed that Marjorie and Jay were divorced on January 2, 1998. But Marjorie said the divorce was just a technicality and they were still living together as man and wife. Everyone in Jay's family believed they were a loving couple. Yet at the same time, Marjorie claimed that their relationship was a farce and that theirs was a platonic arrangement. The two stories contradicted each other. *Which was it?* Butcher wondered.

Larry Weisberg's appearance in this investigation opened up a slew of new possibilities. The man's violent outburst with police was suspect. *Was it possible Jay was murdered because he found out about the affair?* she wondered. *Had Larry killed Jay in a rage?*

Whatever had happened to Jay, Butcher had no doubt Marjorie had the answers. But there was not a shred of physical evidence to prove Jay was dead, much less that it was murder.

Butcher's worst fear was that Jay's body was rotting in a shallow grave somewhere and would never be discovered. She had seen it in other cases where a family member vanished and was never heard from again. It was often worse for the family than knowing their loved one was deceased. The family would be tortured, clinging to the hope that the victim was alive somewhere, while knowing they were likely dead. As tragic as it would be for the Orbin family, Butcher actually hoped Jay's body would turn up. If it never did, the killer would likely get away with murder.

Weeks passed and nothing new was discovered. While the Jay Orbin investigation was never far from Butcher's thoughts and the case file never left her desk, other missing persons cases were stacking up. "Unfortunately, it comes to a point where there's nothing else you can do and you move on to other cases," Butcher recalled.

During the next few weeks, Butcher called Marjorie just

one more time to discuss the case. Toward the end of the conversation, she told Marjorie that if Jay's body was never found, it would be seven years before she would be able to collect on the insurance policies. Butcher meant the remark as innocuous. Later, she would reflect on the comment. It may have triggered a homicide investigation.

CHAPTER 14

The first few weeks of October 2004 passed by with agonizing slowness for the Orbins. Nobody knew exactly what happened to Jay, and the helplessness ate at the family. Jake had grown bitter, angry, and distant. Joann was consumed by despair—hysterical crying spells broken up by moments of quiet anguish. Jake Jr. was doing his best to stay strong for his parents. He served as the family spokesman with detectives and spent his days methodically documenting information he deemed helpful, sending regular e-mail updates to the police. Underneath his composed façade, however, he was reeling in pain.

It had been more than a month since the Orbins had last heard Jay's voice. During that time he had missed his brother's birthday, regular Sunday get-togethers, and business appointments. That simply wasn't Jay.

There was no doubt in their minds that something terrible had happened. Best-case scenario, he was involved in a car accident and was lying somewhere in a hospital bed, unconscious or somehow unable to communicate. But Jay's friends had called every hospital between here and Florida and there weren't any unidentified patients fitting Jay's description. Besides, everything seemed to indicate that Jay had made it home to Phoenix before he vanished. The

Orbins didn't want to face it; they avoided saying it; but they knew Jay was almost certainly dead.

In the past weeks they had learned so much confusing information about Marjorie, they weren't quite sure what to think. Detective Butcher had been keeping the Orbins filled in on the developments of the case, including the detail about Marjorie not being able to collect Jay's insurance for seven years. When Butcher told Jake Jr. about the divorce, he was stunned. The night of the search warrant, when he saw that man outside of his brother's house, Jake Jr. instantly knew something was wrong. Butcher confirmed what Marjorie had admitted to her: She had been cheating on Jay. He wondered if his brother had known.

The divorce, the affair, Marjorie's behavior—it all left Jake Jr. with a sinking feeling in the pit of his stomach. But he still wasn't ready to believe that Marjorie had harmed Jay. It just wasn't possible. "The wheels in my head are spinning but nothing's grabbing on—no, this can't be happening. My brother's still alive, he's out there," Jake Jr. recalled. "You just start thinking, something's going on here. You don't know what it is because nobody's talking."

Speaking to Marjorie was frustrating. She continued to claim she had no idea where Jay was, but she seemed to know more than she was saying. But when the Orbins tried to pin her down on answers, Marjorie became defensive. What had started out as a normal conversation escalated into full-blown accusations. During one phone call with Joann, Marjorie snapped and accused her of feeding information to the police.

"She literally cut my mom off and said, 'you can't see your grandson,'" Jake Jr. recalled. "Marjorie was very controlling. She didn't want to have the family involved anymore. She wanted it all on her own."

Weeks passed and the Orbins weren't able to see Noah. They were used to visiting with him at least once a week and Joann was distraught. She just wanted to hold him in her arms and connect with a piece of her son. Acting as mitigator, Jake Jr. continued to speak with Marjorie for Noah's sake. During one phone call, Jake Jr. told her, "Mom wants to see Noah."

After some coaxing, Marjorie finally agreed and they arranged to meet at Roadrunner Park, a large park with a swing set, playground, and duck pond that the Orbins used to frequent. Coincidentally, it was across the street from Jodi Weisberg's home.

On October 16, Jake Jr. and his mom arrived at the park. While they waited, Joann stood at the edge of the pond—the spot where Jay and Noah used to feed the ducks. She appeared haunted. Her eyes were red and swollen, her skin starkly pale. Joann hadn't been eating and had lost a significant amount of weight.

Around noon, Marjorie arrived with Noah. But when Jake Jr. saw who else was with her, his blood boiled. He recognized the man as the blond bodybuilder who had been at his brother's house the night police served the search warrant. With him were two young boys, one who looked close to Noah's age.

"This is Larry," Marjorie said. "And these are his grand-children."

Larry politely shook each of their hands, brushed past the Orbins, and sat down at a park bench. He didn't say another word to the family, not even the slightest mention that he was sorry to hear about Jay's disappearance. Jake Jr. found this to be totally disrespectful and felt Larry's presence was completely out of place. He had to mask his outrage to carry on a normal conversation.

"Larry's grandkids are around Noah's age," Marjorie explained. "I thought it would be good for him to have someone to play with."

Joann walked over and tried to visit with her grandson, but Noah was running around the park, playing with the other boys. Joann came back to speak with Marjorie and told her about all the hospitals the Orbins had contacted.

"Have you heard anything new?" Joann asked.

"No, unfortunately," Marjorie said.

Joann dropped her head and began sobbing hysterically. Marjorie put her hand on her back for comfort.

"Don't worry," Marjorie said flatly. "Everything will be okay. I'm sure Jay will turn up soon."

Marjorie's words were haunting.

"This sent chills down my spine," Jake Jr. later told Butcher. "All I could think about was that ever since she found out that the insurance doesn't kick in for years that there may be an anonymous call on where he will be found."

Butcher typed up Jake Jr.'s comment and added it to the police report. Jake Jr. asked for Marjorie to be put under twenty-four-hour surveillance, in case she tried to move Jay's body. Ultimately, Butcher did not follow through with the suggestion. Butcher felt horrible for the Orbins. They were a nice family who didn't deserve to be put through such tremendous grief. At this point in the investigation, there was no question in Butcher's mind: Jay was dead. She was determined to do whatever she could to get justice for the Orbins.

For the next few days, Butcher followed up on leads and tracked down surveillance video and financial records. She confirmed that Jay last logged onto his E Trade financial account on September 8, at 5:38 p.m. His total assets: $70,865. Butcher also contacted Jay's physician to try to confirm Marjorie's claim that Jay was impotent. There was no record he was ever treated for any sexual condition.

Butcher spoke with Tom Ellis, Jay's real estate agent. Tom confirmed that Jay was looking to buy a house, but only as a possible investment property.

"So Jay never mentioned anything to you about splitting from Marjorie?" Butcher asked.

"No. Never," Tom said.

CHAPTER 15

On October 23, forty-five days after he went missing, Jay Orbin's dismembered torso was discovered in the northeast Phoenix desert. The gruesome crime scene was lit up that afternoon by the beaming Arizona sun. Homicide investigators scoured the landscape, with no idea what they were dealing with or searching for. In less than three days, the case would collide with Detective Butcher's missing persons investigation.

Detective David Barnes was assigned as the lead investigator. At the time he hadn't heard of Jay Orbin's disappearance and wasn't aware of Butcher's investigation. Tall and athletic with a measured tone of voice, Barnes was a dogged detective with an unflappable demeanor. When politics stood in the way of justice, he was unapologetically outspoken. "I always felt I worked for the deceased victim and their family, not the politics of a big-city department that played games with people's lives," Barnes explained.

A hard-working family man, Barnes had been married to his wife, Trish, since he was nineteen. They had three children, two girls and a boy, the eldest in college. Growing up in Los Angeles, Barnes dreamed of becoming a cop. After he was mustered out of the Air Force he joined the Phoenix Police Department and within three years was promoted to detective. At the age of thirty-six, he became the youngest detective in Phoenix history to make the homicide squad.

When he was first assigned to the Jay Orbin murder investigation, Barnes was an up-and-coming young detective with a promising future. But before it was over his reputation would be tarnished and his career would be in shambles.

The day after the body was discovered, local news broke the story about the dismembered torso in the Rubbermaid tub. The news reports got the attention of the Orbin family. The crime scene was just miles from Jay's home. It seemed too close to be a coincidence. The following Monday, Jake Jr. called Butcher. "Do you think it could be Jay?" he asked.

"I hadn't heard anything, but I will look into it," Butcher replied.

At 10:20 a.m., while the medical examiner was dissecting the torso on the autopsy table, Butcher received a call: Jay's Ford Bronco had been located less than four miles from the Orbins' home.

Butcher grabbed her gun and rushed to the site, calling for forensic support along the way. She arrived about half an hour later to find Jay's 1998 green and tan Ford Bronco abandoned in the Arabian Trails apartment complex parking lot. The remnants of an abandoned vehicle sticker were stuck on the passenger-side window. The doors were locked and the rear window had been rolled down. The rear seat of the truck was folded down and a can of Glade air freshener lay on the center console. The driver's seat was close to the steering wheel, indicating that a smaller person had been driving.

After the evidence technician arrived to photograph the vehicle, Butcher spoke with some of the residents of the apartment complex. One man said he had noticed a white female with long blond hair park across the street, walk toward the Bronco, remove a sticker from the passenger side of the windshield, and leave. It was about two weeks ago, the man said.

"She was slim," he said. "I think she mentioned something about her 'crazy little sister.'"

"Do you think you could identify the woman?" she asked.

"Yeah. I think so."

The Bronco was towed to the police station basement and parked in a forensic examination bay. About four hours later, Detective Barnes was drying out evidence discovered with the torso in that same basement, unaware that the key to unlocking the victim's identity was parked just fifty feet away. Barnes was approached by Detective Tommy Kulesa, who told him about a missing person he had been investigating named Jay Orbin. They decided to test the keys found with the victim on the man's truck.

At 6:25 p.m. Barnes called Detective Jan Butcher: He had found Jay Orbin.

It was a Tuesday morning, October 26, three days after the torso discovery, when Butcher arrived at the Phoenix homicide unit to brief Detective Barnes on the case. For thirty-two days the Jay Orbin disappearance had been *her* case. She worked it day and night, chased every lead, and in the process, became very close with the Orbin family. Now that it was officially a homicide investigation, Butcher was forced to relinquish control. It pained her.

"You can stay on and help out," Barnes said. "I would like you to."

Butcher sighed. She slid a stack of papers across his desk, about six inches thick.

"Here's the copies of all my case files," she said. "Everything you requested."

The tension in Barnes' tiny, cluttered office was obvious. He sensed Butcher's animosity and understood the reason why. Butcher was passionate about the case and she wanted to be the one to solve it. But two lead detectives on one case was a bad idea and now it had to be investigated as a murder.

Butcher left and Barnes spent the rest of the day studying the case files. Reading through the report, one thing was apparent—Marjorie was lying. Every piece of evidence contradicted her story that Jay never came home, especially the body being found just miles from their house. For the next few days, Butcher would assist Barnes on the case as he got up to speed. The Phoenix Police Department didn't follow the partner system, which was common on other homicide squads. Instead, detectives all assisted on each other's cases when needed.

Later that afternoon, Barnes met Butcher at the Arabian Trails apartment complex to determine if any of the residents could pick Marjorie out of a photo line-up. Two residents could not identify anyone. The man who said he had seen a blond woman identified the wrong suspect.

The detectives spent the rest of the evening sorting through Jay's credit card and financial documents. At about five p.m., Butcher was reviewing a stack of credit card statements from Citibank when she noticed a transaction that caught her attention. On September 9, the day after Jay disappeared, there was a $482.31 charge at a Phoenix Target location. What was curious about this purchase was that it was made on a credit card that Jay had used on September 8 at the La Quinta Inn in Tucson. The next day, someone had used this same card in Phoenix. *Was that person Marjorie?* Butcher wondered.

From the credit card statements, Butcher could see how much was spent where, but not what was purchased. Butcher called the Target store, spoke with the security manager, and requested for a copy of the receipt to be faxed to the police station. When Butcher received the fax a few moments later, she nudged Barnes. "Check it out."

That day someone had used Jay's credit card to purchase nearly $500 worth of cleaning products, mops, buckets, rugs, scrub brushes, and men's clothes, as well as some other items.

"It sounds like the kind of stuff you need to clean up a murder scene," Barnes said. He called the credit card company and confirmed that there was only one of these cards issued to the account. This was important. If Marjorie made the purchases, that put her in possession of Jay's credit card, the day after he disappeared.

That evening, Barnes and Butcher went to a local Target store to see exactly what had been purchased. Upon arrival, Barnes spoke with the store manager on duty and explained why they were there. The manager called a few employees over and asked them to gather the merchandise. Meanwhile, Butcher requested an evidence technician to photograph the items.

Twenty minutes later, the employees brought the items to the store's garden shop to be photographed. The amount of cleaning supplies was staggering—four bottles of Tilex, two bottles of Clorox, Liquid-Plumr, seven scrub brushes, two buckets, and a Shark steam-cleaning machine. Before the detectives left, store security cued up the surveillance video. Sure enough, on tape was a woman with platinum blond hair, shopping with her son.

"That's Marjorie," Butcher exclaimed. "We got her!"

After the discovery of the credit card charges, Barnes contacted the Maricopa County Attorney's Office. Veteran prosecutor Noel Levy was assigned the case. In his late sixties, Levy had a long face and salt-and-pepper hair. Behind his round framed bifocals, heavy eyelids draped over his eyes. He had a slow, deliberate manner of speaking. An Arizona native, Levy's father had had a thriving private law practice in the 1930s and had encouraged his son to go into law. In 1955, Levy joined the Marine Corps. After being discharged, he went back to college and married, and he and his wife had three children. While working and raising a family, he attended law school at the University of Arizona in Tucson. But money was tight and the Levy's barely made ends meet. After just one year in law school, Levy took a three-year hiatus and went back into the Marines where he served as an officer from 1961 to 1964. Three years later, he finished his law degree and went into private practice, handling mostly accident and injury cases.

In 1980, he joined the Maricopa County Attorney's Office, where he would work as a prosecutor for the next twenty-five years. Over his career, Levy handled some of Arizona's most high-profile cases. In 1990, he successfully prosecuted the case of Debra Jean Milke, a twenty-five-year-old mother who was convicted of conspiring to kill her four-year-old son for the insurance money. Milke received the death penalty and became one of Arizona's few female death row inmates. A year later, Levy also won a controversial decision in the prosecution of Ray Krone, who was convicted and sentenced to death for the murder of a bartender. Krone was once dubbed the Snaggletooth Killer because forensic dentistry matched his dental records to a bite mark left on the victim. But the match turned out to be inaccurate. In 2002, after spending more than a decade behind bars, a forty-five-year-old Krone became the one hundredth innocent man to be freed from death row. While his role in the Krone case became somewhat of a black mark on his record, Levy came to understand his role in the legal system was not to assign guilt or punishment. "I tend to take the attitude that you present the evidence as openly and honestly as possible and then the jury determines it—that's the way it's supposed to be," Levy explained. "A long time ago I accepted that that's how it's supposed to work"

By 2004, Levy was a grandfather of seven and had technically retired from the prosecutor's office. Not quite ready for a life of leisure, he signed up for an additional yearly contract.

When Barnes first briefed him on the Jay Orbin murder, Levy knew it was going to be a difficult case. But in 2004, he couldn't fathom how complex or drawn out it would become. The Jay Orbin murder would take up the next five years of his life and become the last case of his long career.

Levy assisted Barnes in securing three search warrants for the following day. They were about to aggressively come after Marjorie and Larry. Before conducting the searches, however, detectives had the agonizing task of informing the Orbins that they had found Jay.

By the somber look on the detectives' faces, the Orbins knew the news wasn't good. It was early on the afternoon of October 28. Barnes and Butcher arrived at Jay's parents' house to speak with the Orbins in person. Informing parents that their loved one is dead is one of the most unsettling tasks anyone in law enforcement faces. Because of the condition of the body, this was particularly disturbing.

"Would you like something to drink?" Joann asked as she welcomed the detectives into her home.

They both declined with a polite "No, thank you." Barnes introduced himself; when he said he was with the homicide unit, he noticed the Orbins' expressions change. They all sat down in the living room as Jay's parents braced themselves for news they weren't ready to hear.

"There's no easy way to say this," Barnes said slowly. "We think we found Jay's remains."

"No!" Joann sobbed. She grabbed onto Jake and they held each other, weeping. Jake Jr.'s face twisted with agony. Butcher reached for him and gently squeezed his hand in an expression of sympathy.

"We're ninety-nine percent sure it's him," Barnes continued. He explained about the keys found with the body and told them that DNA tests would be done to ensure it was Jay.

"Can we see him?" Jake asked.

"There's not much to see," Barnes said. "We only found part of him."

As delicately as possible, Barnes told the Orbins that police had not found their son's legs, arms, or head. The color drained from Jake's face. He appeared as if he were about to be sick. Tears streaming down her face, Joann cried in disbelief, "You didn't find his head?"

"He was . . ." Barnes said haltingly, "decapitated. His head is gone."

It was unthinkable.

Joann gasped. "Who could do that to him?"

CHAPTER 16

Brandishing assault rifles and large shotguns, half a dozen SWAT officers, dressed head to toe in heavy black body armor, stormed the quaint one-story home on 317 E. Orange Drive in Phoenix.

Stealthily, they secured the perimeter and advanced in pairs toward the front and back doors. The officers leveled their weapons and, with a sudden forceful blast, shot the hinges off the doors, splintering wood in all directions. The shots rang throughout the quiet neighborhood, severing the calm of the otherwise peaceful Thursday afternoon. Neighbors peered through their blinds, gawking at the dramatic scene with shock and amazement. It was an astonishing and unexpected sight. This was a virtually crime-free neighborhood that hardly ever hosted a raucous party, much less an entire SWAT team. The residents were older, law-abiding folks; the Phoenix mayor lived right across the street.

As the SWAT unit burst inside the home they announced their presence by shouting, "Phoenix Police. We have a warrant." They blew through the house room by room, busting down doors, securing each area "clear." When it was apparent there was no threat, they exited the premises and signaled the detectives across the street with a wave. Larry Weisberg was not at home.

It was 4:07 p.m. on October 28 and the Phoenix Police were serving one of three simultaneous search warrants—one at Larry Weisberg's home, one at the Orbins' home, and one at the business warehouse for Jayhawk International. Larry's home would be the only one to receive such a dramatic, forceful entry. Because of his aggressive behavior when police served the first search warrant on the Orbin house, his was deemed "high risk."

After the SWAT officers cleared the house, seven detectives including Butcher and Sergeant Gilbert Soto, a heavyset veteran detective with a dark mustache and a wry sense of humor. The detectives fanned out to search for any evidence that could implicate Larry Weisberg in the Jay Orbin murder.

From the outside, Larry's house appeared cozy and welcoming—painted light-yellow stucco with a front yard neatly landscaped with trees and grass. Two chairs were situated on the front patio, under the awning. It was an older home, at least by Phoenix standards, built in 1945. Detective Butcher led the way through the front door, which opened up to a family room furnished with a small dining room set.

The home was much nicer than a bachelor pad, but clearly decorated without the touch of a woman. The furniture was mostly mismatched, without any particular theme or style. It looked like the home of a divorcé who was still adjusting to the single life. Near the north wall of the entry way, Butcher noticed a photograph of Marjorie on a small wooden table. Handwritten on the picture: *I'm yours.*

"Check this out." She motioned to Soto.

He glanced at the picture. "Bet the husband would have liked to know that."

Butcher passed through the hallway to the kitchen where more photographs of Marjorie and Noah were attached with magnets to the refrigerator. Carefully, she opened each of the kitchen drawers and cabinets, searching for anything unusual or peculiar. In the cabinet above the stove she removed a large, ominous butcher knife; eleven folding knives; and an out-of-place combat knife. Butcher bagged each item.

The house had three small bedrooms. Situated in the guest room was a white futon mattress, an electronic vibrating chair, and, like in the Orbin home, a tanning bed. Throughout the house dozens of love letters, cards, and notes to Larry from Marjorie were displayed—like a lovestruck schoolboy hanging his girlfriend's picture in his gym locker.

Some of the notes were flowery and romantic: *I love you in so many ways I have never known,* and *There's no escaping the fact that what's happening between us was meant to be.* Others letters were sweet: *You walked in and everything changed, suddenly I found myself smiling almost all the time.* Others still were seductive and sexually explicit: *You hot, sexy love tool,* and *I pleasured myself there, M.*

All of the original notes were impounded.

Meanwhile, Sergeant Soto searched the master bedroom, which consisted of little more than a large bed and chest of drawers. The bathroom was filled with the usual toiletries: hair brushes, gel, soap, toothpaste, lotion, and medicine. When Soto opened the cabinet underneath the sink he was surprised to find a small Ziploc bag containing hypodermic needles, syringes, and a small vial of steroids. Apparently Larry had been "juicing," which could explain his large muscular build and short fuse. Soto confiscated the illegal drugs and then turned his attention toward the shower. With one swift motion, he pulled back the shower curtain.

He paused, took out his cell phone, and called his supervisor.

* * *

Detective Barnes was at the Orbin house when Sergeant Karen Vance got the call from Soto. He told her they had made a "discovery" in Weisberg's bathroom; she put him on speaker phone for the other detectives to hear.

"We found the head and shoulders," Soto said in a dry tone.

Everybody froze; Barnes's eyes were saucer-wide.

"We all about fainted," Barnes recalled. "Until Soto said he was in the shower and that was the shampoo Weisberg uses."

A burst of laughter broke the tension.

"This job, you have to joke and be witty or it will eat you up," Barnes explained. "Soto got the joke for the year and we laughed about that one for many months."

Earlier that morning, Detective Barnes had been busy coordinating officers to serve the three simultaneous search warrants. Each location was assigned seven detectives and forensic investigators. Barnes would be escorting Marjorie and Larry back to the station for questioning. While DNA tests had not yet confirmed the victim's identity, because of the Bronco keys and the close proximity of the tub to the Orbin's home, Barnes had no doubt the torso belonged to Jay Orbin. Now that detectives knew his body had been frozen and viciously dismembered, they needed to know where the murder occurred and with what. With any luck, he hoped they would even find the murder weapon.

"We knew who the suspects were. We knew it was Marjorie and we knew it was Larry," Barnes recalled. "It was just a matter of proving it."

At the Orbin home Barnes approached Marjorie, introduced himself as the lead detective, and told her he needed to bring her down to the police station to take fingerprints and hair and DNA samples. Barnes allowed Marjorie to gather Noah and step out onto the front driveway.

"We need to talk to you about something," Barnes said. "This is not something your son should hear."

*   *   *

When Barnes saw Marjorie for the first time, he felt there
was something off about her. She looked attractive, but
entirely fake. Her hair was unnatural, an almost white shade.
She was overly tanned and sickly thin, with her cheeks
sunken into her face.

Marjorie appeared calm and cooperative as she agreed
to come to the police station. She said she wanted to do
anything she could to help. Marjorie and Noah were put into
the back of a squad car and taken downtown. Meanwhile,
investigators combed over the Orbin home for a second
time. The house was fairly unchanged since the first warrant was served.

Detective Mike Meislish focused mainly on the garage,
where police suspected Jay may have been killed. Meislish
was a husky, gray-haired veteran detective with thick cheeks
and small, quizzical eyes. In his late fifties, Meislish had
been with the department for more than thirty years. One
of the most seasoned investigators in homicide, Meislish
has a passion for solving crimes that has never faded.
Throughout the Jay Orbin murder investigation, Meislish
would work closely with Barnes.

Meislish scanned the garage and noted pieces of cardboard were affixed to the inside of the windows, covering
the panes of glass. Meislish examined the fresh epoxy
paint and hastily patched door, but he quickly realized
something else had changed in the garage. The walls and
ceilings had been freshly painted; not even the faintest
trace of a scuff mark or scratch could be found. Using a
white light technique, he visually examined the garage
floor, but, not surprisingly, there was no trace of blood.

"Jesus," he muttered. "This place is cleaner than most
people's kitchens."

Along the east wall was a large upright Frigidaire freezer.
Meislish opened the door; it was full of various frozen

foods. He set his equipment on the cement floor, grabbed one of the shelves, and attempted to pull it out, but it would not budge. The shelves were affixed to the interior walls of the freezer. If the medical examiner was correct and the body had been frozen, it had not been stored in here. Even without the shelves there was no way it was large enough to store a body.

On shelves along the east wall, Meislish observed something eerily familiar—two jumbo blue Rubbermaid storage tubs. One by one he removed them from the shelves, cautiously peeled off the gray lids, and peered inside. Unlike the box in the desert, these tubs were used to store Christmas decorations, dried flowers, wall sconces, and other knickknacks.

Next to the storage unit in an upright cabinet were some of the cleaning supplies investigators had discovered that Marjorie purchased days after Jay went missing, including the steam cleaner and scrub brushes. Other items were missing, including the mops. Underneath the tool bench was an electric handsaw.

After Meislish finished combing the garage, he went back inside the house. He located Marjorie's brown Louis Vuitton purse lying on the sofa in the family room. He poured the contents onto the dining room table and discovered one of Jay Orbin's credit cards and his checkbook. It appeared to be the same checkbook Jay was known to take with him everywhere he went. As he thumbed through the wallet, looking for receipts, he found something even more curious—an Arizona driver's license with the name Charity Beth McLean.

"Why would she have another woman's driver's license?" Meislish mentioned to another detective.

"Pretty girl," the detective said as he glanced at the license. "Sort of looks like the suspect."

Meislish placed the driver's license in an evidence bag, located the warehouse keys, and headed down the hallway. He walked past the Orbins' home office, where investiga-

Marjorie Kroh was born on October 29, 1961, in Miami, Florida. The daughter of an air-conditioning repairman and a kindergarten teacher, her childhood was wholesome and traditional.

Courtesy of Marjorie Orbin

A beguiling blonde with captivating brown eyes and a sultry smile, Marjorie naturally attracted the opposite sex. By the age of 34, she would marry seven times.

Courtesy of Marjorie Orbin

In her 20s, Marjorie was hired by millionaire strip club owner Michael J. Peter to lead the Vegas-style burlesque dance troupe the Platinum Dolls. With Michael she traveled the world.

Courtesy of Marjorie Orbin

Throughout her life, Marjorie became accustomed to the finer things. She traveled on yachts and private jets, vacationed on tropical islands and lived in mansions.

Courtesy of Marjorie Orbin

During the late 80s, Marjorie lived with Michael J. Peter in his Florida mansion and shared in his extravagant lifestyle—even appearing on an episode of the show *Lifestyles of the Rich and Famous.*   Courtesy of Marjorie Orbin

Born on September 8, 1959, in Phoenix, Arizona, Jay Orbin was the second son to Jake and Joann Orbin, a blue-collar, middle-class Catholic family.
Courtesy of Marjorie Orbin

At first glance, Jay and Marjorie made for quite the mismatched couple. He was casual, down-to-earth and easygoing; she was glamorous, flashy and high-maintenance.

Courtesy of Marjorie Orbin

In late 1995, after months of trying to conceive, Marjorie learned she was pregnant.
Courtesy of Marjorie Orbin

Flipping through their family album Jay and Marjorie appear to be a perfectly normal family.
Courtesy of Marjorie Orbin

Noah Jacob Orbin was born on August 26, 1996. Because of the difficulty Jay and Marjorie had in conceiving, they called Noah their "miracle baby."
Courtesy of Marjorie Orbin

In 2002, Jay purchased a 2,600-square-foot home in an upscale suburb of northeast Phoenix. Marjorie was not a co-signer on the house, for reasons which would be uncovered after Jay's murder.

Author Photo

On September 28, 2004, while police were serving a search warrant on the Orbin home, Marjorie's lover, Larry Weisberg, reportedly attacked a team of SWAT officers and was severely injured.

Courtesy of Phoenix Police

Jan Butcher, a five-year veteran of the Phoenix Police Department, was assigned as the lead investigator on the Jay Orbin disappearance. Author Photo

For veteran Maricopa County prosecutor Noel Levy, the Marjorie Orbin murder trial would be the last case of his career. Author Photo

David Barnes was a nine-year veteran of the Phoenix Police Department and considered an up-and-comer on the force when he became the lead detective on the Jay Orbin homicide. Author Photo

On December 6, 2004, Marjorie was arrested for first-degree murder. In her mug shot she appeared despondent.

Courtesy of Phoenix Police

On trial for murder in 2009, Marjorie bore only a faint resemblance to the glamorous blonde showgirl she once was.

Photo by Ross Mason

Marjorie's defense team, Herman Alcantar (left) and Robyn Varcoe (standing) put on a bombshell defense in court. Prosecutor Treena Kay (front) was appointed to the case halfway through the trial.

Photo by Ross Mason

tors were packing up a black Compaq computer tower and a Toshiba laptop. Packed in evidence bags around the house were various store receipts, checks, credit cards, miscellaneous papers, knives, cleaning supplies, cell phones, journals, letters, packing tape, garbage bags, and rolls of plastic sheeting.

In the master bedroom, another detective was tearing through the dresser. Meislish entered the walk-in closet, which was packed with clothes, neatly organized according to color. On the top shelf, Meislish found an opaque storage box containing XXL polo shirts and pants that would fit a 42-inch waist. The victim's clothes had already been packed up, he noted. Replacing them on the racks were men's sleeveless T-shirts and 36-inch waist pants—Larry Weisberg's size.

In a light brown wooden case on another closet shelf was a white powder, divided into four small piles on a piece of glass, and a razor blade. At first Meislish thought it was cocaine, but the lab would later determine it to be methamphetamine.

Back at Weisberg's home, Detective Jan Butcher had finished the interior search and had moved on to the backyard.

The enclosed back patio was covered with numerous potted plants and a small self-contained fountain, with a screen door that led out to the large grassy area. Tucked away toward the rear of the yard was a small, stand-alone shed with double swing-out doors. Butcher and evidence technician Jerry Yarbrough walked over to the shed. The padlock had already been cut off by the SWAT unit. The shed was filled with gardening tools, fishing gear, hardware, and other tools.

Butcher glanced around the shed as Yarbrough photographed. Hanging on the east wall of the shed was a large metal hacksaw, a blue-handled tree saw, and a chainsaw.

Any number of these tools could have been used to dismember Jay's body, and it was necessary to test each one for blood. On the floor was also an orange electrical cord, a box of black trash bags, and more clear plastic sheeting.

Could this be where Jay's body was dismembered?

Yarbrough did preliminary tests for blood, but he could tell immediately he would not find anything. A thick layer of undisturbed dust and dirt covered the floors, work benches, and most of the tools. Unlike Marjorie's immaculate garage, Larry's shed had not been cleaned for months. There was no possible way Jay Orbin had been butchered in there.

"We've got blood over here," crime scene technician William McMahon hollered across the Jayhawk International warehouse, which was located about twelve miles from Larry Weisberg's home.

He held up the bright pink swab for the other investigators to see before securing it in an evidence bag. McMahon was testing the front metal security door of the warehouse with a substance known as phenolphthalein reagent, which changes to an intense pink color when it comes into contact with blood. It just had.

It was about 6:30 p.m. and McMahon and the six other investigators were combing Jay Orbin's business warehouse, cataloging evidence and processing the scene for blood.

The warehouse was where Jay Orbin had conducted most of his business and stored his merchandise. Now, with the discovery of blood, it was also the location where authorities would come to suspect Jay's body had been dismembered. Investigators had arrived at the warehouse at approximately 4:45 p.m. The spacious rectangular-shaped warehouse was located within a small strip mall, surrounded by other single-story commercial structures. Barbed wire ran along the top of a six-foot chain-link fence, blocking off the business complex from the street. There were five separate suites in the complex, connected with common walls. Jay's business was in the southernmost suite. Plastic decals on the front door read JAYHAWK INTERNATIONAL, and featured Jay's logo: a hawk, with its wings spread broadly.

Along the back wall of the warehouse was a garage door; wooden pallets were stacked along the rear wall. Situated directly behind the warehouse was a six-by-five-foot empty dumpster. McMahon swabbed the interior and exterior of the dumpster and found additional traces of blood.

Inside, Detective Tommy Kulcsa stood in the narrow entryway of the warehouse, observing the building's layout. It was dark. The only light came from the two small desk-top lights in the rear of the building.

After the search of the exterior of the building, Kulesa, McMahon, and another detective went to work on the warehouse, while the rest of the team examined the front office area. Kulesa placed numbered stickers on the shelves as McMahon photographed the scene. Swabs of a reddish-colored substance, believed to be blood, were found on the exterior door frame trim, on the door leading into the office, and on the doorknob leading into the warehouse. Kulesa picked up a trash box near the rear of the warehouse and carefully bagged the torn photographs, rubber gloves, and rolls of tape. As he was digging through the trash, one of the detectives called him over. "I've got something over here."

Kulesa dropped what he was doing and met the detective, who had removed something off one of the top shelves. It was an open package of Skil jigsaw blades. The package originally contained sixteen blades. Two blades were missing.

"You'll find nothing at my place," Larry Weisberg calmly told Detective Barnes as he was fingerprinted. "You guys are barking up the wrong tree."

An evidence technician entered the small police station interrogation room with a swab. Barnes explained to Larry that the warrant compelled him to supply his fingerprints and DNA. Larry was accommodating and cooperative. He opened his mouth wide, allowing the technician to swab the inside of his cheek.

While investigators were serving the warrants, Barnes returned to the downtown Phoenix police station to question Larry and Marjorie. He glanced down at his watch. It was 5:30 p.m. Investigators had been at Larry's house for a few hours now. Curiously, he wondered if they *had* found anything incriminating.

Regardless, Barnes wasn't ready to rule Larry out; his gut told him the man knew more than he was saying. Unfortunately, he wasn't going to talk, at least not tonight. Larry Weisberg had already lawyered up.

Shortly after the SWAT team burst through Weisberg's home, patrol officers arrived at his place of employment, Tri Star Visual Communications, to take him into custody. When Larry was informed his house was being searched, he immediately invoked his right to an attorney. Around six p.m., after his hair and DNA samples were collected, Larry Weisberg was released.

Across the police station, Marjorie was sitting in another interrogation room. She was wearing black yoga pants and a zip-up hoodie, with her hair pulled back under a baseball cap. On the way to the station, Marjorie kept insisting to detectives that Noah not be handed over to the Orbins. "He is not to be taken anywhere, by anyone," she said. After some coaxing, she agreed to let him sit with a female officer while she and Barnes talked.

Coolly, Barnes walked into the interrogation room. He sat at the table across from Marjorie and told her there had been a development.

"We found a body that we believe to be Jay," Barnes said.

At first Marjorie appeared stunned, showing no emotion at all.

"Parts were missing. We didn't find his head," Barnes continued, matter-of-factly. "He had been dismembered."

With that, Marjorie appeared to sob.

"No! No!" Marjorie wept dramatically.

As she cried, Barnes thought her reaction seemed phony. She appeared to be crying, yet there were no tears. She also didn't seem surprised that the remains were found, even when Barnes told her how close they were to her home.

"When were they found?" Marjorie asked, dabbing her cheek with a tissue.

"This past Saturday."

"Why do you think this is Jay?" Marjorie asked.

"We found a set of keys and other things in the pockets of his pants that lead us to believe it is him," Barnes.

Suddenly, Marjorie switched from emotional to defiant.

"You're wrong," she said, shaking her head. "That's not Jay. He never carried anything in his pants pockets. It couldn't be Jay."

Because of his weight, Marjorie said Jay never kept a wallet in his pants pocket. Instead, he always carried things like his credit cards, cash, to-do lists, and a photo of Noah in the front pocket of his shirt.

"DNA testing will be done," Barnes said.

"Has his Bronco been found?"

"Yes," Barnes said. "And the keys found with him opened the truck."

Marjorie shook her head in disbelief, seemingly confused and dumbstruck. Barnes paused and closely monitored her lack of reaction. Marjorie appeared soulless. Her dark eyes were colder than Jay's corpse in the mortuary cooler.

Marjorie told Barnes she needed to talk to her lawyer. She made a call to Levenbaum & Cohen and was told her attorney, Rob Webb, was heading back from Tucson and was on his way to the station. Marjorie said she wanted to sit and wait with her son until Webb arrived, but Barnes told her that Noah had been taken to Childhelp, a child advocacy center, to be interviewed by a victim's advocate. Marjorie was furious. "I specifically told you he wasn't to be taken anywhere."

Barnes left Marjorie in the interrogation room.

At about 6:15 p.m., Rob Webb arrived. He spoke with Marjorie and then with the detectives, who informed him of the developments. When Barnes reentered the interrogation room, Webb was glued to Marjorie's side. Investigators took her DNA and hair samples.

"We have notified Jay's banks and the accounts have been frozen," Barnes said. "All of them."

With that, Marjorie appeared genuinely horrified. Actual tears started running down her cheeks. She seemed devastated and panic-stricken.

"You can't do that!" Marjorie said with dismay. She turned to her attorney. "They can't!"

Webb whispered something in her ear.

"Noah and I will be kicked out of the house!" Marjorie said hysterically.

Unsympathetic, Barnes got up and left the room.

"She never showed any real emotion till I told her the bank accounts were shut down," Barnes recalled. "That's when she got emotional, upset, and angry. That's when you saw the real her."

The search of Larry Weisberg's home was meticulous, but after more than six hours, investigators had found little more than proof of his and Marjorie's sexual relationship. At about 10:10 p.m. Sergeant Soto called Larry to notify him that the search was over and he could return to his home.

"When I get there, are you planning to arrest me?" Larry asked tentatively.

"No," Soto replied.

Larry then asked if officers had confiscated his checkbook.

"We left a report on your dining room table listing all the evidence that was seized," Soto said, without answering his question.

Before hanging up, Larry asked, "Did you search the stand-alone garage in the rear yard?"

"Yes, we did," Soto said.

Larry paused. Over the phone Soto could almost hear him holding his breath. He asked again, "Are you going to arrest me?"

"No, we're not, Mr. Weisberg," Soto said confused.

They hung up and Soto waited for Larry to arrive. About twenty minutes later, a car pulled up to the house. Larry was sitting in the passenger seat of someone else's vehicle. But he didn't get out. Instead he just sat there. Soto drove up next to the car, waved to acknowledge his presence, and drove away. It appeared as if he was waiting for the marked patrol car to drive away before getting out of the car.

It was odd behavior for an innocent man, Soto thought.

CHAPTER 17

At about seven p.m. on October 28, after two miserable hours inside an interrogation room, Marjorie left the police station. Her attorney drove her to the Childhelp center to pick up Noah. On the way, Webb told Marjorie what he had learned through the detectives: three search warrants were served and all of her vehicles had been seized.

"They will be at your house most of the night," Webb said, "so you can't go back there tonight."

"Okay," Marjorie said, calmly.

"They told me it's your husband body," Webb said, as he glanced at Marjorie. "They are pretty sure it's him."

Marjorie nodded. She appeared unfazed. After picking up Noah, Webb asked her where she wanted to be taken.

"You'll have to stay at a hotel for the night if you have nowhere else to go," he said.

"Take me to Larry's daughter's house," Marjorie said.

Webb said he didn't think that was a good idea, but Marjorie was adamant, "Take me to Jodi Weisberg's!"

Marjorie wanted to see Larry. She knew if the cops were searching his house, too, that's where he would be. They arrived at Jodi's about a half an hour later. Marjorie got out of the car, sprinted to the house, and pounded on the front door. Jodi opened it.

"My dad's not here," Jodi said.

Past Jodi, Marjorie could see Larry weaving back and forth in the dark.

"I need to talk to him," Marjorie said. She yelled over Jodi's shoulder to Larry, "I need to talk to you!"

Sullenly, Larry came outside, followed by Jodi and Brad Fritz. Larry appeared dejected. The events of the day clearly had impacted him. The sixty-year-old production manager who was often mistaken for a bodybuilder looked meek. He was trembling. When he saw Marjorie, he began sobbing.

Outside on Jodi's front lawn, everyone began shouting. Marjorie kept trying to pull Larry aside, but Jodi blocked her. "You need to go, Marjorie!"

"I need to speak with you, Larry!" Her voice raised defiantly. "Larry! Larry! Larry! We need to talk."

Larry was stumbling around. He put his head in his hands and cried. Webb grabbed Marjorie's elbow. "Let's go. We need to go." He pulled Marjorie toward the car. "Your son's watching this!"

Marjorie got back in the car and they left. Webb drove her and Noah to a hotel.

"I'll see what I can find out," Webb said. "I'll pick you two up in the morning. We'll take care of this."

That night, Marjorie tried to stay as calm as possible for Noah. After they checked into their room, she tucked him into the hotel room bed and Marjorie went into the bathroom. Vacantly, she stared at her reflection in the mirror for what seemed like hours. When she went back into the bedroom she noticed the glowing digital clock. It was well after midnight. It was officially October 29—her forty-third birthday. There would be no celebration.

At eight a.m. that morning, attorney Rob Webb arrived at Phoenix Police headquarters and called Detective Barnes, who came outside to return Marjorie's house keys. Barnes explained that they would be holding Marjorie's vehicles for several weeks while forensic tests were conducted. Webb provided Barnes a copy of Jay Orbin's last will and testament, as well as a two-page handwritten letter. Webb explained that when his firm was retained by Marjorie, she gave them these documents. Legally, he was obligated to provide them to the police.

Barnes went back to his office and laid out the papers on his desk. The will was dated May 22, 2004, signed by Jay Orbin and witnessed by his friend and an attorney. It bequeathed the majority of the assets to Marjorie Orbin and a few items to Noah Orbin. It also stated that in the event of Jay's death, Marjorie would be the guardian of Noah. If Marjorie was unable or unwilling to serve, guardianship of Noah would go to Jake Orbin Jr.

The handwritten letter attached to the will was more instructions from Jay to Marjorie about how to organize the merchandise. There was also a note that read *Final Card*, directing Marjorie to go to the post office, buy 2,800 prestamped postcards, and have a message printed on them for Jay's customers. The message read: *Dear friends, I'm sorry, but if you are reading this, I have passed away. I left this card with my wife, with instructions to send it out, in case this should happen. I would like to thank you for your business and friendship. I'd also like to ask a favor. My wife Marjorie will still be selling and shipping my catalog items. So if you need our artifacts, jewelry, pewter items, or tribes and symbols posters and postcards, please continue to call and order the products you need. I am grateful for your past and future support and thank you for your continued support of my family. Best wishes and good luck.* The last line stated, *Remember me as Noah's dad.*

Reading the dead man's words was heartwrenching for Barnes. Jay Orbin was clearly a man who loved his family more than anything. It was tragic to think he was he was likely killed by the person he trusted most.

*   *   *

After obtaining Marjorie's house keys, Rob Webb picked Marjorie and Noah up at the hotel and brought them back to the house. The house was torn apart. The cars were missing, the computers were gone, and the bank accounts were seized. Marjorie never expected any of this. All she wanted was for this to be over so she could start putting her life back together.

Marjorie spent that morning frantically trying to put her perfect house back in order. Charity McLean called to wish her happy birthday. When Marjorie heard her friend's voice, she burst into tears.

"I don't know what I'm going to do," she cried.

Around noon, the doorbell rang. Marjorie peered through the peephole. Larry Weisberg scowled back at her. She knew even before she opened the door: Their relationship was over.

For the next few weeks, Detective David Barnes pored through the evidence gathered during the search warrants. The knives, weapons, and tools were tested for traces of blood. Both Marjorie's and Larry's hair and DNA were compared with forensic evidence located on the body. Investigators would comb over the vehicles and scour the computer hard drives for clues. All of this would take weeks.

It was frustrating for Barnes. Although the search warrants had turned up many clues and potential leads, they hadn't found anything that directly linked either Marjorie or Larry to the crime.

Even the blood at the warehouse wasn't compelling evidence. It seemed to indicate that *something* happened to Jay there. But there were just trace amounts on a few doors, not enough to prove a body had been dismembered there. In court that evidence could be argued away. Jay had worked in that warehouse for months and it was possible that he had cut himself or had a nose bleed.

Sitting in his cluttered office, Barnes went over the case

in his head. All he had were theories. He still had no hard evidence to show how Jay was killed, where he was killed, or where he was frozen and dismembered.

Reviewing Jay's credit card transactions and cell phone record seemed to indicate all normal activity had ceased on the evening of September 8. With that, Barnes reasoned that Jay likely died on his birthday. Clearly, Marjorie had lied when she said Jay didn't come home that night. Sometime that day, she had to have seen Jay. During the search, detectives found Jay Orbin's checkbook and briefcase. All of Jay's friends and family said he didn't go anywhere without those. Most damning, however, was that surveillance video of Marjorie using Jay's Citibank card at Target to buy $482.31 worth of cleaning supplies. That purchase was made on September 9 at 5:39 p.m. The day before, Jay had that same card in his possession. Sometime between September 8 and 9, Marjorie obtained Jay's credit card. Still, it didn't prove she was the killer.

Barnes knew that sometime between September 8 and September 22, the day Jay was reported missing, his body had been dismembered and dumped in the desert. But where? And for what purpose? Why cut up a body? Clearly it was not to cover up the crime, because the Rubbermaid tub was left in a place where it would almost certainly be found. Was it cut into pieces so it would be easier to move?

Barnes leaned back in his chair, looked up at the ceiling, and sighed. There was going to be no smoking gun. He was going to have to build his case on circumstantial evidence. He started with the credit cards. Around his office, piles of financial documents were stacked waist high. One of the more tedious, but necessary, parts of the investigation involved going through these documents and reviewing the bank and credit card activity before and after Jay's disappearance. The credit card activity was unusual to say the least. Suddenly, Marjorie had gone from being on a tight $500-a-week allowance to spending a thousand dollars a day.

Barnes picked up one stack of papers and scanned through the hundreds and hundreds of transactions. These records showed when and where the cards were used and for how much, but they didn't show what was purchased. Each and every receipt would need to be obtained individually from each store. Depending on what was purchased, surveillance video would also have to be subpoenaed. It was a daunting task that would take a lot of legwork.

For that job, Barnes enlisted the help of Detective Bryan Chapman, an enthusiastic young investigator with an athletic build and short, dark hair. Chapman was new to the homicide squad and eager to be involved on the case. Excitedly, he began the menial task of tracking down receipts. It was a huge undertaking which would likely take weeks.

Barnes had also requested and received Larry's Weisberg's bank account and credit card records. At first glance, however, it didn't seem like they were going to be that useful to the investigation. "There was nothing in Larry's financials," Barnes recalled. "It's not like all the sudden there's payments to Larry. There's nothing out of the ordinary. There's no change in money."

Meanwhile, Barnes turned his focus toward the cell phones.

In 2004, the technology to trace cell tower records was relatively new in the Phoenix Police Department and only four detectives in homicide were trained to use the pricey equipment. The technology allows law enforcement to pinpoint the approximate location where a wireless phone was used by "pinging" which cell tower the signal bounces off of when in use. Essentially, it lets authorities trace the movements of anyone who uses their cell phone. Each wireless provider keeps the data for a different amount of time, varying between one and three months.

In late October, Barnes got a court order to obtain the cell tower data for Marjorie's, Jay's, and Larry's cell phones. Based on everything he knew about this case, Barnes had a sense of what he could expect to find on Jay's phone, but he was especially interested to see Larry's. Comparing Larry's cell tower records to Marjorie's could show when exactly they were together and if Larry was near the Orbins' house on Jay's birthday.

But when Barnes attempted to obtain those records, he was disappointed to learn that they had been purged. Larry's cell phone provider, Verizon, only kept that data for thirty days. Those records were now lost forever. It was a huge blow to the case against Larry Weisberg. Without that, it would take nothing short of forensic evidence to indict him for the murder.

Unfortunately for Marjorie, her and Jay's wireless provider, AT&T, kept records for ninety days. Barnes had reason to believe it had been Marjorie who was using Jay's cell phone after September 9. Interviews with Jay's business associates indicated she had been returning Jay's phone messages for weeks prior to reporting him missing. At the very least, these records should show that Jay never left town after returning to Phoenix on September 8.

In early November, Barnes received Jay's and Marjorie's cell tower records. He sat down at his desk with Marjorie's in one pile and Jay's in another and perused them page by page. With that information, Barnes was able to retrace Jay Orbin's last business trip from Arizona to Texas into Louisiana and Florida and back. On Jay's birthday, he started his morning in Tucson. Throughout that day, his phone registered in Red Rock, Eloy, and Tempe, Arizona. The last call that afternoon was at 4:31 p.m., registering from a cell tower in Phoenix. This corresponded with surveillance video that showed Jay buying gas at 4:35 p.m. from a nearby Phoenix gas station.

Hours passed and no calls were made from Jay's cell. Then, at 9:44 p.m., someone checked Jay's voice mail. The call registered from a cell tower near the Orbin house. The records couldn't prove the calls were made from inside the house, but it was about as close as it got. Someone had used Jay's phone that night from the house. Because

Noah had no memory of seeing his father, Barnes reasoned that Jay was killed between five p.m. and six p.m. in the garage.

The next morning, between 7:30 a.m. and 1:30 p.m., several more calls were made to Jay's voice mail. All of these calls registered from towers near the Orbin house. For the next two weeks, all of Jay's phone calls were made from Phoenix, near the Orbins' home. This was incredible evidence. The records proved Jay came home on his birthday and never left. Barnes was excited about the discovery, but what he found next nearly knocked him out of his seat.

As Barnes dug deeper into the records, he was able to discover where Jay's phone was on September 20, the day eight people reported seeing his phone number on their caller ID. Barnes believed those calls were made by Marjorie in an attempt to deceive Jay's friends and family and throw investigators off her trail. As expected, Jay Orbin's cell tower records showed these calls were made from Phoenix. In a curious twist, one of these calls registered from a cell tower near Larry's home; four more calls were made near Larry's place of employment.

But as Barnes matched Jay's cell records to Marjorie's, he realized they matched up, practically simultaneously. When a call was made from Jay's phone, a few minutes later, a call was also made from Marjorie's in the same area. When Marjorie made a call at 1:35 p.m., someone made a call from Jay's phone at 1:36 p.m., from the exact same location. The records proved Marjorie was driving around, making calls from Jay's cell, while using her own phone to call Larry and her friends.

My God! She's got his cell phone, Barnes thought.

"This was huge," Barnes recalled. "Very, very incriminating stuff. Now the evidence was starting to stack up."

Barnes sprang up from his desk and headed to the evidence impound. During the search, police confiscated both Marjorie's and Jay's phones. Barnes located Jay's phone and removed the battery to look at the serial numbers, but it didn't match the phone he had with him when he went missing. Marjorie must have had a new phone issued to the same number. Later, Barnes was able to determine she had in fact had a new phone issued to Jay's number on September 28, six days after reporting him missing.

Still, the cell tower records were compelling. Surely it was enough for an indictment. Barnes contacted district attorney Noel Levy and briefed him on the development. The county attorney's office, however, wanted more. This was entirely circumstantial, Levy said. To indict either Marjorie or Larry, they needed more evidence. Barnes would need to dig deeper.

After the discovery of Jay's body, Marjorie's affair with Larry abruptly ended. They spoke a few more times by phone, and saw each other just one more time, but it was no longer romantic. The stress of being entangled in a homicide investigation was too much for their relationship.

Marjorie still spoke with Jake Jr. and continued to profess her innocence. Police, she said, were trying their best to get her, but they were wrong. Jake Jr. asked about Larry, and ultimately Marjorie admitted to the affair.

"You don't understand our relationship. I was lonely!" Marjorie contended. "Jay never touched me anymore."

Marjorie also told him, "Larry is now staying away."

In early November, Marjorie got a call from her old friend Todd Christy. Years earlier, Marjorie had met Todd through Charity McLean. But after Charity moved back to Las Vegas, Marjorie and Todd fell out of contact.

"Charity told me you were going through some tough times," Todd said on the phone, "and that you could probably use a friend."

Todd came to Marjorie's house that night after work. Marjorie was grateful for someone to talk to and some semblance of normalcy. She told Todd the same thing she had told Charity, that her husband had gone missing and that police claimed a piece of his body had been found.

But Marjorie was most distressed by what had happened to her. Marjorie ranted about how the police had seized her car and computers and frozen her bank accounts.

"I don't know how police can do this and leave you so helpless!" Marjorie complained.

Todd felt sorry for her. He offered her his friendship and support.

"I will help you in any way I can," he promised.

The following day, Todd drove her to pick up a rental car.

Marjorie was becoming increasingly concerned about money. With Jay gone, she had planned to manage his business from her house and believed she could easily maintain the sales without him. For the past month, she had carried on making a few deals and shipping out orders. She had also moved much of the valuable merchandise from the warehouse to her home. She had managed to conduct phone and Internet orders relatively smoothly. But now that the computers had been seized, it was nearly impossible.

Almost daily Marjorie was on the phone with her attorney, asking when her property was going to be released. At the very least, she wanted a copy of Jay's "in case of" letter. She needed those instructions to understand the business. Somehow, Marjorie didn't seem to understand the gravity of the situation. She was considered the prime suspect in the first-degree murder of her husband. Marjorie, however, was more concerned about cars, computers, and money.

"I absolutely could not function without a computer," Marjorie said years later. "I began looking for one."

Detective Barnes was consumed by the Orbin case. He worked twelve to sixteen hours a day on the investigation.

Scenarios replayed in his mind: *Did Marjorie kill Jay by herself? Was it Larry who pulled the trigger? Did they plan this together?*

"Even when I wasn't working on the case, I thought about it all the time," Barnes recalled. "She was out there, free, and she didn't deserve to be free. She killed somebody. It was like, what can I do to put her where she belongs? What am I missing?"

Barnes chased down dozens of leads. At the same time, he and other detectives continued the tedious and time-consuming task of combing over financial records and bank account activity. Additionally, Barnes contacted each of Jay's banks and credit card companies to freeze his accounts. The process took days.

On November 12, he contacted Circuit City to inform them of Jay's murder and to have his card "flagged" as fraud if it was used. All of his cards had been seized, but Barnes had a feeling that Marjorie would try to have them reissued. As it would turn out, his hunch was dead on.

A representative from Circuit City informed him that a new card had already been requested by a person who identified themselves as "Jay Orbin." Barnes was certain that person was Marjorie. He informed Circuit City that Jay was deceased. The fraud warning would alert the cashier to call the police. Barnes also placed a "file stop" on Marjorie, which meant he would be immediately notified if she had any contact with the police. Now it was a waiting game. Fortunately for Barnes, he wouldn't have to wait for long.

The next night, Saturday, November 13, Barnes was at home enjoying a rare sit-down dinner with his wife and kids. At about 5:50 p.m., his cell phone rang. It was the night sergeant, Dave Lane, and he had some exciting news—Marjorie Orbin had been arrested. As Lane recounted the details, Barnes' eyes widened and adrenaline started pumping through his veins.

They didn't yet have her for murder, but Marjorie Orbin had just been caught red-handed.

CHAPTER 18

"I need a shower," Marjorie muttered under her breath. "I want go home. I just wanna go home."

She ran her fingers through her hair and nervously glanced across the narrow interrogation room. Paint peeled from the walls; the gray carpet was well-worn and stained with dirt, grime, and old coffee spills. Marjorie squirmed in the cheap metal chair. She was dressed in black boot-cut leggings, a razorback athletic top, and a zip-up sweatshirt.

It was 6:23 p.m. on November 13 and Marjorie was once again in a Phoenix Police interrogation room. But this time she had been arrested on charges of credit card fraud. Earlier that afternoon, after picking up Noah from school, Marjorie had run a few errands and gone shopping for a new computer. Around five p.m., she stopped by Circuit City and headed straight for the computer section, picking out an expensive laptop.

Marjorie was intent on buying a new computer so she could manage Jay's business. Originally she had intended to buy a new desktop, but she started to think a laptop would be better. That way, Marjorie believed she could keep it hidden if police searched her home again. But the laptop was more expensive than the desktop and she wasn't sure she had enough credit available on the Circuit City card. Handing the sales person Jay's card, she asked if he could check the balance. The salesperson glanced at the name on the card and gave a confused look. "Is this you?" he asked.

"Yes," Marjorie lied. "I'm Jay Orbin."

A few minutes later, the salesperson came back and asked for her ID. Marjorie took out her wallet and handed it to him. "Jay's my nickname," she said. Marjorie continued to browse the store, while Noah looked at computer games by the front counter. Suddenly they were approached by a uniformed police officer. "Ma'am, I need to speak with you."

The officer escorted Marjorie and Noah into a waiting area and explained that she was being detained because the credit card she was attempting to use belonged to someone listed as deceased. Marjorie tried to explain it all away as a simple misunderstanding. She confessed that she was actually Jay's wife. "I've been using this card for ten years," Marjorie said.

"Stay here," the officer told her. "Maybe we can get this all straightened out."

Unbeknownst to Marjorie, more officers were already on their way. When Marjorie provided the officer with her ID, he ran it through the system and learned she was a suspect in a homicide investigation. Barnes was notified and several more officers were sent to Circuit City to arrest her. A few moments later, two squad cars were outside. Marjorie was placed in handcuffs and she and Noah were hauled downtown for the second time in two weeks. Suddenly Marjorie found herself at the center of a second criminal investigation.

Marjorie was outraged and humiliated. Despite what officers told her about Jay's credit cards being frozen, Marjorie felt she had the right to use them. These were the same cards she had used every day for ten years. Sitting inside the interrogation room, Marjorie was confident she could explain it all away.

The door of the interrogation room opened and an older-looking gentleman dressed in a crisp blue police uniform emerged.

"My name's Dave Lane," he said as he eased into the chair adjacent to Marjorie. "I want to talk to you a little bit about this mix-up here with this credit card stuff at Circuit City."

Lane was a cool-headed veteran police officer and one of the most highly decorated sergeants in the department. Tall and fit with dapper brown hair, round-framed glasses, and an affable manner, Lane was in his late fifties and had been with the police department for thirty-two years.

"I'm going to advise you of your rights just for your own protection," he began, in a calm, friendly tone.

When he finished reading the Miranda rights, Marjorie asked about Noah. Lane told her that her son was fine, coloring and chatting with officers in another room.

"I don't know why they are saying they've closed Jay's accounts," Marjorie said, indignant.

Marjorie explained how she and Jay had divorced because of the tax lien. She said Jay authorized her to use the credit cards whenever she needed to and explained the letters conveying his final wishes.

"But I guess it says it showed up that he's deceased," she continued. "Umm, I know Detective Barnes has been working on this missing persons thing."

"Barnes?" Lane pretended not to recognize the name.

In fact, Detective Barnes was across the police station gathered around a fifteen-inch color monitor with his sergeant, Karen Vance. Barnes knew Marjorie would not speak with him, so when Lane pulled him aside and said he was actually a family friend of the Orbins', Barnes agreed that it would be wise to let him conduct the interview. Barnes explained the entire case and they concocted a strategy for Lane to befriend Marjorie. "I knew as soon as she saw me that it would be over," Barnes recalled. "I had already tried to interview her once and she knew I was the one coming after her. We used this tactic to get her to talk. We knew this was a long shot but it would be worth a try."

Detectives knew Marjorie was intelligent enough not to implicate herself in the murder, so it was decided that Lane would pretend to focus on Larry as the main suspect. If Marjorie took the bait and attempted to place blame on her boyfriend, she would have to admit she knew what happened to Jay and reveal a level of culpability in the murder.

"We knew she would not confess," Barnes recalled. "The angle we decided was to go into the fraud, firm up that charge, and then try to get Marjorie to talk about Larry Weisberg, putting all the blame on him."

Back in the interrogation room, Marjorie was filling in Lane on what he already knew. "Barnes or Burns . . . Barnes I think," Marjorie continued. "He brought us in to tell us that he thinks that they found my husband."

"Uh-hum." Lane nodded.

"I'm sorry, I still, he's my husband in my mind and they told his parents that they're pretty sure it's him. His parents are in their seventies and just completely distraught. Barnes told them that he's one hundred percent sure that it's him before the DNA test. It's just very irresponsible."

"What'd you think?" Lane asked.

"I don't know," Marjorie cried. "At first, I thought he'd just come walking through the door. I haven't told his son."

Marjorie became emotional and Lane passed her a box of tissues. "I haven't told Noah, but I am sure that something terrible has happened. I don't know what. It might be he had an accident or something. He would not just walk away and forget about us."

"Do you have any other family, you know, for support?"

"I have nobody. I have nobody. Nobody in the whole world knows I'm here tonight," Marjorie wept.

Marjorie asked Lane about what would happen to Noah if she went to jail.

"Lemme tell you my goals are two things right here,"

Lane said. "Number one is your son. We want the best for your son. You know a son needs his mom and . . ."

"He may have lost his dad," she finished his sentence.

"So the number one concern is your boy."

"He's afraid. He saw a SWAT team come through our front door."

"A SWAT team?" Lane feigned surprise.

"A SWAT team comes through my door and Tasers a sixty-year-old man, a friend of my husband that was there, and throws me on the floor, handcuffs me, and I'm screaming. He was traumatized. He's in therapy."

Marjorie tried to direct the conversation back to the credit card issue. She said she was trying to get a computer so she could spend tomorrow paying bills. "I did not know I was doing anything wrong."

"This forgery stuff, we can take care of that, all right? We can sort all of that out," Lane said. "There's some other stuff that, if you'd like to talk to me about, I would like to talk to you. First of all, with this Taser deal, who got tased in your house?"

Marjorie told Lane his name was Larry Weisberg, and after some coaxing, admitted that she had been having an affair with him.

"Larry Weisberg. Okay, umm, let me tell you what I know about your whole situation," Lane said. "I'll just be very straight."

Lane explained to Marjorie that he has known Jake and Joann Orbin for more than thirty years and had met her and Noah a couple of times in passing. He said he was there to help, but first, Marjorie needed to be frank with him.

"Do you have any idea where we can start to look for him?"

"How can I know?" Marjorie said defensively. "I want him back here."

Throughout the interview Marjorie insisted she didn't actually believe the body they found belonged to Jay.

"What makes you so sure that that's not him?" Lane asked.

"I don't want to believe it," Marjorie said. "Noah and I, we have decided that we're just taking a position that he's not dead until someone proves it to us. Maybe that's denial, I don't know if that's the healthy way to do it, but unless someone proves it to me . . ."

Lane shifted the conversation back to Larry Weisberg. "Do you think there's any way that, uh, Larry may be a little bit jealous of you and Jay?" Lane asked.

"No. No." She shook her head, dismissing the thought.

"Maybe want to intercede a little bit?"

"I don't think so."

"You don't think so? Anything's possible," Lane said. "Did you ever see Larry get in a rage of any kind?"

"No."

"Get pissed about anything?"

"No. You're not going to make me say something here," Marjorie said. "I don't want to get anybody in trouble that hasn't done anything."

"Okay, it's up to you if you don't wanna continue." Lane placed his palms on the table as if to stand up to leave.

"I'm just afraid . . ." She stopped him. "I'm just afraid of something I say being misconstrued or taken out of context or read in a way that might not be fact. I don't want my son to lose his mother."

"You know, Marge," Lane said warmly, "I think you're a real dedicated mom. You're really dedicated to your son, and you and Jay did have an unusual, I think is to say the least, unusual living type of a thing."

"How?"

"Well, you're married. You get divorced. He's on the road two weeks, he's home two weeks. I mean that's not normal," Lane said.

"Our relationship was a friendship," Marjorie said. "I don't think that's that unusual."

"Lemme run something by you and don't even make

any comment till I get a chance to run the whole thing by you, okay?" Lane said. "My own opinion, based on all the years I've been doing this and all the cases I've investigated, is I think Larry's involved in your husband's . . ."

"Why?" Marjorie interrupted.

"Now just listen to me, okay?" Lane said slowly. "I think Larry got jealous and in some way he took Jay and removed him from the picture."

"He never said anything. I can't imagine," Marjorie sobbed.

For several moments Marjorie wept loudly.

"Alright," Lane stood up. "Why don't we take a break for a minute. Let me get a drink of water."

"Can I see Noah first," she pleaded. "For just a minute just to reassure him that everything's okay?"

"Yeah. Let me get him," Lane said. "You just sit right there and relax."

Marjorie shifted her posture as Lane left the room. A few moments later he reemerged with Noah, who rushed to his mother's side

"There's my big boy," she said, as she crouched down to his level.

Lane chuckled. "He's doing great. You're having a good time, aren't you, buddy?"

Noah nodded happily.

"Why don't you guys just sit here and visit for awhile, okay?" he said as he closed the door behind him.

Marjorie hugged her son, pulled back and looked him over, "Are you okay? Whatcha been doing?"

"I've been talkin' to 'em," Noah said.

"You're not scared, are you?"

"No," he said, shaking his head. "Did they say that you can use your credit card?"

"No," Marjorie said. "That was probably not a good thing to do because that credit card has Daddy's name on it and not mine and you're not supposed to really use a credit card unless it has your name on it, so I shouldn't have used it even though they know that I have used it before with Daddy's permission."

"Okay. I'm gonna go, okay?" Noah said. "I'm going back over there to see Gram and Grandpa."

"They're here?" Marjorie asked, surprised.

"They're coming."

Marjorie suddenly became very guarded.

"Something funny is going on," Marjorie said more to herself than to Noah. "Somebody's trying to pull a trick. I don't know."

Marjorie pulled Noah close to her, "You don't go anywhere. You do not leave this building with anybody, okay?"

"Okay. See ya, Mom," Noah said.

"I love you," Marjorie said as Noah left the room. Just then, Sergeant Lane reemerged. "He is a pistol, isn't he," he said as the boy brushed past him.

"Yeah," Marjorie said. "So Jake and Joann are here?"

"I think they're on the first floor," Lane said nonchalantly.

"You think we'll be able to go home tonight?"

"Well, you know what? I think we're making some progress," he said. "I've done many, many criminal investigations and I like you. I think you're pretty much straightforward."

Marjorie shrugged. "People either like me or hate me. Or love me or hate me. My friends love me to death. People that don't like me, don't."

"Well, you know what, if I don't like you I'm just gonna walk out and say hell with her, I don't wanna talk to her." Lane smiled.

"Do they, do they know yet if that's Jay?"

"They're pretty sure, but it's all still circumstantial. Like I said the DNA test hasn't come back," Lane said. "I see you're really hurt by this emotionally, totally. I also see the fact that you're torn a little bit between loyalty for maybe your friend and wanting to get on with your life. I wanna see you and your little boy, you know, have a great life. But there's gonna have to be a little bit of accountability on one part. And that's why I gotta come back to Larry."

Marjorie sat silent for several moments, staring vacantly at the table.

"We met casually once, a long time ago," Lane said.

"Sorry, I don't remember." Marjorie looked up and shook her head.

"I'm saying if, you know, when it comes time I'll help you out any way I can," he said in a kind, gentle tone. "And like I said this credit card thing, I think we can probably square that away and get some more clarification."

"Yeah?"

"Listen," he said. "I think Larry's involved because of the way the remains were found."

"Anyone that would do that would have to be an animal." Marjorie shuddered in disgust. She covered her mouth with her hand and jerked her shoulders forward. "I just threw up."

"Calm down, calm down," Lane said. "I know you don't wanna think about it."

"My stomach hurts," she said, wrapping her hands around her midsection.

"So that's why I'm telling you Larry's involved. And we need to focus now. We need to focus on closing this and getting some closure to you and Noah."

"Are you telling him the same thing?" Marjorie asked quizzically.

"Tellin' who?"

"Are you going to have a conversation with Larry and tell him the same thing?" Marjorie repeated.

"I haven't spoken to Larry yet," Lane said.

Marjorie paused for a moment. "It seems to me like this is the kind of conversation that you have with both parties and implicating both sides," she said suspiciously.

"In the room next door, there's nobody there, and I'm tellin' you right now," Lane said.

Lane continued to press about Larry but Marjorie began to cry.

"I'm afraid," she said, her voice lowered to a whisper. "I'm afraid. I'm just afraid."

As Marjorie sat, her head in her hands, Detective Barnes watched her every move from the video monitor in the other room. He slid to the edge of his seat. She was going to crack, he could sense it. Everyone was holding his breath, watching intently. Barnes turned to his sergeant and whispered, "Oh, my God! She's going to talk."

"There's a point when you know someone is about ready to break," Barnes recalled years later. "For a moment, I thought we had her."

But just as suddenly Marjorie snapped back at Lane, "I wouldn't stand a minute caring about someone that could do something like this."

"Listen. Listen to me," Lane leaned forward. "I think Larry's involved up to his ears. And I think Larry's tryin' to come between you and Jay and you and Noah and be the focus of your entire life, trying to take Jay's place."

"I want to know what was done," Marjorie whispered.

"I see that you're very troubled and I think that you're sort of torn."

"I'm not torn." Marjorie looked straight at Lane. "This is what I'm afraid of, you're saying that you're seeing that I'm torn and I'm not torn about anything."

"People do bad stuff all the time," Lane continued. "Larry could easily have been involved in this. Larry could be involved in this, like I said, he could be involved up to his ears."

Over and over Lane tried to encourage Marjorie to finger Larry for her husband's disappearance, but Marjorie wouldn't budge. Larry wasn't capable of harming her husband, Marjorie repeatedly insisted.

"Will . . ." Marjorie hesitated. "Will you agree to resuming this conversation during the daytime with my attorney present?"

With that, Detective Barnes got out of his chair and calmly walked down the hall toward the interrogation room. After speaking with Lane for about two hours, Marjorie had asked for an attorney. Anything she said from here on out would not be admissible in court. Barnes entered the interrogation room and dropped a file folder on the small table in front of them. He knew it wouldn't do any good to try and question her, but he wanted to gauge her reaction to his presence.

"Marjorie, I'm trying to help you out," Barnes said in a measured tone.

"I know you're trying to do a job and it's a job that I want you to do," Marjorie said. "I will tell you anything you want to know, but I have a little boy out there that may have lost his father and I'm terrified of him losing his mother and I don't want to say anything that may be taken out of context."

"A little bit more on the credit card issue," Barnes said matter-of-factly. "Jay last used his credit card September 8 when he left Tucson, okay? There is only one of these credit cards that have been issued, I verified that. This credit card was found in your house, in your possession. And you used this credit card on September 9 at Target."

"Okay."

"So the question is this, how did this credit card come into your possession, because Jay had it on September 8 and you had it on September 9."

Marjorie shook her head, but didn't answer the question.

Lane interjected, "That's what we're talkin' about. Larry had access to your personal effects."

"How'd you get Jay's credit card," Barnes pressed. "Did Larry give you the credit card?"

"Larry's never given me a credit card." Marjorie became defensive. "Can we do this conversation during the daytime? Would that be okay?"

"You have to understand, Marjorie, we think Larry is the one who someway manipulated Jay's credit cards."

"I used . . . I," Marjorie stuttered. "I used Jay's credit cards."

"How do you have Jay's credit card?" Barnes repeated.

"I don't know. I don't know," Marjorie stammered. "There is, there is, umm, cards in my purse all the time."

"There's only one of this credit card," Barnes said firmly.

"Okay, I need my lawyer present in here, okay?" Marjorie said directly. "'Cause you're scaring me."

"You're scaring us, too." Barnes reached for the file folder and removed an eight by ten color photo—the most gruesome of the autopsy photos. He held the photograph of Jay's bloody, dismembered torso in Marjorie's face and coolly said, "We'd like to know where the rest of Jay is and I think you know."

Marjorie wrenched back, shielding her eyes with her hand. Cowering in her chair, she whispered, "Oh god! Oh, no!"

"You're going go to jail tonight for credit card fraud, Marjorie," Barnes turned to leave.

"No, why?" Marjorie wailed. "I don't. I don't believe you just did that. I don't believe you just did that."

As Barnes left the room, Marjorie continued to cringe, seemingly disgusted by the sight of the photo. Barnes wasn't at all affected. He was sure that wasn't the first time she had seen that sight.

"She looked disgusted, but it seemed like she was trying to fake an emotion," Barnes recalled years later. "This was her husband and the father of her child and she could show no real emotion at all."

CHAPTER 19

That night, Marjorie was booked in county jail on forgery charges. She was fingerprinted and photographed; her purse, jewelry, and jacket were confiscated. Meanwhile, Jake and Joann took Noah home for the night. In a frigid holding cell, Marjorie was surrounded by prostitutes and drug addicts. Marjorie stood in the corner, arms crossed, fuming. In her mind she was entitled to use Jay's credit cards. She had used those credit cards for ten years. How could they call that forgery?

After several hours, she was told she was being released. Because she hadn't actually used Jay's Circuit City card, and had only inquired about the balance, they couldn't hold her. Through the secure glass box, a corrections employee informed her that her purse and jacket were too large for a storage locker and she would have to wait till Monday to pick up her property from impound.

"What time is it?" Marjorie asked.

"Three a.m.," the officer said.

Marjorie left the jail, the heavy metal door slamming shut behind her. She was lost and alone with no jacket, money, or cell phone. It was freezing. Marjorie rubbed her arms, shivering. In the dark, all the buildings were forbidding. She walked aimlessly down the south Phoenix streets.

glancing at the homeless people sleeping in the doorways. A strange man started walking toward her. Frightened, she started running.

"I was frantic. I was hysterical," Marjorie said years later. "Everything that happened since the start of this had just closed in on me. I ran and I cried."

Marjorie ran for miles and miles, until she began to recognize the neighborhood. She saw a few phone booths, but she had no one to call. A few cars slowed and the drivers tried to talk to her, but Marjorie was frightened. She kept running. What felt like hours passed.

Marjorie looked toward the horizon. The sun was beginning to break. Suddenly, one car stopped in the middle of the street, made a U-turn, and started speeding her way. She thought she was being followed. Panicked, Marjorie ran faster. In a blind frenzy, she ducked and dove between buildings, climbed over a fence, and ran through a stranger's backyard. Minutes later, she looked back over her shoulder and could no longer see the vehicle.

"After I knew I had lost them, I stopped," Marjorie recalled. "I was so scared. As soon as I stopped I threw up. My heart was beating so fast."

That night Marjorie ran twenty miles from the jail in downtown Phoenix to her home in northeast Phoenix. Her garage had a coded keypad entry. She entered the code and went inside. It was ten a.m. and Marjorie was hysterical. She knew now that she was in way over her head. She picked up the phone and called the one person who had promised to always be there for her: Michael J. Peter.

Detective Barnes had briefly put Marjorie behind bars, but not for the murder of her husband. So far the evidence in the murder case was scant and prosecutor Noel Levy was ＿ried it would not hold up in court.

＿nes continued to sort through records and track ＿s. While perusing Marjorie's cell phone records, he noticed several phone calls were made to a number in Las Vegas. Many of these calls were made on September 7, 8, and 10 to a cell phone ending in 4327.

Barnes contacted T-Mobile with a subpoena and learned that the number belonged to Charity McLean, the same woman whose license was discovered in Marjorie's purse during the second search of the Orbin's house. This woman had been in regular communication with Marjorie before and after Jay Orbin's disappearance and on the suspected day of his murder. Was it possible Marjorie confessed to her the details of the crime? To find out what she knew, it was important to speak with her in person. Barnes didn't have a partner, but Detective Mike Meislish had been helping him substantially throughout the case.

"Hey Mike," Barnes said. "Want to go to Vegas?"

On Tuesday, November 16, Barnes and Meislish arrived in Las Vegas and checked into a suite at the New York-New York Hotel & Casino. At about 9:10 a.m., they drove to Charity McLean's apartment complex off the Vegas strip. Charity came to the door. She had just gotten home from working a long shift stripping at the Spearmint Rhino.

"We wanted to talk to you about your Arizona driver's license," Barnes began. "Do you know where it is?"

"Yeah," Charity said. "I traded it into the DMV when I got a new license in Vegas."

"Well, your Arizona license was found in a house, Marjorie Orbin's house," Barnes said. "Do you know Marjorie?"

"Yes," Charity said. "She's my friend."

Charity told detectives that she had known Marjorie for years and that they spoke frequently by phone. She explained that she knew Jay was missing and that Marjorie was very upset but that she didn't know much else about the investigation. In regards to Marjorie's marriage, Charity described it as an arrangement.

"Do you know if they had an intimate relationship?" Barnes asked.

"No. That's gross," Charity said. "That's like thinking about my parents having sex."

According to Charity, Jay was looking for a house. Marjorie also mentioned to Charity that if Jay died, they would be well taken care of with Jay's living trust, will, and other documents.

"Do you have any idea what may have happened to Jay?" Barnes asked.

"No." Charity shook her head. "I have no idea. I know he was always out on trips."

Barnes and Meislish left. While they didn't learn much from Charity, the trip to Las Vegas wasn't a complete bust. That week there was a police convention in town and Barnes and Meislish were able to meet up with a few of their cop buddies. That night they went out for a nice dinner and stopped by a bar for a few hours of well-deserved relaxation. The next morning they returned to Phoenix.

For the next few days, Marjorie spoke to Michael J. Peter at length. She told him about the search warrants and how the bank accounts had been seized. She explained to Michael how she had been arrested on charges of credit card fraud.

Keeping the promise he had made to her years prior, Michael came to her rescue. He made a few phone calls and arranged for her to meet an attorney he knew named Tom Connelly. In her conversations with Michael, Marjorie had admitted to being in trouble with the law. Not once, however, did she tell Michael that she was a suspect in a murder investigation.

That week, Marjorie met with Connelly and explained everything that had happened. Nearly completely bald, plump with big, bulging eyes, Connelly was a native of Chicago who specialized mainly in business law.

Using funds from Jay Orbin's estate, she paid him a retainer of $7,500. This was money Marjorie had acquired by cashing checks for merchandise she sold while Jay was missing.

The Monday after Marjorie's arrest at Circuit City, Todd Christy took her to pick up her purse and other belongings from the police impound and her rental car, which had been abandoned in the store's parking lot for days.

"I'm so scared, Todd," Marjorie cried.

"How can I help?"

"Will you stay at the house?" she asked. "I just want a man in the house."

Todd felt empathy toward this woman who had just lost her husband.

At the time Todd was working at a Blockbuster Video store. Each night after work Todd came by Marjorie's house. She would make dinner, and they would curl up on the couch and watch pay-per-view movies on cable. At Marjorie's request, Todd began staying the night. He slept on the couch or in Noah's room, when he slept with his mother. Occasionally, Todd's boyfriend, Oscar Moreno, stopped by as well. In his mid-thirties, Oscar was short and slender with black curly hair and a dark complexion.

One night, they were on the couch watching a thriller when a character in the movie was shot. Suddenly, Marjorie burst into tears. Todd moved closer to her on the couch and gave her a hug for comfort. Quietly, Marjorie sobbed on his shoulder.

"This is just so horrible," Marjorie whispered in his ear. "Jay was a wonderful person. He loved that child."

Marjorie had hardly ever been single a day in her entire life. She needed to be with someone. With Jay dead and Larry gone, she glommed onto Todd Christy. Their relationship was never sexual, but Todd became the new man in her life.

* * *

For weeks, while Detective Barnes was busy tracking down leads and sorting through Marjorie's cell phone and financial records, Phoenix crime lab analyst John Knell had been working on piecing together the forensics. The tub in which the body had been discovered had yielded many important clues.

The torso had been neatly packaged, wrapped in heavy black garbage bags and clear plastic sheeting, sealed with duct tape. The plastic and tape were compared to rolls of duct tape and garbage bags obtained during the search of Marjorie's and Larry's homes. Analysis of the duct tape showed it consistent in size and scrim pattern to tape found in Marjorie's home. Clear plastic liner found at Larry Weisberg's home was also a match in thickness, size, and composition to sheeting found wrapped around the torso. However, the sheeting was determined to be polyethylene, a very commonly used plastic.

Additionally, there were minute fibers discovered stuck to the duct tape. Those fibers were found to be consistent with tan carpet fibers from the Ford Bronco. It appeared that it was the vehicle used to dump the body. But the most important evidence was four short hairs adhered to the duct tape. These hairs were light and had been chemically treated. Both Marjorie and Larry had bleached blond hair. Further testing would need to be done to match the hairs to either suspect.

Meanwhile, leads continued to pour in about Marjorie. In November, Detective Barnes was sitting in his office going over documents when he received a call from a woman who wished to remain anonymous. Her voice was trembling and she sounded frightened. She said she had been terrorized by Marjorie.

"For the past year, I've lived in constant fear of her," the woman said. "I'm always looking over my shoulder. I always feel like Marjorie might be following me."

The anonymous woman was Janice Matthews, the

mother from the karate studio who claimed to have been harassed by Marjorie. Janice had heard about Jay's disappearance through the studio and, after much soul searching, contacted the cops.

Barnes listened intently as Janice told him her shocking story about the defamatory letter, the mysterious phone calls and Marjorie's harassment over the last year. Before they hung up, Janice told Barnes something else. There was another woman, one of Marjorie's neighbors, who told Janice that she had watched Noah overnight sometime in mid-September, around the time Jay went missing. Her name was Jan Beeso.

The following Monday, Barnes went to see Jan Beeso. Jan knew Marjorie, Jay, and Noah through her son, Christian. The two boys attended the same school and were friends. Barnes asked Jan about what he had learned through the anonymous phone caller. Jan confirmed that on September 16, Noah spent the night at her house.

"Marjorie called, sort of last minute, and wanted me to watch her son," Jan said. "It was kind of strange because it was a school night and Marjorie didn't normally allow sleepovers."

Jan said she didn't know Marjorie that well and Noah had never before spent the night at her house. After school that night, Marjorie brought Noah over. She told Jan she was going out with some friends, but she didn't say with whom or where. Despite Noah's "rowdy" reputation, he seemed happy and content. Noah and Christian played for hours and went to bed. Not once that night did Marjorie call to check on her son, nor did he ask about his mom.

The following morning, Jan was getting the boys ready for school when she realized Marjorie had forgotten to pack a shirt. On the way to school, Jan stopped by Marjorie's house. When they arrived, Marjorie seemed agitated and distressed, complaining about "Noah's father." At the time, Jan didn't think much of it. She retrieved the shirt and left.

The next week, Jan heard Jay was missing.

Detective Barnes spoke with several more parents from the karate studio, confirming the letter and Marjorie's strange behavior. Almost everyone told Barnes there was someone else he needed to speak to: Sharon Franco.

CHAPTER 20

"I know Marjorie killed Jay," Sharon Franco told detectives. She paused, "Or had someone kill him for her."

When Sharon saw Jay's picture on the news, she knew right away that Marjorie had murdered her husband. Reluctantly, she contacted police. In mid-November Detectives Barnes and Meislish met Sharon at her job. Having heard her name through several parents at the karate studio, Barnes was anxious to hear what she had to say.

When Barnes approached Sharon, he could tell she was nervous. Like Janice Matthews, Sharon said she had been threatened by Marjorie. She told detectives that she had moved and changed her name because she was so scared of her former friend.

Throughout their friendship, Sharon said, Marjorie complained about her husband—calling him fat and disgusting. Marjorie would speak at length about Jay's small penis and lack of sex drive. Marjorie also claimed that Jay was infertile and that Noah wasn't even his biological son. According to Sharon, Marjorie hated Jay and wanted him to die.

"She would say things like, 'Jay is so lucky that nothing has ever happened to him, like an accident or robbery,' and 'Someone has to cut that fucker's brakes sooner or later. Something's got to happen,'" Sharon said.

Marjorie was hanging on for the money, just waiting for Jay to die so she could sell everything, get her money, and move on, Sharon said. Over time, Marjorie's threats became more direct. One day while ranting about Jay, Marjorie asked an alarming question: "Do you know someone who would kill Jay?" At first, Sharon thought it was a joke. She knew Marjorie was unhappy, but Sharon didn't honestly believe she would do something to hurt Jay. But the more Marjorie talked, the more Sharon began to worry.

Sharon told detectives that in early 2004, toward the end of their friendship, Marjorie was talking of leaving Jay. But there was no way Marjorie would ever give up Noah. According to Sharon, Marjorie would say things like, "No one will ever take Noah from me. I'd kill 'em. They would find themselves without a head or wrapped in a blanket in the desert."

Sharon said Marjorie wanted to kill Jay. Her favorite method would be to "cut his brake lines or shoot him in the face, wrap him in a blanket, and call it a day."

Eyes wide, Barnes glanced at Meislish. This was huge for the investigation. Both detectives were thinking the same thing: *This was a premeditated, calculated murder.* Apparently, Marjorie had carried through with her threats, killing Jay using a method similar to what she had discussed months prior.

Sharon also told detectives about Marjorie's relationship with Michael J. Peter. Marjorie had bragged that Michael had the mafia connections and financial means to help her get rid of Jay. If she had to, Marjorie said, she knew exactly what to do. "Marjorie told me she got the idea from Michael Peter. She said you shoot them in the face, wrap them up and put them in the desert,'" Sharon said. After she learned of Jay's death, Sharon told police she began to believe that Michael J. Peter had likely helped her hide the crime. "I think Marjorie covered her tracks so well, the murder can't ever be pinned on her."

Barnes made a mental note of the name Michael J. Peter. So far in the investigation, that name hadn't come up. *What role would he come to play in this increasingly tangled case?* Barnes wondered.

Sharon told detectives how her friendship with Marjorie had come to a tumultuous end in March, when Marjorie called her out of the blue, claiming to have slept with her boyfriend, Jessiah Rueckert. After that encounter, Sharon said, Marjorie started stalking her and obsessively calling her cell and work phone. Looking back, Sharon wondered if Marjorie had started to plan the murder of her husband at this point and, realizing how close they were, decided to cut off all communication to avoid having Sharon as a potential witness. To Sharon it made sense of Marjorie's ending their friendship suddenly, for no reason. Marjorie was aware of how much *she* knew, Sharon said. Because of this, Sharon was afraid for her safety.

Meislish asked Sharon about Marjorie's relationship with her son. He also asked what she would think if Marjorie let Noah spend the night at a friend's house—someone she didn't know very well. Sharon said if she did, it must have been the night she killed Jay or disposed of his body.

"There's no way in hell Marjorie would allow Noah to spend the night anywhere," Sharon insisted.

Before they left, Barnes asked Sharon once again if Marjorie had ever said she wanted to kill Jay.

"All the time," she said, without hesitation. "She would say if he ever tried to take her son, she would kill him."

"In your opinion is Marjorie capable of murder?" Barnes asked.

"Absolutely. Not a question," she said. "Marjorie had no feelings for anyone but Noah."

After interviewing Sharon, Barnes contacted Jessiah Rueckert. According to Sharon, Jessiah was present for one of

Marjorie's rants against Jay. Jessiah was eager to help. He mentioned to Barnes that he had always wanted to be a Phoenix cop and had applied to the academy.

He told detectives he had last spoke to Marjorie in June or July, when she had called to tell him she was divorcing Jay. Marjorie wanted to see him but Jessiah said he had refused. The last time he saw her was in March.

As far back as the beginning of the year, he had heard about Marjorie's threats against her husband through Sharon. On one occasion, Marjorie mentioned directly to Jessiah that she hoped Jay's brakes would go out on the road.

He told detectives that Marjorie would flirt with him constantly and lead him on like she wanted to have an affair. Several times Marjorie told him she wasn't happy with her marriage. "She was jealous that I was with Sharon," Jessiah said. "She was always implying that she wanted to have a threesome with everyone."

"Did your relationship with Marjorie ever turn sexual?"

"No." He shook his head as he glanced down at the floor. Barnes studied Jessiah's face closely—he had a strong suspicion Jessiah was lying.

Jessiah had in fact had an affair with Marjorie. Soon his secret would be exposed.

On the evening of November 21, Jessiah's father, Steve Rueckert, and his girlfriend were running errands when they were suddenly ambushed. Emerging from the darkness, an armed man approached their vehicle and fired six shots, striking both Steve and his girlfriend. Both were seriously injured and were rushed to the hospital. For several days it was unclear if either one would survive and the case was considered a potential homicide.

Rookie homicide Detective Jason Schechterle was assigned to investigate the assault. Years prior, Schechterle had miraculously survived a car accident while on patrol and was severely disfigured from burns that had covered his entire face. In March 2001, while Schechterle was working a night shift, an out-of-control taxi cab slammed into the back of his Crown Victoria cruiser at more than one hundred miles per hour. Instantly, Schechterle's car burst into flames, trapping him inside the inferno. Firefighters pulled his charred body from the wreckage in time to save his life, but not his face. He received fourth-degree burns to his face, arms, and upper body. The burns consumed the skin on his head, face, and neck; his hands were seared down to the tendons. Schechterle lost his nose, ears, eyelids, and three of his fingers. Remarkably, he survived and returned to work a little more than a year and a half later. The story of his courage made national news and he became a beloved local celebrity. After returning to duty, Schechterle rose through the ranks of the Phoenix Police Department and, by 2004, he achieved his dream of becoming a homicide investigator.

When Sharon Franco received news of the shooting of Jessiah Rueckert's father, her first thought was that it was Marjorie. Because of Jessiah's link to the Orbin investigation, Barnes briefly looked into the case. Days after the shooting, Barnes met with Schechterle and Jessiah at the police station.

When Schechterle told him the facts of the shooting, Barnes could tell it was unrelated to his investigation. The shooter was described as a male and there were dozens of potential leads, including the girlfriend's jealous ex-husband. When Barnes spoke with Jessiah, however, he did learn new information about Marjorie. Jessiah said he received a text message from Marjorie the day after his father's shooting. The message read: *Want to Play?* He said he was disturbed and didn't respond.

"I don't know what that was supposed to mean," Jessiah said.

Again Barnes asked if he had ever had a sexual relationship with Marjorie, but again Jessiah denied it.

Steve Rueckert and his girlfriend both survived the shooting, but were left with permanent injuries. Steve was left blind in both eyes; his girlfriend was a paraplegic. Schechterle did his best to investigate the case but none of the leads panned out. Years later, the shooting remained unsolved. As a cold case, it had been forgotten. Because it was not a homicide, it would likely never be looked at again.

As for the Jay Orbin case, Sharon Franco and Jessiah Rueckert were added to the witness list. At the time, however, Jessiah's connection to Marjorie didn't seem to have much significance. Months later, that would all change. Barnes got a call from a sergeant at the Phoenix Police Academy inquiring about Jessiah Rueckert. Barnes told the sergeant that he was a witness at an upcoming trial.

"Did he have an affair with the suspect?" the sergeant asked.

"He told me no, but I always had my doubts," Barnes said. "Why?"

The sergeant told Barnes that Jessiah had mentioned to another recruit that he had lied to a detective during a criminal investigation. Jessiah admitted to this recruit that he had slept with the suspect, Marjorie Orbin. The recruit told his class sergeant, who called Barnes.

Barnes re-interviewed Jessiah. Caught in a lie, Jessiah admitted to the affair and said he had slept with Marjorie numerous times, behind Sharon's back. He was discharged from the academy for lying during a criminal investigation and barred from ever serving as a Phoenix cop.

Jessiah also had to admit to Sharon about the affair. Sharon was devastated.

CHAPTER 21

As November was winding down, the Orbins began to wonder if there would ever be justice for Jay. It had been more than two months since he was reported missing and there had still been no arrests.

Meanwhile, what was left of Jay's body remained on a cold metal slab at the morgue. DNA tests hadn't yet positively confirmed the corpse was Jay, meaning his body couldn't yet be released to the family. Secretly, the Orbins were still clinging to the flimsiest shred of hope that Jay was alive and this was all some bizarre mistake. They just wanted to wake up from this nightmare.

Jake Jr. continued to speak to Marjorie for Noah's sake. With each passing day, however, contact became less and less frequent. Jake Jr. worried that Marjorie would try to completely cut the Orbins out of Noah's life.

Meanwhile, Barnes felt the case was finally coming together. The interviews with Sharon Franco and the parents from the karate studio provided tremendous insight into Marjorie's character. Barnes came to believe that Marjorie had hated her husband and wanted him dead. She no longer wanted to be with Jay but she wasn't willing to give up the house, the money, or custody of Noah.

Through the evidence, Barnes developed a theory of

what had happened to Jay. He believed Jay was shot and killed in his garage, probably with his own weapon. Jake Jr. had informed Barnes that ten years prior he had given his brother a .357 Smith & Wesson revolver, which was consistent with the .38 caliber bullet found in the Rubbermaid tub. That gun was missing. It was not found in the home or warehouse during any of the searches. When Jake Jr. asked Marjorie about the gun, she said she had given two guns to Larry's son-in-law, Brad Fritz, to pawn. Jake Jr. relayed that information to Barnes.

Barnes wasn't sure yet who pulled that trigger. He reasoned that either Marjorie ambushed her husband in the garage or persuaded Larry to do it for her. Either way, Barnes believed that Marjorie had orchestrated the crime.

Barnes wondered if Jay had been able to look into the eyes of his killer. His mind flashed to an image of Jay bleeding to death on his garage floor. Jay's last thoughts were probably of his son. As he lay dying, did Jay have any clue that his wife had betrayed him? The man who was so afraid of dying on the road didn't seem to realize that the biggest danger was in his own house.

As for the dismemberment, Barnes thought Jay's dead body had been frozen somewhere while Marjorie cleaned up the crime scene, epoxy coating the garage floor and painting the walls so well that not even the slightest trace of blood could be found. Jay's thawed corpse had then been transported to the warehouse and grotesquely hacked apart with a jigsaw. Because of all the plastic found with the body, Barnes envisioned plastic sheeting spread out on the floors and walls to prevent blood splatter in the warehouse.

To test out his jigsaw theory, Barnes purchased the same make and model of jigsaw and blades as the ones that had been discovered at the warehouse. During the search, a package of sixteen jigsaw blades had been discovered, two of which were missing. At the medical examiner's office, Dr. Alex Zhang gathered old human bones that had been donated for research. One by one, Barnes and Zhang tested each blade in the package attempting to saw through the bone, but each blade would either jam or stop short of slicing clean through. Then Barnes tried a blade like the ones that were missing from the warehouse package. That blade was designed for "fast metal cut."

"It was like a hot knife through butter," Barnes recalled. "The blades that were missing from that jigsaw package were the only two blades in that whole package that could cut through bone. We tested every one of them."

Zhang closely examined that bone under the microscope and compared it to Jay Orbin's bone. It was the exact same cut pattern.

However, none of the jigsaws seized during the search warrants had any trace of blood. Whatever saw was used to dismember Jay's body was never recovered.

Meanwhile, a confused Noah was asking his mom questions she could not answer. When Jay went missing, Marjorie had told him his dad was never coming home and Larry was his new father figure. But soon after the body was discovered, Larry vanished from Noah's life. Then Marjorie suddenly didn't believe that the body in the tub could be Jay. She and Noah were holding out hope that Jay was still alive, Marjorie said. Depending on when Noah would ask, Marjorie would tell him alternating stories about his father.

When Noah asked why the police had arrested her, she assured Noah that everything would be all right. No one would take her away from him, Marjorie said.

"Everyone loved your dad so much. They just really want to find out who hurt him and they can't figure it out," Marjorie said. "They think it might have been me. But that's just a mistake. It will get straightened out soon."

In the mind of an eight-year-old, it all must have been impossible to process.

* * *

Meanwhile, the money was running out. Marjorie was three months behind on the mortgage and she had no access to Jay's bank account or credit cards. While she tried to maintain Jayhawk International, she was finding it increasingly difficult. With Jay gone, Marjorie had thought she could seamlessly take over the sales. Soon she discovered it was not so easy. So much of the business information was inside Jay's head and many of the sales were because of Jay's outgoing personality. Marjorie found it overwhelming. She complained to Todd Christy.

"I need money for groceries and everything," Marjorie sobbed. "I need an income!"

Todd offered to help her with the business. At the time he was working a nine a.m. to five p.m. shift at Blockbuster, but Marjorie said she didn't like being at the warehouse after dark. To accommodate her, Todd changed his work schedule to nights. For weeks, Todd assisted Marjorie at the warehouse filling orders and packing boxes. To Todd, it seemed disorganized. Marjorie had always bragged to Todd about how instrumental she was in building Jay's business. But to him it appeared that this was the first time she had ever done such laborious work.

"Oh my god!" Marjorie exclaimed as they toiled away at the warehouse. "I have never realized how much work this man did."

Todd stopped and stared at Marjorie. She looked so out of place. To him, Marjorie was a pampered, high-maintenance housewife. It was funny to see her packing boxes in a dirty warehouse.

"How did you ever wrap boxes with nails like that," Todd teased.

With Todd's help, Marjorie was able to make a few sales. She directed all of the customers to make out the checks to her name. Marjorie had opened a checking account in her name where she deposited the checks. After the arrest at

Circuit City, Marjorie scraped together enough cash together to buy a laptop. Even with a computer, however, she was hardly able to muddle through Jay's business. Marjorie's source of income was evaporating before her eyes.

While Todd was staying with Marjorie, they didn't talk much about Jay. Todd knew Jay was gone, but any time he asked questions, Marjorie would burst into tears. Todd later said he never suspected Marjorie of any wrongdoing. Marjorie never seemed afraid that she would be arrested for Jay's murder, but "just in case," she drew up a power of attorney form granting Todd Christy the power to act on her behalf.

"If things go bad," Marjorie said, "if something goes wrong, I want you to take care of things."

Marjorie told Todd she wanted him to stay at the house and take care of Noah. Todd would need to take him to Copper Canyon and pick him up at the end of the day. Noah got out of school at 2:30 p.m., Marjorie explained.

"I don't have a problem with that," Todd said. "With my schedule I can work out anything."

Todd was concerned that there would be a legal issue because he was not a family member. Marjorie, however, assured him that with her power of attorney, he could take care of Noah.

On Thanksgiving, Marjorie prepared dinner as she had every year. While she usually celebrated with Jay's parents, Marjorie and Noah spent the holiday with Todd and Oscar. They all gathered around the dining room table for turkey, dressing, and all of the fixings. Todd carved the turkey and Marjorie made homemade pumpkin pie. Afterward, they all went to see a movie at the theater.

A few miles away, Jake and Joann Obin had a quiet dinner at their house with Jake Jr. It was a somber celebration. This year, they had little to be thankful for.

On December 1, DNA tests finally confirmed what detectives had known for weeks—the torso in the tub was Jay

Michael Orbin's. Detective Barnes went back to the Orbins' house to tell them the development in person. Joann sobbed. It was still impossible to accept that her youngest son was really never coming home.

At nine p.m. that night, Marjorie, Todd, and Noah were eating dinner in the living room. Todd was sitting on the love seat while Marjorie and Noah were on the big couch. Suddenly, the evening news came on and a reporter read the lead story: "A dismembered torso discovered in the North Phoenix desert has been positively identified as belonging to local art dealer Jay Orbin." Todd turned to Marjorie. Her eyes went wide and a look of panic flashed across her face. For a moment, neither said a word. The sounds of Noah's cries broke the silence.

Marjorie dropped her plate on the coffee table, scooped up Noah, and took him into the bedroom. Todd was stunned. He sat quietly on the couch. About fifteen minutes later, Noah and Marjorie came back into the living room. Noah's eyes were red and puffy, but the boy's sadness had turned to anger.

"Whoever did this to my daddy," Noah fumed, "I'm going to get 'em. I'm going to get 'em."

A few days later, Marjorie told Todd that the stress of everything had become too much. She wanted to take Noah and go to Florida to live with Michael J. Peter.

"Will you come with me?" Marjorie asked.

"I don't know," he said. "What about Oscar?"

"He could come too," Marjorie said.

Todd had lived in different places across the country and was the type who liked to relocate every seven years. For months, Todd had been feeling antsy and was interested in a change of scenery. He told Marjorie he would consider it.

During a later conversation with Jake. Jr., Marjorie mentioned Florida. Jake Jr. became fearful she was planning to take Noah and flee the state. Alarmed, he told Detective Barnes. Suddenly, there was a new sense of urgency in his investigation. If Marjorie were to disappear, they might never apprehend her.

Barnes thought he had enough evidence to make an arrest, but the county attorney still wanted more. They just didn't have anything to definitively connect Marjorie to the crime. Barnes needed DNA, a witness, a murder weapon, something. If that one big piece of evidence was never found, the case could still go to trial, eventually. But would the cell tower records, Jay's credit cards, and Marjorie's bizarre behavior be enough to get a conviction?

Then in early December, there was a breakthrough. For weeks, rookie Detective Bryan Chapman had been tracking down receipts from each purchase made on Jay's credit cards following his September 8 disappearance. So far, most of the purchases appeared unrelated to the murder. Aside from the large number of cleaning supplies purchased at Target on September 9, it seemed that Marjorie had mainly bought clothes, cosmetics, electronics, and home decor.

Then, while scouring though transactions made on Jay's American Express card, Chapman noticed a $175.46 purchase at a Scottsdale Lowe's on September 10. On Saturday, December 4, Chapman drove to Lowe's to obtain the receipt and learn exactly what was purchased.

After reviewing the receipt, the security manger cued up surveillance video from the time of the purchase. As the video played, Chapman saw a woman fitting Marjorie's description calmly push her cart up to the cashier and place merchandise on the register. But when Chapman realized what was in her cart, he quietly gasped. Immediately, he called Detective Barnes.

"You're not going to believe this," Chapman told Barnes. "We've got her buying the tub. It's on video!"

"You've got to be kidding me," Barnes said with an astonished laugh. "Where are you?"

A moment later, Barnes was in his car, headed toward Lowe's. Upon arriving at the store, Barnes met Chapman inside the security room to review the tape. Sure enough, he saw a blond woman, hair tucked into a ponytail, in a red tank top and black pants. It was clearly Marjorie Orbin. In her cart were two fifty-five-gallon Rubbermaid containers.

Barnes was floored.

"Holy cow!" Barnes turned to Chapman. "You found the smoking gun."

This was better than forensics. The tape showed Marjorie, alone, buying Jay's Rubbermaid casket.

"This was the biggest discovery of the investigation," Barnes said years later. "Here we've got her, on video, buying the tub he's found in with his credit card—two days after he went missing. It was incredibly damning."

After reviewing the tape, Barnes and Chapman grabbed a cart and went through the store collecting the items from the receipt. Marjorie had purchased two of the fifty-five-gallon containers. They were both the exact same size and exact same color as the one in which Jay Orbin's remains were found.

"This is very interesting," Barnes remarked to Chapman. "You know, we never found a second tub."

Barnes wondered if the other tub contained the rest of Jay's body. Was it out there somewhere in the desert, waiting to be discovered?

This was powerful evidence. Barnes and Chapman bought every item Marjorie had purchased on September 10. These included a nine by twelve roll of plastic, disinfectant, floor cleaner, mop pads, and a box of fifty-five-gallon black trash bags that looked similar to the bags found inside the container.

"Now everything is finally coming together," Barnes recalled years later. "The cell tower records, the financial records, and finally the discovery of the tub."

The case was like a puzzle. On their own, some pieces were small and seemingly insignificant. But taken together, they formed one persuasive picture of murder.

On Monday, at the police station, Barnes went down to the main evidence storage room to compare the tub from Lowe's with the one in which Jay's torso was discovered. The tubs weren't just similar—they matched exactly. The dimensions, size, and color were all the same. The UPC sticker on the tub in which Jay was found was an exact match to the bar code number on the receipt. Later another detective contacted the Rubbermaid Corporation about the distribution of this type of container and learned that Lowe's sold it exclusively. In fact, that particular Scottsdale Lowe's was one of the few locations in the Phoenix area that sold the container.

Detective Barnes brought the evidence to prosecutor Noel Levy and a warrant was obtained for Marjorie's arrest.

At 7:22 p.m. on December 6, Detectives Barnes and Meislish, as well as five other officers and sergeants, arrived at Jay and Marjorie's house armed with an arrest warrant. Marjorie answered her front door while on the phone with her attorney, Tom Connelly. She appeared annoyed and inconvenienced.

"Marjorie Orbin," Barnes said authoritatively, "you're under arrest for the first degree murder of your husband."

Marjorie didn't say a word. Calmly, she hung up the phone and put her hands behind her back as detectives placed her in handcuffs. Moments later, she was in the back seat of a patrol car. She stared out the window of the car as detectives retrieved Noah from the house. As the car drove off, Marjorie watched Noah until he disappeared from view. It was the last time she would see her son.

Detectives took Noah to the police station to be released into the custody of Jake Orbin Jr. Barnes had already

called the Orbins to inform them of the arrest and to arrange to place Noah into their charge.

At the police station, Barnes attempted, one more time,
to interview Marjorie, but again she asked for her attorney.
Marjorie did have one request—she wanted to speak to
Jake Jr. "I didn't do this," Marjorie told him. "I didn't kill
Jay. I would never hurt the father of my son."

That night Marjorie was booked into the Estrella Jail,
where she was fingerprinted and photographed. In her
mugshot, Marjorie was expressionless. Her eyes were vacantly cast down toward the floor. Her makeup was flawless but her brittle, electric blond hair was a wild, tangled
mane. She was dressed in a designer gray sweatshirt and
matching pants. After what was likely the least glamorous
photo shoot of her life, Marjorie was searched and ordered
to change into standard prison garb—a baggy, black-and-
white stripped uniform with neon pink slip-on sandals.

That evening, from the cell block phone, Marjorie used
her one free phone call to contact Todd Christy. She got his
voice mail. Todd had recently gone to Texas to visit a
friend. When his plane touched down, about twenty minutes after Marjorie's arrest, he checked his voice mail.
Marjorie's message was frantic: "Todd, I have been arrested for first-degree murder. I will call you later this evening. Answer the phone!"

That night, Todd's phone rang again. "Marjorie?" he
asked.

"Yeah, Todd," Marjorie said. "Listen. I need you to get
some of my stuff."

CHAPTER 22

That night of Marjorie's arrest, as instructed, Todd Christy and Oscar Moreno drove to her empty house. Slowly, they crept up to the garage and typed in the security code on the key pad. Using the house keys Marjorie had provided him, Todd entered the laundry room through the garage and headed straight for the home office. Todd knew exactly what to get. He and Marjorie had discussed this several times before her arrest.

Rummaging through the office closet, he located several storage tubs full of silver, turquoise, and gold jewelry—Jay's merchandise. The tubs were heavy, each one weighing close to a hundred pounds. One by one, Todd and Oscar loaded the tubs into the SUV Marjorie had rented. Todd also found a backpack, a briefcase, and a duffel bag, which he packed with Marjorie's things. From the bedroom dresser, Todd grabbed Marjorie's jewelry and her diamond engagement ring.

The next day, Marjorie called and he told her he got the stuff.

"Hide the jewelry," Marjorie instructed, "Or *they* will get a warrant and seize it."

Marjorie instructed him to return to the house and get a few more items. Specifically, she wanted him to find the laptop computer she had purchased. Several times she reiterated that it was very important that Todd find the laptop.

"I need you to do something else," Marjorie said. "Withdraw all the cash from the checking account."

Todd needed to act quickly before the account was frozen. This was Marjorie's only remaining money. The balance—about $7,500—was money Marjorie had acquired by cashing checks made payable to Jayhawk International. Marjorie knew the police would come after all her assets. In preparation, she had already given Todd her debit card and the pin number to the account she had set up. But Todd was concerned. "What if I get caught?" Todd asked. "I can't lose my job."

"Michael will keep you out of harm's way," she said. "If you ever need a job, he'll hire you in a second."

The next day, Todd withdrew the cash.

This was Marjorie's insurance policy. If she got out of jail on bond, she could collect the jewelry and money and flee to Florida.

In the days following the arrest, local news outlets were buzzing with details about the case. A brutal dismemberment, a beautiful suspected killer—it was one of those tantalizing news items that made the front page of the paper and led off nightly newscasts.

The bizarre murder also mirrored another famed Phoenix case. In 2000, a Scottsdale hairdresser and wannabe socialite named Valerie Pape was arrested for killing and dismembering her husband and dumping his torso in a dumpster behind a grocery store. It became a celebrated case; local TV stations dubbed it "The Torso Murder." Ironically, Pape's husband was a successful local businessman and she was a pretty, petite blonde.

For the Orbins, the media coverage was surreal. Three months ago, they had had a nice, normal life. Now they were entangled in a murder mystery.

After the arrest, Detective Barnes sat down with the Orbins and told them the evidence they had against Marjorie. Once Jake Jr. heard all they had, any doubt in his mind was gone. As difficult as it was to comprehend, he knew that Marjorie had murdered Jay.

The weekend of Marjorie's arrest, hundreds of Jay's loved ones flocked to the church for his funeral. In his will, Jay's final wishes were to be buried, no open casket: With so little of his body remaining, his torso was cremated. At the service, dozens of Jay's friends and business associates stood up and delivered emotional speeches about how Jay had touched their lives. Many recalled watching Noah grow up through photos over the years. Jay was remembered as a proud and loving father.

No one was more devastated than Jay's mother. Joann sat in the front row clutching Noah's hand, sobbing. Noah, meanwhile, still seemed unable to comprehend the loss of his father. He sat through the services, despondent.

Detective Barnes and Sergeant Karen Vance returned to Jay and Marjorie's house the week of Marjorie's arrest. With layered, dark blond hair and a sweet, inviting smile, Vance was a petite veteran sergeant in her mid-forties. As Barnes's direct supervisor, Vance had been supporting his investigation throughout the case.

At about 4:30 p.m., Jake Jr. arrived at the house to let the detectives inside.

"I found some legal documents you need to see," Jake Jr. said. While Marjorie was in jail, Jake Jr. was granted temporary custody of Noah. But while retrieving Noah's belongings from the house, he found something disturbing. He led detectives through the house to Jay's office and produced four power of attorney documents, granting four separate people the power to act on Marjorie's behalf, as well as granting them guardianship of Noah. The four people listed on these forms: Michael J. Peter, Charity

McLean, Bryan Todd Christy, and Larry Weisberg. Larry's form, however, was unsigned.

"It's like she wanted Noah to be with anyone but me or my family," Jake Jr. said.

Jake Jr. left to get dinner while Barnes and Vance searched the house. In Jay's office the detectives discovered several uncashed checks to Jayhawk International from Jay's clients, four blank checkbooks, and more credit cards.

In the spare bedroom, dozens of pictures of Marjorie and Michael J. Peter were strewn across the floor. In the garage, a Skil jigsaw and Black & Decker jigsaw were also discovered, as well as a package of jigsaw blades similar to the ones found at the warehouse. Those items were seized for forensic testing.

The following afternoon, Marjorie called Todd Christy from jail.

"Did you get the laptop?" she asked.

"We went back to your house," Todd said. "The cops were there."

Marjorie was furious that the police were traipsing around her house again. They were probably planting evidence, Marjorie claimed. She told Todd the cops had nothing against her. Todd informed her he had withdrawn $6,300 from her bank account. He said he was worried he would get caught, but Marjorie assured him everything was all right and that the power of attorney documents permitted him to act on her behalf.

Marjorie instructed Todd to deposit some of the cash into her jail account so she could purchase food and toiletries. Marjorie also asked him to add money to four other inmate accounts and provided him with their booking numbers. This way, Marjorie said, she would have access to a lot of funds through different people.

As for the jewelry, Todd said he had secured it in a safe place. "Don't tell anyone that you have the jewelry or that you took it from the house," Marjorie said. "Not even my attorney."

While Todd had been staying at the house, Marjorie frequently told him that if anything happened, Michael would take care of her. After her arrest, Todd called him.

"Marjorie was arrested," Todd said.

"Oh, my god," Michael said. "For what?"

"Well, umm, murder," Todd stammered.

"What do you mean, murder?" Michael said, astonished.

Prior to the arrest, Michael had thought Marjorie was only in trouble for forgery for using Jay's credit card. At most, Marjorie would only have to spend three to five years in prison. Michael felt there had to be some mistake. He had known Marjorie since she was eighteen and didn't believe she was capable of murder.

Although Michael hadn't actually seen Marjorie in a decade and they only spoke occasionally by phone, he came to her rescue. He flew down to Phoenix and personally met with Tom Connelly. Without hesitation, Michael cut Connelly a check for $150,000, with the promise of up to $400,000 for her defense.

Michael spoke to Marjorie and assured her he would do everything he could to help. "I love you and I believe in you," he said.

CHAPTER 23

Marjorie Orbin was behind bars, but Detective David Barnes's job was only half done. His gut told him that Larry Weisberg was involved in either the murder or the cover-up. Larry had practically been living in the dead man's house and sleeping in his bed just days after Jay was killed. His reaction to the SWAT team was suspicious, as was his concern about being arrested following the search of his home. But for months, detectives had not found a shred of evidence against him. Then in December, Phoenix crime lab analyst John Knell made a discovery: Initial tests on the hairs found with the tub were a match for the two suspects—Marjorie Orbin and Larry Weisberg.

"We've got Larry!" Barnes told Noel Levy. "Let's go get him."

But Levy still had doubts. Under a microscope, Knell had compared Larry's hair to the hair found with the tub and determined that it had the same features and characteristics. But he hadn't actually proved that the hair was Larry's, only that they looked similar. The hairs found with the tub had roots attached, which meant they could be further tested for a DNA match. To arrest Larry, Levy wanted DNA. The hairs were sent to the Phoenix bureau of the FBI crime lab for further testing.

In the meantime, Levy pressed Larry's high-priced defense attorney, John Callahan, for an interview with his client. But Callahan would only permit Larry to speak if he was offered immunity from prosecution. With some reluctance, Levy agreed to offer Larry a "free talk," which would grant immunity from anything they learned through Larry during one interview. It was a risk, but Larry's attorney wouldn't let him speak without it. Barnes was against the agreement.

"He could have confessed to the crime and said Marjorie had nothing to do with it and we would not have been able to arrest him or use anything in the free talk against him," Barnes recalled. "Larry knew he could confess everything and walk away free."

Still, both lawyers settled on the terms of the agreement and days after Marjorie's arrest, Barnes, Levy, Larry, and his attorney met at the police station for the free talk.

As they prepared to speak, other detectives gathered around a monitor in another room to watch the interview. After months of investigation, all of the detectives who had assisted on the case were anxious to hear what Larry had to say. The anticipation grew as Callahan and Levy went back and forth on specific wording in the legal agreement. Larry sat in silence, glancing around the room. It was the same interrogation room that Marjorie Orbin had sat in twice. Finally, at about four p.m., with the agreement signed, Levy read aloud the rules of the immunity deal: Any information provided by Larry, during this interview only, would not be used against him in any criminal proceedings regarding the murder of Jay Orbin. They could still bring about later charges based on other evidence or information. With all the legalese out of the way, Barnes began.

"Okay." Barnes motioned toward Larry. "I'll just leave it with you and let you start."

Larry leaned forward in his chair, looked Barnes straight in the eye, and assertively said, "I don't know anything about what had happened to Jay Orbin. I never met

Mr. Orbin. I have never spoken to Mr. Orbin. I've never been around him or anything else. The only way wherever I ever got information about Jay was through Marjorie Orbin."

Larry sat back and gave a slight chuckle.

"Okay, so what you're telling me is you had nothing to do with his disappearance or his murder?" Barnes asked.

"Absolutely zero! Nothing!" Larry exclaimed. "I never ever would have ever even thought about anything like this."

"Has Marjorie ever mentioned anything to you about the disappearance of or murder of Jay?" Barnes asked.

"We discussed the disappearance."

Larry explained that in early September Marjorie made a casual mention that Jay hadn't called the house in a couple of days. At this point in their relationship, Larry was a frequent overnight visitor at Marjorie's. He noticed that every morning in August, the phone would ring. It was always Jay calling to speak with his son. Then suddenly in September, the calls stopped. Larry found it very strange.

"I told her you better get in touch with the police and tell them he's missing," Larry said to Barnes.

Marjorie disregarded his advice, saying she had to wait forty-eight or seventy-two hours because he was an adult. A few days later Larry asked if she had heard from Jay. Marjorie said she had not. At that point, Marjorie indicated to him that she had called the police to report Jay missing. This was a least a week and a half before Marjorie actually reported Jay missing on September 22, Larry said.

"Did Marjorie ever tell you she was involved with his murder?" Barnes asked.

"No." Larry shook his head.

Barnes wasn't swayed. Forensic evidence seemed to indicate that Larry knew more than he was saying.

"I believe your attorney already knows this," Barnes said in an authoritative tone. "We have a hair that was found on his remains. Preliminary results are the hair matches your hair. Now, we're doing further test with DNA and if this hair comes back that it matches your DNA, how would you explain that?"

"I have no idea," Larry said. "Now, it could've been from the individual, who had done this atrocity, could've been on their clothes, it could've been anywhere. I don't know."

"But if that's your hair . . . ," Barnes pressed.

"Again," Larry interjected, "I know I have no idea. I am saying to you and I'm saying to Mr. Levy that there is no way that I know anything about Mr. Orbin's death, disappearance, or anything."

Barnes brought up the plastic sheeting found with Jay's body and explained that it was consistent with plastic found in Larry's house. Larry said he had no way to explain that either. Barnes then reminded Larry of the statement he made to officers after they searched his house.

"We called you and said we're done, you can come home now," Barnes said. "You made a statement to one of our sergeants asking if you were going to be arrested."

"What?" Larry looked puzzled. "Why would I ask that?"

Larry denied making that statement and said he didn't recall speaking with a sergeant that night.

When asked about his relationship with Marjorie, Larry explained how they met in mid-July at L.A. Fitness. According to Larry, Marjorie came on to him, "quite big time." At first, Larry said, he was hesitant because he thought Marjorie was married but she assured him that she was divorced. They began an intimate relationship.

"Did she ever mention anything about Jay Orbin to you?" Barnes asked.

"That he was her ex-husband," Larry said. As far as Larry knew, Jay was a traveling salesman who was on the road most of the year. Larry said he didn't even realize Jay was living at the house until later in their relationship, when he started coming over.

"She said, 'After so many years on the road, I'm surprised that he isn't dead from statistics,' or something to that effect," Larry continued. "And she did state that she wished he were dead."

"How'd that make you feel?" Barnes asked.

"Very strange. Very strange," Larry said slowly. "That was about the second time that we had met in the gym."

"Did she ever mention that she wanted him dead or wanted to kill him?" Barnes asked.

"Not to kill him . . . no," Larry said. "Just mentioned statistically she's surprised that it didn't go off a cliff someplace, that's all."

Marjorie told him Jay returned to Phoenix the first week of September but left town again for a short trip. She never mentioned anything about his birthday.

"Did you ever notice a change in her behavior—her stress level, anything like that in September? Anything strike you as odd?"

"No. Don't think so."

"Do you remember toward the first part of September, her and Noah ever being ill or sick?" Barnes asked.

"Yes. Uh-hum. Yeah," Larry stammered.

"Did you see her during that time frame?" Barnes asked.

"No. No," Larry said.

Larry distinctly remembered that Marjorie had been sick for about three or four days in early September. During this time period, he said he never saw her because he, too, had the flu.

"I wouldn't go over there period! I was sick. She was also." Larry paused. "She *said* she was also sick."

According to Larry, Marjorie had no relationship with Jay beyond occasionally letting him sleep on the couch when he was in town. Larry said he didn't start sleeping at the house regularly until August.

"Where do you think Jay was during these times?" Barnes asked.

"She said he was out of town."

"Okay, have you ever asked her if she was involved in Jay's murder?" Barnes asked.

"Yes, I did," Larry said matter-of-factly.

There was a pregnant pause as everyone waited to hear Larry finish that statement.

"And how'd she react?" Barnes said.

"We were sitting on my couch and I asked her, 'Do you know anything about Jay Orbin's disappearance or anything else?' And she looked me square in the eye and she says, 'I don't know anything,' and I said, 'Are you sure?' And she said, 'Yes.' "

"Did you believe her?" Barnes asked.

"To a point, yes." Larry shrugged.

"What part of you didn't believe her or why?"

"She was concerned that he was missing, but if I had a relationship like that with somebody, I'd be more concerned than she had showed."

Larry told the detective how, after Jay disappeared, Noah started asking questions about his father. He also related the incident when Noah had called *him* dad.

"Did that strike you as odd?" Barnes asked.

"It floored me."

Larry said that a few days later, he pulled his daughter aside to tell her about it. He said it made him very uncomfortable and his daughter was clearly bothered.

"Okay, did it seem like Marjorie was trying to move you in as a father figure to Noah?"

"I believe so, yes," Larry said.

"What makes you believe that?"

"Because she said we looked alike." Larry smirked. "And I said we do not look alike. The only thing we have in common is this color hair."

"Were you talking marriage?" Barnes asked.

"No," Larry said. "Just living together."

Larry told Barnes that they were considering purchasing a house together in the same neighborhood so Noah could stay in the same school.

Larry didn't say much about Marjorie or her behavior that was incriminating, but when pressed, he did recall one peculiar incident. One night, when his daughter was watching Noah, he and Marjorie went back to her house. They were sitting on the couch in the living room, discussing their future, when Larry asked her what she expected to do with her life. Marjorie was confused and asked, "What do you mean?" Larry said, "Well, you know, Noah is eight years old. What do you expect to do, you know, when he's older?" Marjorie's reply was, "I'm going to be a soccer mom." Larry was puzzled. He found it odd that Marjorie had no ambitions beyond being a stay-at-home mom. "I understand Noah's a little young yet," Larry continued. "But from that point onward, you know, you're going to have to give to the household if we plan to do, you know, continue on." At that, Marjorie balked and told Larry to go to hell.

"And she got a little annoyed at that and I said, 'I don't need this B.S.,'" Larry told Barnes. "I got up and I walked out of the house. The next thing I know, my daughter's calling me."

Jodi told her father that Marjorie had come to her house, scooped up Noah, and left in a huff. Larry was embarrassed. He told his daughter about the disagreement. Larry decided to let the tension die down. A few days elapsed and Marjorie called. She apologized and they picked up where they had left off.

Barnes asked Larry if he thought that Marjorie ever displayed symptoms of drug use.

"Would she stay up for long periods of time?" Barnes asked.

"Stay up? At times she wouldn't even go to sleep!" he said.

Often, Larry said, he would wake up in the middle of the night, reach for Marjorie, and find her gone. Larry would explore the house looking for her and would find her on her hands and knees scrubbing the kitchen floor. "What are you doing?" he asked her. Marjorie just said she was cleaning. She explained to Larry that she suffered from insomnia and had difficulty sleeping. A few times, Marjorie stayed up until dawn.

To Barnes, this sounded like typical drug abuser behavior. It tied in to the methamphetamine found in the house and Marjorie's gaunt appearance.

"What is your relationship with Marjorie right now, today?" Barnes asked.

"I wouldn't go next to her with a ten-foot pole!" Larry exclaimed.

"How about a week ago, before her arrest?" Barnes asked.

"I told her to keep away from me!" Larry exclaimed.

Following the search warrants, Larry said, Marjorie kept calling him saying, "I have to see you." Eventually, Larry broke down and went to her house. There, Marjorie led Larry outside to the backyard and said, "I want to run away, I want out of here."

Larry looked at her, dumbfounded. "What? Are you crazy? No way." Larry said he had done nothing wrong. "I don't know what the hell is happening, and you want to run away?" Larry asked, flabbergasted. "That would cause all sorts of complications."

Marjorie started to cry and said, "Well, I'll make dinner." Larry told her to forget it and left.

That was the last time Larry said he saw her.

"Did she say why she wanted to run away?" Barnes asked.

"She was scared," Larry said.

"Okay, what do you think about all this now?" Barnes asked.

"You mean at the present right now? This minute?"

"Yes." Barnes nodded. "What do you think about all this now?"

"If I could go back to July, I wouldn't, I wouldn't, I wouldn't even speak to her," Larry stammered.

"You seem very intelligent and smart to me." Barnes grinned.

Barnes asked one more question about something Larry had mentioned earlier in the interview. "When you asked her pointedly do you have anything to do with this and she answered no, you said you didn't completely believe her?" Barnes asked. "Why is it you didn't completely believe her?"

Larry thought for a moment. "There was hesitation there, if I remember correctly. That's why I asked her twice," he said. "She didn't appreciate the second time I asked. She really didn't appreciate the first, but the second time . . . it unnerved me a little bit."

Continuing his investigation into Larry Weisberg, Barnes also questioned Larry's daughter, Jodi Weisberg, and her husband, Brad Fritz. Like her father, Jodi said she had believed that Marjorie was divorced and that Jay did not live in the house. Although Jodi was around Marjorie during the first part of September, she didn't recall anything unusual in her behavior. Marjorie mentioned in September that she had reported Jay missing, but she didn't act like anything was wrong, Jodi said.

"At times she would act like she knew Jay was never coming back," Jodi said. "Other times she would say Jay's just missing and he does this often."

After Jay disappeared, Jodi said that Marjorie would tell Larry that she was scared and wanted him to stay the night. Marjorie claimed that people were following her and that she and Noah were afraid. To Jodi, it appeared Marjorie was putting on a "good show."

"I never believed her," she said. "I never saw a tear, no emotion, no concerns at all for Jay."

Jodi said her father was devastated by everything that had happened. One day, in front of Jodi and Marjorie, Larry broke down and cried. Marjorie just turned to Larry and snidely said, "I wish you would just get over it." Jodi was shocked. "This is serious!" she exclaimed. "I can't

believe you're acting this way. A man could be dead!"
Marjorie became very defensive. "What am I supposed to
do?" she snapped.

Jodi said this was the first time in her life that she had
seen her father so upset. Normally, Larry was not an emotional person; he didn't even act this way through his divorce. Now he cried almost every day, Jodi said.

"Do you think your dad may have been involved?"
Barnes asked. "That he might be acting this way because
he has something to hide?"

"No," Jodi insisted. "He would have told me if he was
involved in any way."

Jodi's husband, Brad Fritz, didn't have much to add, except some insight into the guns that had disappeared from
the house. Through Jake Jr., Barnes had learned that Marjorie had given Brad two guns to pawn.

"Why did she say she was giving them to you?" Barnes
asked.

"She said she did not want them," Brad replied. "That
she didn't like having them around the house."

Months later, Jodi contacted Barnes with new information. She remembered that on her son's birthday in September, she had seen something strange. Her father was in her
back alley dumping trash. She didn't know what it was or
why he would have that much garbage. In hindsight, it
seemed bizarre.

Was Larry Weisberg a naïve boyfriend ensnared by a manipulative seductress or an accomplice to a heinous murder? The interviews with Larry and his family had done
little to further the case.

During the free talk, Larry had seemed convincing, but
he also had an immunity deal and a seasoned criminal
defense attorney by his side. Barnes wasn't ready to dismiss Larry Weisberg as a suspect. "Larry came across as

believable but I felt his answers were well rehearsed and prepared," Barnes recalled. "It seemed like he was coached by his attorney about what to say and how to behave."

By Larry's own account, he was staying frequently at the Orbins' house throughout August and September. He would have had to be quite gullible not to have noticed a murder had taken place. Larry *had* to have seen something. He *had* to know more than he was saying.

Noel Levy, however, felt quite the opposite. To him, Larry seemed like a reserved, responsible grandfather who kept to himself and minded his own business. While Larry's actions during the investigation seemed suspect, Levy evaluated his behavior as that of a man who had a finger pointed at him as a murderer. "You could tell that he was very upset that he was accused," Levy recalled. "But he seemed to be forthright. He described nothing to implicate her, certainly nothing to implicate himself."

Larry freely admitted to the affair with Marjorie. It certainly seemed possible that Jay came home and caught Marjorie with another man and a fatal altercation ensued. But Levy was beginning to feel that scenario was not very likely. There was simply no motive for Larry to murder Jay Orbin and dismember his body. "He gained nothing out of this. Every bit of the assets would have gone to her. Nothing ever would have come to him, whatsoever," Levy said. "Marjorie knew how to manipulate men. Larry seemed to be an honest person who unfortunately hooked up with her."

If Detective Barnes was going to build a case against Larry, his only hope was the DNA. Barnes was anxious to learn if the hairs sent to the FBI crime lab were a DNA match to Larry. Those results, however, were still weeks away.

CHAPTER 24

The Orbins were paralyzed by crushing, empty despair. Their grief wasn't eased by Marjorie's arrest—they said that they found little joy or relief in the realization that Jay was murdered by his son's mother. Essentially it meant that Noah had lost both parents. Jay was dead and parts of his body were still missing. The family felt lost and emotionally drained. Their only comfort was that they had Noah.

As difficult as it was, the Orbins had to pick up the pieces. Despite Marjorie's four power of attorney documents, the courts ruled that temporary custody would remain with Jake Jr. Never having had any children of his own, Jake Jr. had to learn to be a father. Noah, meanwhile, seemed to be quietly adjusting. At first he didn't talk much about his father or what had happened to him, saying only that his mom had told him his dad was shot. Eventually, Jake Jr. had to delicately explain what had happened. Noah was also put into counseling to work out his grief. "We explained that she would go on trial and there's evidence that said she did do it, but we just have to wait because she's innocent until proven guilty," Jake Jr. recalled. "He understood all that."

For the first few months that Marjorie was behind bars, she was still very much a part of Noah's life. She spoke to her son frequently by phone and wrote to him obsessively. In the letters, Marjorie maintained her innocence and assured Noah that they would soon be reunited. At first Jake Jr. let Noah read all the letters. But over time, they became increasingly worrisome. One letter read, *You know in your heart that your Mommy didn't do anything wrong. I have some really good friends that are helping me. It has been very hard because of the other people around that could be helping but choose not to. If you want to you can ask anyone that says they love you why they are not helping you get your Mommy back. I think daddy would be ashamed of them for not helping.*"

As the letters became increasingly manipulative, Jake Jr. thought it best that Noah didn't read any more.

Weeks after taking custody of Noah, the Orbins discovered something else disturbing. When Noah was first born, he had a little tuft of brown hair like his father, but when he was just a few months old his hair lightened to a golden blond, similar in shade to his mother's. The Orbins figured it was natural, as children's hair often changes color. But while living with Jake Jr., Noah's hair grew out dark. They realized that Noah was never a blond; Marjorie had been bleaching his hair since he was a baby. That was utterly sickening to the Orbins. What kind of mother would do that to her son?

Jake Jr. handled the management of Jay's estate. The house where his brother had lived, and likely died, felt eerie. He decided to put it up for sale. For weeks Jake Jr. went through the house, separating Marjorie's belongings from Jay's and Noah's. Sorting through his brother's things was emotionally draining. Every baseball card or piece of memorabilia Jay had painstakingly collected brought back fond memories from his life. It hurt to think no new memories would ever be made.

Marjorie's clothes, furs, mink stoles, jewelry, cosmetics, and her collection of Louis Vuitton bags were packed up in boxes, along with photos from her life as a dancer and videotapes of her brushes with fame. It was all moved into a storage unit, which the Orbins paid to maintain. Until the trial, Jay's estate would be in limbo. If Marjorie was not convicted, all of Jay's assets would still go to her. She would collect the million dollars in insurance polices and regain custody of Noah. If she were convicted, everything would revert to Noah.

As Jake Jr. tried to make sense of his brother's finances, he discovered that many of the bills hadn't been paid since September. All of Jay's credit cards were behind and the mortgages on his house and business warehouse were past due. When Marjorie called from jail to speak to Noah, Jake Jr. asked why she had let everything go into default.

Marjorie told him there was not much equity in the warehouse and she had planned to let it go into foreclosure. As for the credit cards, she explained that all of Jay's creditors were "screwed." "They can't collect anything once a person is dead," she said.

"Why didn't you have your attorney handle any of this?" Jake Jr. asked.

"I wasn't prepared for this. I was busy taking orders, feeding Noah, and cleaning the house."

Jake Jr. asked Marjorie about the $10,000 piano. She said it was a mistake and claimed she tried to return it. In a subsequent call with Todd Christy, however, Marjorie said the piano was hers and, "No one is to liquidate it!"

During one of Jake Jr.'s conversations with Marjorie, he confronted her about the evidence. He said that police believed she had had Jay's cell phone the entire time. To Jake Jr. this aspect of the crime was particularly cruel. Marjorie had intentionally prolonged the Orbins' grief by attempting to fool his family into believing Jay was still alive. Marjorie, however, denied this and claimed, "Cell towers bounce all over the place."

Marjorie told Jake Jr. that the police were fabricating evidence. She even claimed that the keys found on Jay's body were planted by the cops. Marjorie had an explanation for everything—none of which made any sense to Jake Jr. *It was all so ridiculous*, Jake Jr. thought. He gave up trying to get answers from Marjorie. He no longer believed anything she had to say.

On December 27, Marjorie stood in front of a judge with Tom Connelly at her side as the formal charges were read: first-degree premeditated murder.

"How do you plead?" the judge asked.

Confidently and defiantly Marjorie uttered the words, "Not guilty."

Marjorie was wearing black-and-white prison stripes with her booking number, P031041, stenciled across the back in pink. She wore her hair straight; her makeup, purchased from the jail commissary, was still flawless. Because of the heinous nature of the crime, the judge deemed her ineligible to receive bond. Marjorie would remain in jail until the trial.

Arizona jails are notorious for their squalid conditions. Maricopa County Sheriff Joe Arpaio, who promotes himself as "America's Toughest Sheriff," has garnered national publicity for housing inmates in tents, forcing prisoners to wear pink underwear, and running the country's only female chain gang. Human rights groups regard it as the harshest jail system in the United States.

In secure lockdown, Marjorie would be housed in an eight-by-twelve-square-foot cell twenty-three hours a day with another inmate. There she would be fed meals consisting of moldy cheese and green bologna twice a day. There would be no organized recreation. Marjorie could mail letters, but would be unable to receive any in return. Loved ones were only permitted to send inmates postcards. Visitors would only be able to speak to her through thick plate glass or over a video link.

Throughout her life, Marjorie had become accustomed to the finer things. She had traveled on yachts and private jets, vacationed on tropical islands, and lived in mansions. Jail was quite a change. At first, she seemed withdrawn and kept mostly to herself. Over the next few weeks, however, Marjorie seemed to adjust to life in jail fairly well.

Correction officers recalled how she would do karate moves and yoga in her cell. Every morning she would make her bed and apply her makeup. She read books and made friends with some of the other girls. Marjorie was first housed with a petite, forty-five-year-old brunette named Lissa Sherman, who was in jail on charges of credit card fraud. Lissa was very crafty. From her cell, she made flowers out of magazine pages and created ceramics out of a wet paste she made from stale bread. Marjorie shared stories with her about her various home improvement projects.

One afternoon they were in the jail day room, flipping through the pages of a home decor magazine, when Marjorie came across a picture of Martha Stewart standing in her kitchen. That's when Marjorie told Lissa about one project of which she was particularly proud.

When Lissa later told Detective Barnes what that "project" involved, it took the case on another strange detour.

Aside from Todd Christy, Marjorie did not have many jailhouse visitors. Todd would come to the jail to see her every Tuesday, occasionally accompanied by Oscar Moreno. On a few occasions, Charity McLean flew in from Las Vegas to see her. The day after Charity's visit, Marjorie called Todd and told him about Charity's "bad plastic surgery" and how awful she looked.

During her first month behind bars, Marjorie spoke to Todd Christy three or four times a week, continuing to instruct him to hide her property.

"We need to protect my assets," she said.

During one conversation, Todd brought up the news coverage of her case. Marjorie said that everything that had been reported was lies, and that "The police have no case."

On January 3, 2005, Detective David Barnes received recordings of all of Marjorie's jailhouse phone calls from her past month behind bars. In Maricopa County jails, as in most jails across the country, inmate phone calls are digitally recorded and readily made available to police and prosecutors.

In the Phoenix Police Department, it is not policy for detectives to listen to all of these recordings. The process can be tedious, time consuming, and often unnecessary. But in many cases these phone calls can also be helpful in uncovering previously unknown facts about a crime. As he did with all of his murder suspects, Barnes listened to every single one of Marjorie's phone calls.

The calls to Noah, Jake Jr., and Charity McLean were mostly irrelevant. But her conversations with Todd Christy got his attention. Through their conversations, Barnes was easily able to put together the details of Marjorie's brazen jailhouse scheme. She was stealing from her dead husband's estate.

Based on what he learned through the phone calls, Barnes called Marjorie's attorney, Tom Connelly, and informed him that all the jewelry, cash, and anything else taken from the house needed to be returned. On Wednesday, January 5, Connelly called Barnes and said Todd agreed to return the jewelry. Of the $6,300 he had withdrawn from the account, Todd said there was only about $3,000 left. Todd arranged to return the property in one week's time.

Meanwhile, quite foolishly, Todd and Marjorie continued to conspire. In a subsequent conversation, Marjorie told Todd to turn over some of the jewelry to Connelly—but not all of it. She listed some of the more expensive items she wanted Todd to keep. Don't leave it at your house, she said, hide it somewhere else.

"What do you want me to do with the cash?" Todd asked.

Marjorie told him to get rid of the money before police took it. Don't turn it over to the cops, she instructed. She said that she planned to use all of the commissary money on her books before it was seized.

"I need you to take care of me," Marjorie pleaded. "I need you to protect me."

On January 10, Connelly informed Barnes that Todd had returned three boxes of jewelry but no cash. Based on the cash not being returned, Barnes drafted a search warrant for Todd Christy and Oscar Moreno's apartment. At about 5:20 p.m. that evening, Barnes and Detective Richard Polk arrived at their place to search for the cash, laptop, and jewelry.

Detectives knocked on the door but no one answered. Barnes tried their home phone. From outside the apartment he could hear it ringing, but again no one answered. Eventually the apartment manager opened the door using the master key and the detectives made entry.

"Phoenix Police," Barnes shouted, one hand on his gun holster, as they slowly entered the apartment. Suddenly, Oscar and Todd emerged from their bedroom. Neither seemed surprised, but they both appeared nervous. Barnes explained why they were there and showed them a copy of the search warrant.

"I don't want any trouble," Todd said timidly.

"Okay, we can search your place but it would make it easier if you would just hand over the property," Barnes said.

Todd told Barnes he would cooperate. From the bedroom he collected a black backpack, a brown Louis Vuitton handbag, and a Ziploc bag full of miscellaneous jewelry. He also produced $1,600 in cash. Todd admitted to originally withdrawing $6,300 but said that was all that was left.

"Is there anything else?" Barnes asked.

"No," Todd said. "That's it."

"What about the laptop?"

"I never got the laptop," Todd said.

At about six p.m., Barnes went back to Jay Orbin's house with another search warrant. They searched the home for three hours but could not find a laptop.

On February 4, Noel Levy announced the state's intent to seek the death penalty due to the heinous nature of the crime and other aggravating factors in the case. Over his career, Levy had prosecuted many types of dangerous criminals. He had come to believe that Marjorie was one of the most conniving, manipulative sociopaths he had encountered.

To Levy, Marjorie's motives were clear: She was driven by greed and lust. Levy believed that when Jay penned his "in case of" plan, he was signing his own death certificate. Jay had essentially outlined for Marjorie how to acquire all of his money and property. The first step—Jay had to die. "Jay wrote out everything she needed to do to collect about a million dollars worth of assets," Levy said years later. "For a woman like that it's like an invitation. It was like a treasure map."

In 2005, there were just two other women on death row—one of whom Levy put there for the murder of her son. It would likely be difficult to convince a jury to sentence a mother to death, essentially making a young boy an orphan. But considering the vast amount of evidence and the viciousness of the dismemberment, Levy felt the punishment was warranted.

A potential death sentence upped the ante for Marjorie's defense. Arizona law required that on capital cases, a team of death penalty–certified attorneys represent the defendant. Because Tom Connelly wasn't qualified, the court appointed John Canby, a Maricopa County public defender who had been practicing in the state for two decades. Because Connelly had already been retained by Michael J. Peter on Marjorie's behalf, he stayed on as part of the defense team.

The trial was originally slated for April 2005, but over the next four years the trial date would be delayed nearly a dozen times.

When Marjorie learned the death penalty was being sought, she was incredulous. She told Todd Christy that she couldn't believe that this was a capital case when there was no evidence that there had even been a murder.

By February, Jay and Marjorie's house had been sold. When Marjorie found out, she was furious. She expressed her outrage in a subsequent conversation with Noah.

"They sold my house!" she told her son. "I have no place to live."

Noah didn't seem to understand.

"Uncle Jake came to court to make sure Mommy stays in jail," she said.

Noah didn't reply. Marjorie asked Noah if he had been in any trouble and when Noah said no, she seemed surprised. "How can that be?" Marjorie asked.

Toward the end of the conversation Marjorie repeated, "I can't believe they sold *our* house."

In a later conversation, Marjorie told Todd she wanted him to go the house, enter through the back gate, and see who was living there.

From her jail cell, Marjorie studied the thousands of pages of police reports, which by law had to be provided to her through her attorney. Despite the vast amount of evidence against her, Marjorie truly believed the prosecution had no case and that she would be vindicated. Over the course of their many conversations, Marjorie told Todd that there was no evidence against her and that she would soon be free. In one conversation, she mentioned that one of Larry Weisberg's hairs was found on Jay's body.

"I don't know how Larry could be involved," she said.

CHAPTER 25

From behind bars at the Estrella Jail, Marjorie had become something of a jailhouse celebrity. She told her cellmates about her glamorous life as a dancer, her millionaire ex-boyfriends, and her brushes with fame. The majority of these inmates were being held on drug, theft, and prostitution charges; others were there for petty crimes but couldn't afford to pay their bail. Marjorie's extraordinary life and whispers about her crime attracted much attention.

Even in jail, Marjorie was something of a mother hen. She befriended many of the other inmates and took several of the younger women under her wing, sharing her toiletries and commissary food. She gave them advice about men and told everyone about Todd Christy and Oscar Moreno and how they were helping her from the outside. Marjorie even promised several inmates that she would arrange to pay for their bail through Todd.

As she had a tendency to do, Marjorie made up fantastical stories about her past. She told several women that she had a pilot's license. At one point, Marjorie even claimed that she was a journalist who was only in jail for a writing assignment.

The other inmates were bewitched by Marjorie's charms. She made a lot of friends, although her focus was mainly on one person at a time. And because Marjorie could no longer have a man in her life, she satisfied her sexual cravings with women.

A month after she first arrived, Marjorie met a pretty blond inmate in her mid-thirties named Kate McDonald. They began a lesbian relationship and soon Marjorie was referring to Kate as her girlfriend. Each day they would have sex in Marjorie's bottom bunk. Marjorie became very fond of Kate. At one point, she told Kate she was rewriting her will to include her in it.

Soon after, Marjorie received a new bunk mate. Sophia Johnson was a twenty-four-year-old former amateur model. With golden blond hair, deep blue eyes, and full lips, Sophia was a stunning beauty with a troubled past. Since she was a teenager, Sophia had had problems with the law ranging from minor theft to assault charges. According to Sophia, she had been involved in an abusive relationship with her ex, with whom she had two sons. Frightened, Sophia took her children and fled. Sophia's ex claimed she had kidnapped the children and she was arrested on charges of custodial interference. Sophia was booked into jail on December 2, four days before Marjorie.

Housed in the same tiny jail cell as Marjorie, Sophia opened up emotionally about her abusive relationship. Something about Sophia's plight must have touched Marjorie. They became close friends. At first, Marjorie told Sophia few things about her case. She spoke only of her career as a stripper and choreographer and about Noah's karate classes. They bonded over stories about raising sons.

As usual, Marjorie's truths came with a healthy dose of lies. She told Sophia about her seven ex-husbands but claimed one of them had died in a car accident in Florida. Marjorie also told her that she had a pilot's license. "When everything happened," Marjorie said, "I should have just taken my son, got on a plane, and left the country."

Marjorie and Sophia sat and ate meals together, exercised together, and talked about their sons. Marjorie lent

Sophia her shampoo and gave her some of her commissary food. She even offered to bail her out with an $8,000 diamond ring she had stashed for safekeeping. Sophia was shrewd and street smart but lacked a formal education. Marjorie began helping her by teaching her grammar and vocabulary. Each day they would go through the dictionary and make lists of new words for Sophia to learn. Marjorie taught Sophia proper silverware placement, using the cheap plastic utensils in the mess halls.

Marjorie said she would inherit Jay's estate and be able to collect from his insurance policies when she was found not guilty at trial. After her release, Marjorie planned to go back to running Jay's business and offered Sophia a job.

"You and your boys could live with me and Noah. We could raise our children together," Marjorie said. "We'll have a great life with a lot of money. And we won't have any men in the picture."

Marjorie grew to trust Sophia and began to open up to her about her husband and his death. Then one day Marjorie slyly pulled Sophia aside. Her voice lowered, Marjorie leaned close to Sophia and whispered a shocking secret.

Throughout February, Detective Barnes continued to investigate the Jay Orbin murder. Most investigations come to a halt once the suspect is behind bars. But as news spread of Marjorie's arrest, Barnes began receiving calls from across the country providing fresh leads.

One call of interest was from Marjorie's fifth husband, Ronald McMann, who contacted police with an alarming story. Toward the end of their two-year marriage, they argued constantly. During one particularly nasty fight, Ronald had threatened to kick Marjorie out of the house. The next day, Ronald heard Marjorie on the phone with a friend, talking about how she planned to get rid of him by luring him into the bathtub and throwing a television set into the water. A few days later, in the kitchen of the couple's home,

Marjorie came up behind Ronald and hit him in the head with a frying pan. Ronald was dazed, but remained conscious enough to defend himself. They divorced soon after. Ronald never reported the incident to the police.

Barnes took down Ronald's statement. It was unrelated to Jay Orbin's murder, but it certainly spoke to Marjorie's violent temper.

On February 7, Barnes was contacted by a defense attorney named Michael Urbano. His client, Lissa Sherman, had been housed in the same cell with Marjorie during her first thirty days in jail. Urbano said Lissa had information that could be relevant to his investigation.

That afternoon, Barnes met with her. Lissa informed Barnes about Marjorie's lesbian relationship with Kate McDonald and her friendship with Sophia Johnson. Both women, she said, would know more than she did.

"The only thing I know firsthand," Lissa said, "was one day Marjorie said something about the kitchen island."

Marjorie had spoken at length about moving the kitchen island from one spot to another. Lissa thought she had heard Marjorie say, "It is under the kitchen island."

"What do you think she was referring to?" Barnes asked.

"Her husband's head," Lissa said. "Or other missing body parts."

For a moment, Barnes was struck with the possibilities. *Was it possible that Jay's body had been in the house the entire time? Could Marjorie have buried his head in concrete underneath the kitchen island?* Barnes had been through the house several times, and he and dozens of other detectives had traipsed through the kitchen. They may unknowingly have been walking on Jay's grave.

Barnes got ahold of Jake Jr. to discuss the possibility that something was buried under the house. Jake Jr. recalled that when he had last visited in the summer of 2004, the kitchen island was in two pieces. When Jay went missing, he returned to the house and noticed the two small cabinet islands had been fused together to create one large six-by-eight-foot center island. "It looked like just one of her home improvement projects," he said.

Barnes needed to search the house one more time. This time, however, he wouldn't be looking for what was in the house; he'd be looking for what was underneath it.

Barnes spent the next few days assembling a team and securing a new search warrant to excavate the kitchen floor. The house had been sold and the new homeowners were planning to move in the following weekend. Barnes explained to them the situation and they agreed to put off the move until the police were finished. Barnes also located a company in Colorado called Necrosearch, which specialized in ground penetration radar. The company flew in two geologists to assist with the search.

Days later, the Necrosearch team arrived from Denver and Barnes briefed them about what they were looking for and where. They would need to search the kitchen floor under the island, the dirt area in the backyard, and the entire garage. The team would use radar to determine if anything had been buried under the house.

At eight a.m. on February 12, detectives arrived at the former residence of Jay and Marjorie Orbin. Detective Barnes, Noel Levy, Sergeant Karen Vance, and four other detectives were on the scene, along with the geologists from Necrosearch.

They started their search by examining the kitchen. Barnes crouched down to inspect the island. It was obvious that at some point it had been moved. The tile and grout around the island were different than the rest of the floor and several tiles had been replaced. The crew pulled up the island, revealing a slab of concrete. Using the radar device, the geologists hovered over the spot where the island had been. "We've got an anomaly."

Barnes's eyes went wide; his heart started pounding. The geologist showed Barnes that there was something buried about two feet under the concrete. The area of the anomaly was about two by three feet. *We found Jay*, Barnes thought.

The team next searched the entire garage and outside the house but nothing was found. The only anomaly was right where Lissa Sherman said it would be—under the kitchen island. Barnes called the station.

"We found something," he said breathlessly. "We're going to need cadaver dogs down here."

An hour later, two detectives and their K-9 partners arrived to search the entire property. The dogs sniffed through the front yard, the back yard, the kitchen, and every other square inch of the property. Neither dog indicated any scent of a body. Regardless, Barnes gave the order: "Let's dig!"

A Phoenix concrete cutting crew was called in to dig up a section of the floor. In addition, a forensic anthropologist arrived to assist with the recovery. More than a dozen people crowded Jay and Marjorie's former kitchen. The concrete crew worked for hours into the night digging up the floor. At about eight p.m., twelve hours after beginning their search, the crew raised last chunk of concrete. They had reached the spot of the anomaly. Everyone anxiously gathered around the hole in the foundation, not knowing what gruesome sight to expect.

The anticipation was palpable. All eyes were focused on the hole. Everyone seemed to be holding their breath. In a moment, the dust cleared. But there were no body parts. There was no grisly, dismembered head. There was nothing.

The anomaly, as it turned out, was simply a leak. The PVC plumbing attached to the pool, which ran under the corner of the house, had cracked. The two-by-three-foot anomaly was water. The following day, the crew dug up a spot in the front yard entryway where the front water fountain had been placed. Nothing was found. No anomalies were detected in the garage.

The whereabouts of Jay's body would remain a mystery.

CHAPTER 26

"She told me that she did it," Sophia Johnson said bluntly. "She murdered him."

It was February 19, and Sophia was at the Phoenix police station with her attorney Michael Urbano and Detective Barnes. After the interview with Lissa Sherman, Urbano learned that Sophia had been housed with Marjorie for more than a month; Sophia had since been relocated. Urbano spoke with Sophia and learned she knew quite a bit about her former cellmate. Sophia was scared of Marjorie but willing to talk. Urbano brought her to Barnes's attention and Sophia was escorted from the Estrella Jail for questioning.

Sophia's story was astonishing. In late January, after she and Sophia had been housed together for more than a month, Marjorie started to open up about her husband's murder. During one conversation, Sophia was discussing her abusive ex-husband when Marjorie pulled Sophia aside, away from the other inmates, and calmly whispered, "I did it."

"Do you know what she meant when she said she did it?" Barnes asked.

"That she murdered him," Sophia said. "She didn't say that, but that's what I'm assuming." Marjorie never said, "I shot him," saying only that "He was shot," Sophia explained.

"What did she say she did with the body?" Barnes asked.

"She said he was shot. Frozen. And his head was decapitated," Sophia said, her voice unwavering. "His arms were cut off. And his legs. And they found his torso in the desert. I think she said it was in the desert."

When Marjorie told her this, Sophia said she was shocked. She just stood there, unable to move, not knowing what to say.

"And she said she did this?" Barnes asked again.

"Yeah, she said 'I did it,'" Sophia said. "She didn't say 'I killed him,' she said 'I did it.'"

Barnes was taken aback. The details of the crime were rushing through his mind. He asked if Marjorie told her what she did with the rest of Jay's body, but Sophia said she did not know. Marjorie only said, "Not a single person knows where his body is."

"Did she ever say what her motive was for doing it?" Barnes asked.

"She was going on about how disgusting he was and overweight and just like she was just repulsed by him."

Marjorie felt trapped with Jay, Sophia explained. She was "dying inside" and needed a way out. She had a lot to gain financially if she got away with the murder, and she would live very comfortably. Marjorie wanted the money and the house, just not her husband, Sophia said. "She mentioned that she would want to have that money and live a lifestyle and not be tied down and that sort of thing."

Marjorie believed police had no evidence against her, Sophia continued, and that she would regain custody of Noah. "She said the only thing that you guys had on her is the fact that the container found had the same UPC code."

"Does she ever mention Larry in this?" Barnes asked. "That Larry knows?"

"She didn't mention him." Sophia shook her head.

Marjorie never indicated that anyone helped her kill Jay, Sophia said, but she did brag that Michael J. Peter was paying for her defense.

"Did she say why Michael's now back in the picture?" Barnes asked.

"From what she's telling me, she plans on getting back with Michael into a relationship and she says that he wants to get married and he wants her to move down to Florida with him," Sophia said. "She talks about how Noah is just going to love Michael. How they're going to get along so well and that they're going to be able to start a new life."

Sophia also mentioned that Marjorie told her in the '90s Michael went to prison, but she didn't know what for. During Michael's trial, Marjorie claimed that she lied in her testimony on his behalf.

Barnes believed Sophia. She seemed honest and forthright and her statements corroborated many of the facts of the case. Jailhouse informants often come forward, usually looking for a deal in their own case. But to Barnes, Sophia seemed different. She wasn't looking for a plea agreement; Sophia believed she was innocent of the charges against her and wanted to go to trial.

Sophia said she was willing to help police by finding out more information about Marjorie. With any luck, she might find information about where the rest of Jay's body was. Barnes arranged for Sophia to be moved into the same cell as Marjorie. For the next month, he would meet with Sophia for weekly debriefings.

The next day, Sophia resumed bunking with Marjorie in the same eight-by-ten-foot cell. At times it was unnerving. At night, Sophia slept in the top bunk directly above the woman she believed to be a violent murderer. During the day, Marjorie would flip through the pages of her case files, at times becoming uncomfortably irate. Gingerly, Sophia would ask questions about her case. As she had before, Marjorie freely opened up to her.

A week later, Barnes discreetly brought Sophia back to

the police station, under the guise of a legal visit with her attorney. Sophia told Barnes that Marjorie didn't seem to suspect anything.

"I asked her if they'd found the body parts, the rest of the body parts, and she said, 'Let's just say the dogs ate good that week,'" Sophia told Barnes. Marjorie had owned a twelve-pound Maltese named Sasha. The dogs that Marjorie claimed ate Jay, however, were four Doberman Pinschers. Marjorie said that once the dogs get a taste of human flesh, they will always want it. When Marjorie made this statement, Sophia was lying in her bunk, holding her breath. She had no reply. The statement brought their conversation to a halt.

In early March, during a subsequent interview with Sophia, she mentioned a fight between Marjorie and another inmate. In the jail's dining hall the inmate yelled at Marjorie, "You cut your husband's head off." Marjorie snapped back, "Yeah, bitch! You're next!" A fight ensued, which was quickly broken up by corrections officers.

Sophia also informed Barnes about the latest developments in Marjorie's lesbian trysts. Her relationship with Kate McDonald had ended and Marjorie had a new girlfriend. Lately, Sophia said, Marjorie had been preoccupied with her new lover. She was considering ways to help her get her child back and had offered to pay for her attorney.

"What is Marjorie's and Kate's relationship right now?" Barnes asked.

"It's not too good," Sophia said. "Not good at all right now."

Marjorie's new girlfriend was in the cell right across from them. Marjorie was "throwing her new relationship in Kate's face, every chance she gets," Sophia said. Marjorie said she no longer trusted Kate and was afraid she would turn against her and testify at trial. She said that she would "slaughter" her if she testified.

The following week, Sophia told Barnes that Marjorie's

story was starting to change. Marjorie had heard through her attorneys that Larry had been given some sort of an immunity deal and she seemed very concerned. Marjorie told her, "Larry has something to hide." Marjorie was now suggesting that Larry killed Jay during a fight but would not go into detail. She claimed Jay had learned of her affair and had been following her for weeks prior to his death. There was some sort of violent confrontation in which Jay was accidentally shot and killed.

"She ever mention anything about a hair that was found?" Barnes asked.

"She mentioned that they found a hair on his body that was hers," Sophia said. "She also told me that she took her extensions and flushed them down the toilet."

By mid-March, Sophia said Marjorie's story was become increasingly bizarre. She was now claiming that she had proof that Jay was not dead.

"She was saying that Jay was actually alive two weeks after the police pronounced him to be dead." Sophia snickered. "It doesn't really make a lot of sense to me, but that's what she said."

"Those were her words?" Barnes asked. "He was still alive?"

"Right," she said.

Lately, Marjorie had become very paranoid, Sophia said. She now believed her jail cell was bugged and seemed leery about discussing her case. Marjorie also mentioned her attorney told her to fabricate things to help build a defense.

Detective Barnes had been keeping prosecutor Noel Levy apprised about the Sophia Johnson interviews. Barnes contacted Levy and told him that Marjorie was becoming wary about discussing her case. They decided it was time to move Sophia away from Marjorie and into protective custody.

On March 16, Sophia, Barnes, and Levy met at the police station for another interview. Sophia reiterated to Levy what Marjorie had told her about shooting her husband, freezing his corpse, and dismembering his body.

"Have you read the police reports?" Levy asked.

"No," Sophia said.

"Have you ever been told what's in them by any source?"

"No," she repeated.

"Do you think she's fabricated anything to you?" Levy asked.

"She does fabricate things," Sophia said frankly.

Sophia told Levy about Marjorie's bizarre stories, including her claims of having a pilot's license. Recently, Marjorie had mentioned that during the investigation she was escorted to Jay's warehouse by police on motorcycles. The things she lied about, Sophia said, were basically to "make her look high class, like she's important." "But as far as things that she's told me about her case, in the murder, I believe her one hundred percent on what she was saying," Sophia said.

"Why do you think she's telling you these things?" Levy asked.

"I think that deep down inside she's scared," Sophia said. "And I think that she needs to get some things off of her chest and she needs to talk to somebody."

Marjorie could be vulnerable, Sophia said, but she also had a very cold, callous side. She said that when she was first housed with Marjorie, they also had a roommate named Jan Marty. One day Marjorie was cleaning the cell, bragging about how she was so neat and organized. Jan made a joke about how Marjorie was so organized that she even dismembered her husband's body in "alphabetical order," meaning A for arms, H for head, and L for legs.

Jan and Marjorie both broke out in laughter. A chill ran down Sophia's spine as she stood a few feet away. Marjorie looked at Sophia and tried to force a smile so as not to seem suspicious.

"They were laughing about this," Sophia told Levy. "And I was pretty shocked."

"Why cut him in parts?" Levy asked. "Did she explain that?"

"She mentioned that he was very heavy. That he was a very big guy." Sophia told Levy that Marjorie had used a jigsaw and that his blood was drained out of his body. "She said, this is disgusting, but she said his guts were hanging out."

"Has she ever talked about the death penalty?" Barnes asked.

"Yeah. She says that you guys are seeking the death penalty if she's charged guilty with this," Sophia said. "She mentioned to me that she's not scared of death."

Sophia told Levy about how Marjorie began to change her story in March, claiming that "Larry did it." "She mentioned that he gave a 'free talk' because he's guilty and he wants to get off of this," Sophia said.

"Those were her exact words," Barnes asked, "because he's guilty?"

"Yeah, because he's guilty," Sophia paused, "of Jay's murder."

CHAPTER 27

On March 17, a deflated Larry Weisberg skulked into the Phoenix police station, his attorney at his side. Larry was haggard. His skin was sickly pale; his eyes looked dull and lifeless. He was trembling and muttering under his breath.

Despite his apprehensive appearance, Larry was not in handcuffs. He was not about to be interrogated as a murder suspect and he was not under arrest for any crime. He had been called back to the police station simply to obtain a new set of fingerprints. When he was first brought down to the police station in October his prints were taken, but were later determined not to be suitable for comparison purposes. The forensics lab needed another set.

At about 12:30 p.m., Detective Mike Meislish met Larry and his attorney at the station. When Meislish first saw Larry, he was astonished. Larry was unrecognizable. He appeared to have aged ten years in just a few months.

"Are you okay?" Meislish asked. "Are you sick?"

"I'm, I'm just nervous," Larry stammered. "I, I haven't eaten anything."

Meislish escorted Larry down to the records and identification bureau. As he waited, Larry swayed back and forth, his eyes rolling back in his skull. To Meislish it looked like he might faint in the middle of the police station. Concerned, Meislish asked, "Do you want something to eat?"

Larry just shook his head. "I can't eat. I don't think I'd be able to keep anything down."

The latent print examiner gently grasped Larry's shaking palm, dabbed each finger in ink, and pressed it against a card.

Suddenly, Larry stumbled, grabbing onto the wall to brace himself.

"I need to sit down," he muttered.

Larry slumped into a chair and dropped his head.

"Are you sure I can't get you anything to eat?" Meislish asked.

"Maybe some water," Larry said.

Meislish left and returned a few minutes later with a bottle of water. Larry took a few small sips and stood back up, and they finished taking his prints.

That same week, Detective Barnes heard from the FBI concerning the hairs he had sent for DNA testing months prior. Bureau crime lab analyst Joseph Nunez had some surprising results.

"We're not going to proceed with DNA testing," Nunez told Barnes.

"What? Why?" Barnes asked perplexed.

"Because neither of those two hairs are anywhere close to matching your two suspects."

"You've got to be kidding me!" Barnes exclaimed.

Nunez told him that the FBI lab did their own hair comparison tests on the evidence, and that their findings contradicted that of the Phoenix lab. There was no possible way those hairs were a match to either Marjorie Orbin or Larry Weisberg.

"We're not even going to waste the time testing," Nunez said. "We're that positive."

Barnes was outraged. This was just the latest in a series

of screw-ups by the Phoenix crime lab. Phoenix had the fifth-largest police department in the country and the city's crime lab handled evidence for hundreds of investigations. The lab should have been one of the most efficient and technologically advanced in the country. The reality was quite the opposite. Disconcertingly, botched testing, lost evidence, untrained technicians, and a massive evidence backlog were common at the lab.

According to the lab's own audit report, the Phoenix crime lab was typically unable to meet the legal requirements to complete forensic analysis within forty-five days on certain cases and routinely sent out letters requesting six-month extensions, which had resulted in a contentious relationship between police investigators and the lab.

In 2003, it was discovered that Phoenix crime-lab technicians blundered the analysis of DNA that linked suspects to crimes in nine criminal cases, including a homicide case that brought a conviction and two other investigations in which suspects pleaded guilty.

At this point in his career, Barnes had been with homicide less than a year but was already well familiar with the problems at the lab. Barnes was outspoken about the problems and how they were jeopardizing his investigations. Often Barnes complained to his supervisors in person and in e-mail. Those complaints would eventually create problems for Barnes and lead to serious complications at trial.

For Barnes, the most recent incident was particularly bothersome. It seemed unfathomable that the Phoenix lab could get the evidence so wrong. If the hairs didn't belong to either Marjorie or Larry, was it possible that they came from her hair extensions? Marjorie's hair pieces were made of real human hair. It seemed plausible that this hair had wound up on the body. Barnes called Levy to tell him of the development.

"This is a mess!" Levy said. "Who are we supposed to believe?"

Levy decided that the hairs needed to be sent to a private

lab for DNA analysis, at the cost of more than $8,000. Weeks later the results came back, confirming the FBI findings. The hairs were not a match to either Larry Weisberg or Marjorie Orbin. It was a devastating blow to the case against Larry. "That was our last hope to get Larry," Barnes recalled.

After several months behind bars, Marjorie's court-appointed defender, John Canby, contacted Barnes. Marjorie was now willing to reveal "the truth," Canby said. According to Marjorie, Larry had murdered Jay. She claimed that when Jay came home unexpectedly on his birthday, Larry confronted him in the garage and accidentally shot him. Larry then threatened Marjorie's life if she revealed the truth.

This was similar to a scenario Barnes had once envisioned. Except, according to Canby, Marjorie was not involved in the murder or the dismemberment. She was placing the blame entirely on Larry. That didn't match up with the facts. Marjorie had bought the tub and used Jay's cell phone and credit card.

Barnes suspected that Larry was involved in some way and might have actually pulled the trigger, but that didn't mean Marjorie was innocent. If Larry killed Jay, Barnes believed he did so at her urging.

Still, if Marjorie was now flipping on Larry, Barnes wanted to talk to her. Through Marjorie's statements, Barnes could possibly build a case against Larry as well. But there would be no interview. Marjorie would not speak to police without some sort of immunity deal.

"That is not going to happen," Barnes told Canby.

No charges would ever be brought against Larry Weisberg. With no evidence against Larry, the case shifted completely toward Marjorie. As the trial approached, Levy instructed Barnes to refer to Larry only as a witness, not as a suspect or an investigative lead. Levy knew the defense would try to pin the murder on Larry to deflect guilt from their client. After all, they had created Marjorie's defense with the investigation of Larry.

Later, Noel Levy made the controversial decision to offer Larry Weisberg full immunity from prosecution in exchange for his testimony against Marjorie at trial. "I made the decision because we could find nothing to implicate him," Levy recalled. "We had no forensic evidence on him, no eyewitnesses. Nothing."

Through Larry's statements, Levy knew he would not provide any information at the trial that would help to incriminate Marjorie. The decision to offer immunity was strategic. Instead of having this mysterious, faceless figure at the trial, Levy was going to parade Larry out in front of the jury to explain firsthand that he didn't kill Jay.

"I wanted to present him to the jury, 'Here he is, folks. Let's not have any mystery hour here,'" Levy explained years later. "That could be a risk. That could be interpreted that the prosecutor was so intent on getting Marjorie convicted, he's willing to give up an accomplice to a murder. It was actually quite the opposite. I'd rather keep working to nail Weisberg and have her as the accomplice, it just wasn't there. There was no evidence on him, whereas there was plenty of evidence on her."

Still, years later, Detective Barnes had doubts. He continued to believe it was not only possible, but quite plausible that Larry got away with murder. There were four hairs found with the body. The Phoenix crime lab only tested two. Because of those two mysterious, untested hairs, it remained unclear if there was any evidence that could link Larry to the crime.

"I still believe Larry was involved," Barnes said years later. "Here we still have these unknown hairs—who do they belong to? What if they are Larry's hairs? The crime lab refused to test them. Today, I don't think we'll never know the truth."

CHAPTER 28

In the spring of 2005, Detective Barnes received more recordings of Marjorie's jailhouse phone calls from the past few months. Not surprisingly, Marjorie continued to instruct Todd Christy to "hide the jewelry" even after his apartment was searched. Despite direct orders from police and Marjorie's attorney to return all of the property, Todd was cooperating in the scheme.

In one conversation, Todd indicated that he had found the laptop. Marjorie told him to tell Jake Jr. and anyone else who asked that the laptop was actually his and that he had left it in the house. In another conversation, Todd told Marjorie that detectives had been to his place but he had only given Barnes "some" of the money and that he still had $2,200 hidden. Marjorie told Todd not to give the money to police and that she would find someone to collect it. Todd said he was worried about a theft charge, but he would do what she wanted him to do. Todd also said he had stashed the jewelry.

"I only gave them the cheap costume stuff," Todd said. "The other items are on their way to 'MJP.' And they are insured."

It didn't take much detective work for Barnes to figure out that 'MJP' was Michael J. Peter. Barnes had first heard of him through Sharon Franco and later saw his name on one of the power of attorney forms Marjorie had drawn up prior to her arrest.

In April, Barnes contacted the United Parcel Service and learned a package had been sent from Phoenix to Michael J. Peter's Fort Lauderdale business address. It had been delivered on January 19, just a week after Todd Christy's apartment had been searched. Based on Marjorie's phone calls, Barnes determined that the package likely contained jewelry from Jay's estate. Suddenly the name Michael J. Peter was all over this investigation. Barnes needed to find out what connection he had to the case.

On May 9, Detective Barnes, Sergeant Karen Vance, and Detective Mike Meislish flew to Fort Lauderdale to track down Michael J. Peter. That night they checked into their suites at the Seminole Hard Rock Hotel & Casino. The following morning they met with Detective Tom Anderson, a tenacious, gray-haired veteran investigator in his late fifties with the Broward County Sheriff's Department. As Barnes explained the reason for their visit, Anderson's ears perked up.

"Michael J. Peter?" Anderson said. "I know Michael J. Peter and I know Marjorie—she's nothing but a pole bitch. She's just a stripper."

The Sheriff's Department had been investigating Michael J. Peter for years. In the early '90s, Anderson said, both Michael and Marjorie were infamous among Florida authorities.

The Sheriff's department explained that in 1991, Michael and Marjorie were engaged to be married and living together in his Fort Lauderdale mansion. At the time, Michael's business was at the height of its success. He had built, opened, and operated 106 nightclubs, restaurants, and country clubs, as well as various nationally and internationally renowned companies.

In his business dealings, Michael was known to be ruthless. He had been accused of strong-arm tactics, and investors in several cities claimed he didn't repay thousands of dollars in loans. While there were allegations, however, there was no evidence and Michael's team of high-priced attorneys was able to squash each and every charge.

Then in 1991, Michael J. Peter was arrested on charges of kidnapping and extortion. A business rival claimed that Michael had forced him into his white Rolls-Royce and threatened him for attempting to recruit his most beautiful dancers. Michael, however, said he was set up by Fort Lauderdale police who were bent on running him out of town. "There are good cops and bad cops, good strip joint operators and bad strip joint operators," Michael told a Florida newspaper. "This time, the bad cops went after the good strip joint operator."

Because of Marjorie's connections to Michael, authorities questioned her concerning the investigation. In an attempt to pressure Marjorie to testify against her boyfriend, she was even arrested on trumped-up indecent exposure charges while dancing one night at Thee DollHouse.

But once again, Michel would slip through the legal system unscathed. In the trial, the business rival refused to testify against him. It took a jury only an hour to find him not guilty of the charges. Months after his arrest, Michael and Marjorie's relationship ended. Marjorie moved out of his mansion, although they continued to be involved in each other's lives.

Even after the not guilty verdict, rumors about Michael J. Peter's connections to the Mafia continued to swirl. In 1993, a federal report was released concerning Michael's businesses. In the report, a confidential informant claimed that the mob had a stake in his clubs. According to the informant, a reputed leader of the Gambino family was a secret part-owner of Thee DollHouse III. Michael also reportedly employed the wife and sons of a reputed mobster.

The informant's claims were never verified, but the report brought about an investigation by the county's Organized Crime Intelligence Unit, which led to a ten-count racketeering indictment against Michael. He was formally charged with allowing members of the Gambino family to keep a hidden interest in his three South Florida clubs and accused of making routine $500 payments to a high-ranking captain in the crime family.

If Michael had been convicted on all counts, he would have faced forty years in prison and the forfeiture of $17 million in assets. But the government's case was weak. Eventually, both sides compromised and Michael pled guilty to one count of mail fraud for failing to list a connected mobster on his liquor license. Michael, who was in his fifties at the time, was sentenced to two years in prison and forced to sell several of his gentlemen's clubs. He was released from prison in May 1998.

By this time, Marjorie had already moved to Phoenix and was married to Jay. She was not with Michael during the bulk of his troubles with federal investigators. It remained unknown if she knew anything pertinent about his business dealings or connections to the Mafia.

Years after Michael's release from prison, Detective Tom Anderson explained, authorities continued to investigate his business dealings. There were more allegations of money laundering and mafia ties, but authorities could never find any solid evidence and no new charges were ever brought. Suddenly, Barnes thought back to something Sophia Johnson had told him. During one interview she had mentioned something about Marjorie lying under oath during a criminal trial. *Was Michael J. Peter paying for Marjorie's silence in his own criminal investigation?* Barnes wondered.

When Barnes explained that they built a solid case against Marjorie for murder, Anderson was thrilled.

"She killed someone and you got her? Good!" Anderson exclaimed. "Too bad for the vic but she's getting exactly what she deserves."

Barnes explained about the package sent to Michael and his connections to the case.

"Could you tie Michael Peter into all this?" Anderson asked. "He's a piece of work."

Michael J. Peter had become something of a nemesis to Florida detectives. Anderson knew all of the players involved in Michael's business and was eager to assist in the investigation. The next day the Phoenix detectives met with Anderson in order to obtain a warrant to search Michael J. Peter's place of business. It would not be easy to get a judge to sign off on a warrant. The jailhouse phones calls had been made months prior, meaning the information was stale.

While their search was delayed, Barnes, Vance, and Meislish enjoyed their stay in Fort Lauderdale. On May 11, two days after their arrival, the detectives located a judge to authorize the search. The following morning the detectives met Anderson at Michael's business, but he was not there. His business manager, Deenie Hale, told the detectives that Michael's mother was ill and he had been in New York for the past month caring for her.

Situated inside the office were an elaborate dark wood desk and several leather couches. On the walls were photos of Michael shaking hands with any celebrity he had ever come in contact with—from Mötley Crüe to Sylvester Stallone. The detectives rummaged through Michael's file cabinets. They could not locate any package of jewelry. The only items of relevance were a few letters from Marjorie to Michael.

Barnes plopped down at Michael's desk and called him on his cell phone. Barnes explained that they were in his office and told him what they were searching for. Michael confirmed that he had received a package of jewelry from Todd Christy, but he wasn't sure what he did with it. He estimated the value of the jewelry at about $20,000 to $30,000.

"I'm not sure where it is," Michael said. "I think it may be in a safety deposit box in Orlando."

Barnes asked about Todd Christy, but Michael said he was just a liaison between him and Marjorie and that they had never actually met. He confirmed he was paying for her defense because he believed she was "one hundred percent innocent."

"Okay, the jewelry—where is it?" Barnes asked.

"I know it's not at my business," Michael said. "I would need to make some phone calls."

They hung up. About fifteen minutes later, Michael called back. He thought the jewelry was in Orlando and he said he would fly there and return it in about a week. Barnes relayed that information to Anderson, who took the phone.

"Michael," he said. "It's Detective Tom Anderson. Remember me?" Michael said he did remember him and sounded irritated that he was meddling in his business.

One week wasn't good enough, Anderson said. "If the jewelry is not in your business, then it's in your house. We're going to get a warrant and search your house next."

Anderson slammed down the phone.

It was a bluff. Detectives were barely able to obtain a warrant for Michael's business and it would be unlikely that they would find a judge to authorize a search of his house. But Anderson knew Michael wouldn't want detectives rummaging through his house. Michael took the bait. A few moments later he called Anderson and said he would find a way to return the jewelry within hours. At around eleven a.m., they left Michael's business.

That evening, Barnes invited Anderson to dinner to thank him for his help. Hours later, Anderson showed up at the Seminole Hard Rock Hotel & Casino with a wide grin plastered across his face. He walked up to Barnes and tossed him a box.

"I got the goods," Anderson said proudly.

Michael told Anderson that he had one of his employees fly a private jet into Miami and retrieve the jewelry. That afternoon, Michael's business manager personally delivered it to the sheriff's office. Barnes sorted through the jewelry. It was all personal items—earrings, two rings, and a wedding set. None of it was Southwestern Native American jewelry.

The following morning, the detectives returned to Phoenix. Michael J. Peter was never charged with any crime related to the Orbin Case.

Numerous times, Barnes gave Todd Christy the opportunity to return the stolen property. Instead, Todd lied to police and flaunted the fact that he was withholding evidence in a murder investigation. Perhaps, like Marjorie, Todd didn't fully comprehend the seriousness of the situation. Todd was willingly aiding a murder suspect in a complicated scheme to defraud a dead man's estate. It wasn't just appalling; it was criminal.

If Todd had turned over all of the property, criminal charges would have likely never been pursued. But Barnes had to chase Marjorie's watch and wedding ring across the country, all the way to Florida. Plus, Barnes suspected that Todd had more stashed.

After Todd had turned over several totes of jewelry to police, Barnes contacted Jake Jr. and two of Jay's business partners. Together they sorted through Jay's records and inventory. Based on Jay's past orders and what he had ordered prior to his disappearance, they were able to determine Jay should have had about fifty kilograms worth of jewelry on hand. Only about four kilograms had been recovered. The estimated retail value of the missing jewelry: $330,000.

None of that merchandise had been recovered through the Florida trip. That meant that Todd was likely hoarding hundreds of thousands of dollars worth of jewelry. On

Wednesday, May 18, Barnes obtained a warrant for Todd Christy's arrest. At about two p.m. Todd was at work stocking the shelves at Blockbuster when police barged into the store and told him he was under arrest. As Barnes read the charges, Todd looked dumbstruck. He was being arrested for burglary, theft, fraudulent schemes, and hindering prosecution. In front of his colleagues, Todd was handcuffed and placed into the back of a police cruiser.

Back at the police station, Barnes questioned Todd. Arrogantly, Todd swaggered into the interrogation room and lounged in the chair. Throughout the interview he cracked jokes and made flippant comments.

"I just want to talk to you about your relationship with Marjorie," Barnes began.

"Well, we've been lovers for years. No kids." Todd laughed. "Joking! . . . I don't think it's a secret that I'm gay."

Todd explained that he had met Marjorie through his friend Charity McLean. Throughout November, he said he had been staying with Marjorie because she didn't want to be alone.

"I truly believe Marjorie's innocent," Todd said. "I had a great deal of empathy, seriously. I cried with this woman. I felt terrible about her husband being gone. She would say what a wonderful father he was to her son."

"Do you think Marjorie killed Jay?" Barnes said.

"I honestly do not," Todd said.

Todd knew that Jay and Marjorie were divorced. He believed their relationship was an arrangement and that they hadn't had sex for about eight years. He wasn't aware that it was a secret. "It wasn't your typical husband and wife deal. That wasn't how it was," Todd said.

Barnes found this statement interesting. With Jay's family and friends, Marjorie had portrayed herself as a loving housewife. Barnes informed Todd that no one in Jay's life was aware of the divorce. "I mean they led on to most people that they were man and wife."

"No they didn't. Did they?" Todd asked. "I mean, Marjorie had men all the time. He had women all the time. He had a woman he was seeing frequently in Tucson."

While Jay did make several phone calls to an exotic dancer in Tucson, detectives had never been able to find any evidence of an affair on Jay's part. Barnes humored Todd.

"Do you think they knew about each other's affairs?" Barnes asked.

"Honestly, with his death, I wonder," Todd said. "I honestly wonder if something didn't go wrong from maybe Marjorie was seeing someone and someone got a little too jealous."

Barnes asked why Todd followed Marjorie's instructions from jail. Todd explained that he believed in Marjorie's innocence and thought he was helping out a friend. "I look at this on both sides of the coin. The child lost his father in what, you know, was an accident, murder, whatever, I don't know. And now possibly losing his mother to the prison system and growing up by himself. I have great empathy for that."

Freely, Todd admitted to breaking into Marjorie's house the night of her arrest and removing the jewelry and personal belongings, as per her instructions. Todd, however, contended that this was permitted because he was living in the house at the time. Todd also admitted to using Marjorie's ATM card to withdraw money from her personal account. "I don't feel I've done anything wrong. I have not stolen anything knowingly, willingly. I have not taken anything, so I truly don't feel I've done anything wrong. Nothing."

Barnes confronted Todd with the fact that he had not returned all the jewelry or cash and instead sent some of the property to Florida. Todd contended that he had returned everything that belonged to the estate of Jay Orbin and that the pieces of jewelry Todd sent to Florida were Marjorie's personal possessions.

"Is there any property that belongs to Marjorie or the estate of Jay Orbin that is anywhere in your possession?" Barnes asked. "In your house? Out of state? Anywhere?"

"The only thing I have that Marjorie gave me is the laptop," Todd said smugly.

Barnes asked where that was, but Todd just smirked. Cavalierly, he said the laptop belonged to him and he wasn't willing to tell Barnes were it was.

"You realize you're withholding evidence, though?" Barnes said.

"I do have a laptop that Marjorie *gave* me," Todd said.

"You could be digging yourself a deeper hole, Todd," Barnes said.

Over and over Todd maintained that the laptop was his and refused to tell Barnes where it was.

"What's the big deal about this laptop?" Barnes asked.

"'Cause I feel I deserve the laptop," Todd said. "Seriously! All the work, you don't understand what I did."

Barnes, however, told Todd that the laptop was stolen property because it had been purchased with the proceeds from Jay Orbin's estate.

"Okay, are you going to tell me where the laptop is?" Barnes asked.

"Ummm, no." Todd chuckled.

"Well that's fine," Barnes said. "So what's going to happen is you're going to jail tonight."

"Okay," Todd said, unfazed.

"You're looking at four charges," Barnes said. "They're all felonies. Burglary, theft, fraudulent schemes, and hindering prosecution."

"You're really grabbing at straws, aren't you?" Todd remarked.

"No, not really," Barnes said. "I mean, this is a big case."

"I understand," Todd said. "That's fine. You have to do what you have to do."

* * *

That afternoon, Todd Christy was booked in jail. Todd was facing serious criminal charges, which carried a maximum of twenty years in prison. From jail, however, Todd was still haughty and arrogant. In one call to his sister, Todd said that he had known he was going to be arrested and had a "back-up plan in place."

"There's nothing in the apartment except for receipts," Todd told his sister. "If they search my place, they won't find a thing."

Todd said that he knew the things Marjorie wanted him to do weren't lawful and admitted to deliberately lying to the police, stating, "I did the things they are accusing me of."

Two months passed, and Todd remained behind bars. During that time, Todd seemingly had a change of heart. His brother came down to the police station to speak with Barnes: Todd was now willing to cooperate completely with detectives.

On July 15, Todd was interviewed by Barnes and Levy one more time. This time, he was no longer arrogant and condescending. Jail had clearly had a humbling effect on him. Meekly, Todd lowered his head and admitted to stashing the laptop as well as another crate of jewelry that police were unaware of. Marjorie wanted those items hidden so she could purchase a car if she got out of jail, Todd said.

"Where is all that stuff?" Barnes asked.

"Umm. Well. I don't know the address," Todd stammered. "But I can tell you it's at Oscar's family's. Where Oscar's family lives in Tucson."

"Okay, so we're going to have to go on a trip?" Barnes asked.

On July 20, Detective Barnes drove up to Oscar Moreno's parents' house in Tucson. Parked in the driveway was a junked-out black Ford Escort covered with a dusty brown tarp. Barnes approached the vehicle and, using a key he obtained through Todd's brother, popped open the trunk. Inside was a large burgundy trunk locked with a padlock. Barnes cut off the padlock and pried open the lid. Inside, as Todd said he would, Barnes found a clear tote full of silver and turquoise Native American–style jewelry and a laptop computer.

Back at the police station, the jewelry was inventoried. It was not just a measly couple of rings. There were over fifty-five-kilograms of jewelry, all merchandise from Jayhawk International. The retail value: $374,220.

Forensic experts later examined the laptop but found nothing incriminating. Marjorie wasn't trying to hide evidence; she was too busy making plans for her future. She wasn't worried about the death penalty or spending the rest of her life in prison; she was more concerned with how she would run Jay's business upon her release. Unfortunately for Marjorie, it was looking increasingly like that would never, ever happen.

Later, Barnes interviewed Oscar Moreno. Begrudgingly, Oscar admitted to helping Todd take the jewelry and the laptop from the house.

"What was his reason for taking it to Tucson?" Barnes asked.

Oscar did not respond.

"Did he think the police were going to come back to the apartment and find it?" Barnes pressed.

"I think so." Oscar sulked. "He said he was holding it for Marjorie so in case she gets out, she'll have something to fall back on."

Oscar said that prior to November, he had never met Marjorie. He never wanted to participate in taking the jewelry, but he said Todd gave him a "guilt trip."

Detective Barnes still couldn't comprehend why anyone would go out of their way to help a murder suspect. "All this stuff he did for her was just out of the kindness of his heart?" Barnes questioned. "Why do you think he's helping her so much?"

" 'Cause he's an idiot!" Oscar said. "That's why!"

Todd Christy would spend a total of eleven months behind bars. In exchange for his testimony against Marjorie, he received a generous plea agreement. Three of the charges were dismissed and Todd received just one felony count of burglary on his record. Because Oscar was forthcoming, he was never charged with a crime.

With all of the additional information discovered, Marjorie's murder trial was postponed until October 2006.

In addition to first degree murder, Marjorie was charged with four additional felony charges for theft and fraudulent schemes against the estate of Jay Orbin. Each charge carried a maximum of five years in prison. At this point in the investigation, it was just icing on the case against Marjorie.

CHAPTER 29

By late 2005, the Jay Orbin murder had become a lesser priority than some of Detective Barnes's more recent, unsolved homicide investigations. At that time he had been investigating the murder of a seventeen-year-old methamphetamine dealer who had been strangled to death with a zip-tie in a flop house. Three people had been arrested for the murder including a troubled nineteen-year-old drug addict named Charity Marie Hill. Two witnesses had placed Charity at the flop house the night of the boy's murder and weeks later, she was arrested while trying to flee the state. During the interrogation, Charity gave a full confession.

In September 2005, Charity was booked into the Estrella Jail on first-degree murder charges. For Barnes, his investigations into Charity Hill and Marjorie Orbin were about to collide.

On December 1, Barnes was at his desk listening to recordings of Charity Hill's jailhouse phone calls. Toward the end of one twenty-minute phone call with her mother, Charity remarked, "This other lady is in here for chopping her husband into little pieces and they never found his head. She is real nice, too."

Suddenly, Barnes stopped the tape. *She's talking about Marjorie Orbin!* he thought. There are a lot of women in jail for murder, but the details of Marjorie's case were highly unusual. After all, not many women are charged with "chopping her husband into little pieces." Barnes checked jailhouse records and sure enough, Charity had been housed in the same pod as Marjorie during her first thirty days behind bars. Barnes contacted Charity's lawyer, and on December 9 they met at the police station for questioning.

"I want to talk to you about some information you might have that is unrelated to your case. I'm sure the attorney has explained everything to you on how this is going to work. Marjorie Orbin—do you know her?" Barnes said as he showed Charity a photograph of Marjorie.

"Oh, Marjorie." Charity nodded. "The lady who chopped her husband up in pieces and lived in that house."

"That's what I want to talk to you about—it's kind of that statement you just said to me how she chopped her husband up into pieces. How do you know that?"

"Because she told people that," she explained. Charity said she was sitting at a table in the mess hall with Marjorie, her current girlfriend, and a few other inmates when Marjorie casually made the confession. "She said that she couldn't stomach chopping him up basically, she couldn't handle it."

"Did she ever say *why* she chopped him up?" Barnes asked.

"She said, 'men are all dogs.'"

"Men—we are all dogs?" Barnes chuckled. "Did she mention what she did with the body?"

"She hid it," Charity said. "I know she hid it. I don't know where she hid it. She said she chopped him up in little pieces, she said she had to hide him, she hid him in different spots."

"How much contact did you have with Marjorie?" Charity's attorney asked.

"Not that much. I didn't really like her; I was kind of scared of her."

"Okay, are you still scared of her?" Barnes asked.

"Fuck yeah, she is creepy!" Charity exclaimed.

It was a short interview, but for Barnes it was another thrilling "got ya" moment in his investigation that could help convince a jury of Marjorie's guilt. Charity signed a plea agreement and agreed to testify in court about what she knew. Charity should have been a simple addition to a growing list of witnesses set to testify against Marjorie. Unfortunately, it would not turn out that way.

When word spread among the other inmates that she was a "snitch," Charity was assaulted in jail. She attempted to recant her testimony and withdraw her plea but a judge would eventually compel her to testify. Her testimony would end up becoming a complicated and confusing aspect of the trial.

There seemed to be a never-ending pool of jailhouse informants willing to come forward to testify against Marjorie. Each snitch told a different story. Some inmates, including Marjorie's former lover Kate McDonald, claimed Marjorie was innocent and her boyfriend had committed the murders. Others said Marjorie confessed to committing the crime alone.

The state's best witness was still Sophia Johnson. She had been in jail with Marjorie during the first few months and appeared to be the first person Marjorie opened up to. Barnes believed the initial story Marjorie told Sophia was the truth.

Sophia was placed in protective custody. In a later hearing, Barnes and Levy attended court on Sophia's behalf, arguing that she was a silent victim because of the abuse she had suffered at the hands of her ex-husband. Because of their support, Sophia was released on bond.

CHAPTER 30

By 2006 Marjorie Orbin had spent two years behind bars at the Estrella Jail. Aside from her attorneys, she no longer received many jailhouse visits from friends or family members. Marjorie had never had a close relationship with her parents—her stepfather had not been a part of her life for years and her mother was now suffering from Alzheimer's disease. From jail, Marjorie wrote her sister Colleen, and they occasionally spoke by phone, but that was the extent of their relationship.

As for Marjorie's friends, Todd Christy was an inmate himself and unable to do her bidding from the outside or stop by for weekly visits. Charity McLean wrote occasional letters but she had since moved on with her life. In fact, everyone had moved forward with their lives, aside from Marjorie. The day of her arrest, Marjorie's world essentially stopped. Stuck in 2004, Marjorie studied every police transcript and wrote exhaustive accounts of her version of events, disputing every witness statement. According to Marjorie, everyone who claimed that she hated Jay or wanted him dead was lying. She was now adamant that Larry Weisberg murdered her husband.

Marjorie's only active remaining supporter was Michael J. Peter. Not only was he paying for her defense, he also made regular deposits to Marjorie's jail commissary account. Because of his financial support, Marjorie was still able to partake in scant jailhouse luxuries—better food, cosmetics, and stamps to mail letters.

Every week Marjorie wrote to Noah, but each letter went unopened. Noah was now ten years old. His hair had grown back to its natural shade of brown, and he resembled his father more than ever. Considering the circumstances, Noah had adjusted well to life in the custody of the Orbins. Jake Jr. and his girlfriend Shelly had since married and she had become a nurturing and supportive stepmother. Both did their best to provide Noah with some sense of normalcy.

Each morning as Jake Jr. walked down the hallway to rouse Noah, he thought of his baby brother. He prepared Noah's breakfast, sent him off to school, and helped him with his homework and school projects. On Saturdays, he and Shelly took Noah to baseball practice and football games. For the past two years Jake Jr. had been doing everything Jay would have done for his son, if he were still alive.

For Detective Barnes, the initial thrill of the Jay Orbin murder investigation had faded. Occasional leads trickled in, but Barnes had since moved on to other cases. In 2007, he was investigating the death of a Phoenix man who was struck and killed by a truck his wife was driving. The wife claimed it was an accident, but the evidence pointed to murder. Blood smeared down the center of the windshield, the hood, and under the cab of the truck indicated that the man was hit intentionally head-on. At the crime scene, DNA swabs were taken and submitted to the lab for testing. During a meeting with crime lab technicians, Barnes argued that to prove his theory fourteen swabs needed to be processed; the lab wanted to test only three. When they couldn't agree, Barnes left the meeting and sent an e-mail to the county attorney assigned to the case, explaining the issue. His superiors claimed that by sending the e-mail Barnes had displayed "unprofessional conduct."

Unbeknownst to Barnes, there was a target on his back. For months, Phoenix police officials had been discussing ways to silence him about his criticism of the crime lab. In one e-mail the assistant police chief wrote: *Dave Barnes is a repeat offender and it is my hope that his specific conduct be addressed formally, rather than informally. Mark my words, if Dave is dealt with, others will think twice about lab bashing.*

Just months later, Barnes was demoted from the homicide squad to patrol. Instead of cleaning up the crime lab, Barnes believed he was made an example of. He decided to fight what he saw as unfair labor practices by filing grievances with the city. The Phoenix Police Union, on Barnes's behalf, went on the offensive with accusations that he was wrongly targeted because of his past reputation as a whistle-blower. A lengthy court battle would ensue. What happened next would threaten to derail the entire case against Marjorie Orbin.

For the Orbins, justice crept along at a snail's pace. Marjorie's attorney John Canby was forced to withdraw due to a conflict of interests. Another court-appointed public defender withdrew because he couldn't agree with Marjorie in forming her defense. The constant delays were frustrating for the Orbins. Each continuance delayed any sense of closure and prolonged the grieving process.

In January 2007, Jake Jr. took a leave from his job in San Diego and returned to Phoenix to inventory the Jayhawk International warehouse. For three years Jay's merchandise had sat on the shelves in his warehouse collecting dust. Until there was a conviction in the case, the Orbins would be unable to sell the warehouse or collect any assets on Noah's behalf.

Meanwhile, forensic testing was complete on the vehicles and they were released. In 2007, Jake Jr. picked up the white cargo truck and was headed back to the warehouse when the front tire of the truck began to squeal. He got out and examined the vehicle. The front wheel had turned into the truck and was facing sideways. It was undrivable. Jake Jr. called the Phoenix police.

Detectives later inspected the truck and determined that the tie-rod, a piston that controls the steering on the front tires, had been cut. They could not determine when or where, but sometime over the past few years it appeared to have rusted and broken loose. If sliced with better precision, the rod would have likely broken loose on the road and resulted in an awful crash.

Suddenly the witness statements concerning Marjorie's threats took on a new connotation. Repeatedly, to dozens of people, Marjorie had said she didn't know how Jay was still alive considering how often he was on the road. Now police suspected that she was not just referring to a statistical likelihood of him being involved in an accident. Marjorie had sabotaged the tie-rod, expecting it to fail on one of Jay's business trips. She didn't appear bothered that it could have resulted in a horrific crash where other innocent victims lost their lives. She just wanted Jay dead.

When her plan failed, Marjorie had found another way to get rid of Jay, detectives reasoned. This new evidence would come to play a pivotal role in the trial when trying to prove that the murder was premeditated.

Meanwhile, Prosecutor Noel Levy was working to build his case against Marjorie. Every piece of evidence and each new jailhouse witness added to the complexity of the case and changed the dynamics of his prosecution. Over his career, Levy had tried some of the most high-profile cases in the state of Arizona. Marjorie's case was becoming one of the most complicated of his career.

Just sorting through Marjorie's various stories was a heavy task. Marjorie was a skilled liar and was adept at mixing each one of her lies with enough sprinkling of the truth to seem believable. For instance, Marjorie had told nearly all of her friends that Noah was not Jay Orbin's biological child. She claimed that Jay was the reason they were forced to use in vitro fertilization and that his genes had to be somehow reduced to the point where he and Noah were no longer biologically linked.

The truth was that Jay and Marjorie did seek out fertility treatments, but not because of Jay. Levy had reviewed Jay's medical records and found no history of impotence or any other sexual deficiency. Marjorie, however, was diagnosed as infertile at an early age, long before she met Jay. Levy also requested paternity tests on Noah and it was determined that Jay was in fact Noah's biological father.

For Levy, this was a very stressful case. While the evidence was strong, it was still entirely circumstantial. There were no eyewitnesses or forensics that tied Marjorie to the crime. A murder weapon was never discovered, and they couldn't even determine the manner of death. Levy was building a first-degree murder case on cell phone records, financial documents, credit cards, the storage bin, and a jailhouse of snitches. It would be a lot of information to convey to a jury. "The case was no slam dunk," Levy said years later. "It weighed heavily on my shoulders. The evidence seemed so compelling. It would have been a travesty if my presentation of the evidence lost this case."

For Levy, this case had become personal. He had devoted years to the investigation and delayed retirement to see it through. Levy wanted to deliver justice for Jay. "His parents were good people. Jay was a good person," Levy said years later. "I am generally pretty cool and collected but I got pretty well into that case, emotionally."

* * *

In the fall of 2007, two new attorneys were appointed to Marjorie's defense team. Herman Alcantar, a seasoned criminal defense attorney who had worked in private practice in Arizona since 1981, became the lead defense counsel. In his late forties, Alcantar was stocky, with a plump face, distinguished salt-and-pepper hair, and a jovial disposition.

Throughout his career Alcantar handled private contract work for Maricopa County. Progressively, the complexity of his cases escalated, and soon he was handling death penalty cases. By 2007, capital cases had become his specialty. Capital cases can be consuming. A death sentence comes attached with mandatory appeals. Between mistrials and appeals, often the cases will stretch on for more than two decades. "A death penalty case is so much more different and complicated than a regular murder trial," Alcantar explained. "I don't think there is any real comparison because there are so many factors that you have to look at." With Alcantar appointed to represent Marjorie, the trial was postponed until May 2008.

Robyn Varcoe, a young Phoenix attorney with an independent practice focusing on criminal defense, was appointed second chair to the defense team. Varcoe was attractive and petite with a slender face, delicate features, dark shoulder-length hair, and a self-assured demeanor. In court she was considered a convincing and well-regarded counsellor. This would be the first capital case of her career. While the stakes were high, Varcoe was confident. "It was a little scary, but it's just like a regular case." Varcoe paused. "Except they're trying to kill your client."

Tom Connelly also remained on the defense team.

The defense had a mountain of circumstantial evidence to overcome. But when the attorneys first met with Marjorie and heard her version of events, they realized there was a very clear defense strategy. Marjorie told a convincing tale about how Jay had come home unexpectedly on his birthday and Larry confronted Jay in the garage. There was an altercation and Jay was accidentally shot and killed. Marjorie claimed she never saw the body or participated in the dismemberment.

The attorneys felt that Marjorie came across as persuasive and sympathetic and her story seemed believable. It seemed impossible that a 135-pound woman could dispose of the body of a 260-pound man. Larry, on the other hand, was very muscular and apparently on steroids. In addition, it didn't seem to Varcoe that Marjorie had any motive to want her husband dead. As for the insurance policies, Varcoe reasoned that they weren't that much when you consider the lifestyle Marjorie was living. "I just never believed she wanted him dead. He was worth more to her alive than dead," Varcoe recalled. "To take her son's father away from him, I don't think she would have done that. I still don't."

Marjorie's story hadn't changed at all since she had first confessed to her previous attorney, John Canby. For Alcantar, Marjorie's version of the crime explained some of the unknowns in this case. Alcantar surmised that after Larry shot and killed Jay, he began to panic. Larry had only known Marjorie for a few months and wasn't about to go to prison for her. Alcantar believed that as the pressure mounted and he became a suspect, Larry decided to frame Marjorie for murder. "That's when it hit me that this slimeball decided to focus the crime on her. That's why the torso was dumped by her house, in a place where it was likely to be found," Alcantar explained. "Marjorie's not a dummy, that's for sure. There's no such thing as the perfect crime but she could have done a lot better than that."

Of course, the problem with Marjorie's story was why she hadn't reported Jay's death sooner. In court, it would be a tremendous obstacle to overcome. Detectives gave Marjorie plenty of opportunities to implicate Larry, but she never even hinted that he had anything to do with the crime until she was behind bars. Marjorie was far from innocent. Even in her own story, she admitted lying to police and helping cover up a crime. Marjorie was facing a potential death sentence. Numerous times Marjorie's defense team encouraged her to take a plea deal, but she refused.

"I'd rather be put to death," Marjorie told her attorneys, "than admit to something I didn't do."

In early 2008, believing the trial was just a few months away, Jake Jr. took a deferred retirement from his dream job in San Diego. He, Shelly, and Noah uprooted their lives, sold everything they owned, and bought a new place in Phoenix. The Orbins believed it was important for someone to represent the family in court and that task fell to Jake Jr. For the next few months he planned to live off of his savings so he could attend every meeting and be there for every day of the trial.

As May rolled around, however, Herman Alcantar filed a motion to continue. Alcantar had only been on this case for less than a year and during that time he was preoccupied with another trial. The judge granted the motion and the trial was moved to January 2009. That date would stand firm.

Meanwhile, Marjorie continued to haunt the Orbins' lives. Until there was a conviction, a feeling of uncertainty lingered over their future. Nothing would ever bring Jay back. Never again would Jake and Joann enjoy Sunday brunch with Jay and Noah. Without him, each holiday, birthday dinner, and family get-together would be forever incomplete.

On September 8, 2008, the Orbins began a new family tradition. Jay's family and friends celebrated what would have been his forty-ninth birthday. In honor of Jay, they cut a cake and everyone recounted fond memories. The celebration was bittersweet. It had been exactly four years since Jay had been stolen from their lives. September 8 would forever be remembered as Jay's birthday, and as the anniversary of his murder.

CHAPTER 31

A modest, oak-paneled courtroom on the eleventh floor of the downtown Phoenix courthouse would be host to one of the most drawn-out and delay-ridden trials in Maricopa County history. With nearly as many bizarre twists as in the preceding homicide investigation, the trial would be marred with convoluted snags, lengthy delays, and bombshell accusations.

In the first of many unusual decisions, the trial was scheduled for just four hours a day, four days a week. While originally estimated to last three or four months, the trial would stretch on for nearly a year.

Perched at the bench in the center of the courtroom sat Judge Arthur Anderson, a gray-haired, middle-aged man with a round face and high forehead. Behind his square-framed glasses, Anderson peered down on the crowd gathered before him with a dour expression.

To the judge's right, Herman Alcantar, Robyn Varcoe, and Tom Connelly crowded the heavy oak table around Marjorie. It had been more than four years since Jay's murder and Marjorie bore only a faint resemblance to the glamorous blonde she had been at the time of her arrest. Her hair had gone brown; she had gained about fifty pounds and wore thick-framed eyeglasses. For most of the trial,

Marjorie, dressed in demure collared shirts and dark-colored sweaters or baggy business suits, took notes on a legal pad that she slid back and forth to Varcoe and Alcantar. Throughout testimony, she spoke almost constantly to her attorneys. Occasionally, she would become visually rigid; her face flushed and twisted with anger in response to testimony she perceived as false.

Adjacent to the defense, Noel Levy sat solo at the prosecution table, wearing traditional gray suits and quiet ties. Behind a barrier, divided by a center aisle of blue Berber carpet, were just three short rows of benches for family and spectators. For each day of the trial, Jake Jr. was planted sternly, arms crossed, in the back row behind the prosecution. Jay's friends and family also regularly attended court. At least two rows of the wooden pews were consistently occupied by a revolving number of Jay's loved ones.

On the opposite side of the courtroom sat a handful of reporters. Noticeably absent from the courtroom was anyone in support of Marjorie. Not one of her close friends or family members attended the trial. Occasionally, an older, overweight gentleman dressed in cut-off jeans attended the proceedings. However, the man, an old acquaintance of Marjorie's from the gym, seemed to attend the trial more out of curiosity than support.

For Marjorie, the stakes couldn't have been much higher. If convicted, Marjorie could face death by lethal injection. If she was found not guilty, she stood to gain more than $1 million in insurance payouts and assets.

On January 29, 2009, opening arguments began. During his statements, Levy presented the state's theory of the murder. When Jay returned home on September 8, Levy said, Marjorie shot and killed her husband in the garage while the couple's eight-year-old son slept in his bedroom. Marjorie then used a hand-held electric jigsaw to hack the corpse into pieces. The motive for this heinous crime:

money. "There was a whole lot of insurance and other property and if he was dead, she would have it made for life," Levy said in a commanding tone.

Throughout the trial, Levy told the jury he would present compelling testimony from Marjorie's lovers, jilted friends, and former cellmates. They would tell the story of a cruel woman who had planned her husband's death. Marjorie was a greedy, manipulative seductress. She hated her husband and had multiple affairs outside of her marriage. "She talked about Jay Orbin, that he was fat and that he could hardly get around, there was no sex between them," Levy told the jury. "She said she hated him. She wanted him dead."

The beginning of the prosecution's case focused as much on the crime as it did on Marjorie's character. Testimony was as steamy as a soap opera.

Among the first witnesses: Larry Weisberg. By February 2009, Larry was no longer a muscle-bound bodybuilder. In court, he looked deflated. Now retired and in his mid-sixties, Larry had shed nearly fifty pounds of muscle and gained thirty pounds of fat. His hair had gone gray and deep wrinkles marred his face. On the stand, Larry appeared nervous and agitated.

For the jury, Larry recounted his summer romance with Marjorie. According to Larry, Marjorie had seduced him. He said that the first time they had sexual relations, Marjorie initiated the contact. "She grabbed my hand and said, 'Why don't we go into your bedroom.'"

When Jay went missing, Marjorie didn't seem concerned. After his torso was discovered and her and Larry's homes were searched, however, she began acting peculiarly. She wanted to run away to Florida, Larry said, and she asked him to come with her. "She said, 'I'm scared, I'm real scared. I want to run away and I want you to come with me,' and I said, 'What?'"

"Do you know anything about what happened to Jay Orbin?" Levy asked in a measured tone.

"Absolutely not." Larry shook his head.

"Did you have any involvement whatsoever in the murder of Jay Orbin?" Levy asked.

"God, no," Larry grimaced.

During cross examination Alcantar immediately took an accusatory stance, attempting to portray Larry as a man crazy enough to confront a SWAT team and confrontational enough to shout at detectives investigating Jay Orbin's disappearance. Alcantar also played the phone call where Larry swore at Detective Jan Butcher.

"That was your voice?" Alcantar asked.

"In the background, yes," Larry said.

In a dramatic courtroom moment, the defense wheeled out a large blue Rubbermaid tub. It had been weighted to the exact heaviness of Jay's torso. In front of the jury, Alcantar asked Larry lift the tub. Larry got down from the witness stand, knelt and grabbed the tub on both sides. "This is awkward," he said as he lifted the tub.

After Larry was dismissed from court, he nearly fainted. He stumbled anxiously out of the courtroom. In the hallway, away from the jury, Larry grabbed his chest. He told Levy he thought he was going to have a heart attack. After a few moments of deep breathing, he calmed himself and left without incident.

Marjorie's former lover Jessiah Rueckert later testified about their steamy fling. After Jessiah came clean to Sharon about his affair, she forgave him and they were later married. On the stand, Jessiah admitted to sleeping with Marjorie while in a committed relationship with her good friend. The testimony appeared to make a strong impression on the jury. When they heard the details of Marjorie and Jessiah's affair, several of the jurors appeared visibly disgusted. Sharon also testified at trial about Marjorie's threats against Jay.

Among the most compelling witnesses was Sophia

Johnson. For the jury, Sophia related Marjorie's chilling
jailhouse confession. "She started going off about how he's
fat and disgusting. Then she starts talking about how I did
it. I did it," Sophia said. "She said he was shot, frozen, de-
thawed, and his arms, legs, and head were cut off."

Although Marjorie's lawyers attempted to dismiss Sophia as just another jailhouse snitch, her testimony seemed
to dampen the defense. Sophia had painted a powerful image for the jury.

Then, in late February, Charity Hill took the stand. A
year after confessing to Barnes that Marjorie had admitted
to "chopping her husband into little pieces," Charity had
recanted her testimony and attempted, unsuccessfully, to
withdraw her plea. Charity had also changed her story about
her own murder case. She was now pleading not guilty although her trial was still years away. In the meantime,
Charity had spent the last four years in jail on non-bondable
status. At Marjorie's trial, Charity told the jury that Marjorie had never confessed to the murder or dismemberment
of her husband. Charity claimed she had lied to broker a
deal in her own case.

"That's not what you told detectives in 2005," Levy
pressed. "Marjorie threatened you—isn't that correct?"

Charity remained cool and collected. She said repeatedly that she had lied to get a deal. Her repeated denials
irked Levy. He confronted her about her changing story, but
Charity stayed firm. Freely, she admitted to lying to everyone to get her deal. Levy would later say that Charity's demeanor got to him personally. "That's what started me to
get all emotional about this whole thing," he recalled. "She
wouldn't deviate. There was something about her manner
that she was saying, 'I'm lying to you.' To me it was just a
bit too brash and bold."

As he questioned her on the stand, Levy became emotional. It became so heated between Charity and Levy that
the jury became noticeably uncomfortable. The judge
asked Levy and the defense to approach the bench. While

Charity was on the stand, Levy mentioned to Varcoe, "I wonder if I shouldn't go forward with a perjury charge." In earshot of Charity, Levy continued to comment about the maximum penalty for a person convicted of lying under oath.

The defense pounced. They proceeded with charges of prosecutorial misconduct, claiming that Levy was attempting to coerce Charity with the threats. The trial was delayed while the defense filed motion after motion accusing Levy of misconduct and attacking his credibility. Over time it began to eat at Levy. Later he would say that he never dreamed that it would go further than just a casual remark. "They would say it's not a personal attack. And to an extent you can accept that but I didn't," Levy sighed, "because it was too personal."

The judge overruled charges of prosecutorial misconduct. But after the Charity Hill debacle, Levy seemed to lose his cool. He appeared absentminded and forgetful. Gradually, he lost his grasp on the case. At one point he even forgot Jay Orbin's name in court.

The trial continued. But for Levy, it was about to end.

For the first few months, Barnes showed up for every day of the trial. Although he was no longer a homicide detective, he wanted to do everything in his power to ensure that Marjorie was convicted. He even arranged his schedule as a patrol officer to attend every day of testimony, at times without pay.

Then in March, Barnes was working out at his gym when he got a call from his wife: The police were at their home with a search warrant. At first, Barnes thought it had to be some sort of mistake or a nasty prank. But he soon learned it was far more serious. The police—Barnes's colleagues—were rifling through his belongings. They seized computers, recorders, disks, external hard drives, and other electronics. They even confiscated a laptop computer belonging to his son, whom was home from college with his girlfriend.

The search warrant was sealed and for months the criminal charges for which Barnes was being investigated would remain unknown. The day his home was searched, Barnes learned he had been placed on administrative leave for undisclosed reasons.

Barnes was the one person who knew more about the Jay Orbin murder investigation than anyone else. He had been the lead homicide detective for the past five years and his testimony was vital to the case. But he would not testify. His attorney, Craig Mehrens, advised him not to take the stand until the scope of the search warrant was revealed. It seemed obvious to Mehrens that Barnes was being unfairly persecuted. If Barnes was going to testify, his attorney required immunity. For Levy, it was unfathomable that the lead investigator would testify under immunity from prosecution because he would immediately lose all credibility with the jury. With his once promising career seemingly destroyed, Barnes was removed from the Orbin case. Detective Jan Butcher, who had since been promoted to homicide, took over as the lead detective.

Without Barnes's testimony it was uncertain that Levy could get a conviction against Marjorie.

Then, on March 8, the trial came to an abrupt halt for two weeks when Levy fractured his ankle while hiking. Levy needed surgery, but the judge ordered him to postpone the operation and continue the trial. Levy's ankle was put in a cast too soon, which caused swelling and bleeding. A plate was put around his leg to stabilize the fracture, and he continued to try the case from a wheelchair.

On April 1, Levy was suddenly rushed to the hospital for immediate, emergency surgery. He was forced to recuse himself from the case. For Levy, it was difficult. It was the last case of his career and he had stayed on past retirement to finish out this trial. In the hospital, Levy came to the realization that it was impossible to continue. "I just felt that I could no longer function," Levy recalled. "I knew it would be better to bow out than to let the case go downhill because I was trying to stay with it. I related it to a battlefield casualty. I had to make the decision to back off."

CHAPTER 32

By April, the trial was in shambles. The prosecutor had been forced to withdraw and the lead detective was being investigated for criminal charges. It was uncertain if a mistrial would be declared. Weeks passed with the trial in limbo.

Then, in mid-May, a new prosecutor was assigned to the case. Treena Kay was a bright, headstrong young prosecutor. Slender with long blond hair, soft green eyes, and striking features, Kay was attractive and stylish. In court she typically dressed in bold, designer tailored suits.

The judge gave Kay just two weeks to read through 10,000 pages of discovery and 2,000 pages of previous testimony. She quickly got up to speed. By May 24, she had streamlined the witness list to lay down the facts and soon the case was back on track. Kay was very effective in court. Her aggressive, confident demeanor earned her the nickname "Ice Princess" among the defense.

For the next month, Kay called witness after witness disputing Marjorie's original story that Jay never came home on his birthday. Computer experts testified that Jay accessed his e-mail from the warehouse the afternoon of September 8. That evening, Jay's e-mail and other Web sites he frequented were accessed from the home computer. Other experts testified that Jay's cell phone bounced off towers in Phoenix for the few weeks following his disappearance.

Jake and Joann Orbin also took the stand to explain Marjorie's behavior following Jay's disappearance. In addition, Jake Jr. testified about the incident with Jay's truck and the tie-rod. It was powerful and emotional testimony. In court the family came across as extremely sympathetic. Noah would not testify. Against Marjorie's wishes, the family fought a long legal battle to keep him off the stand.

Kay helped build a compelling circumstantial case. In June, after nearly six months of testimony and delays, the prosecution rested.

It was time for Marjorie's attorneys to present her defense. In preparation, Robyn Varcoe crammed the courtroom with colorful props including a reciprocal saw, a model of a skeletal spine, and a blue tub that was identical to the one in which Jay's torso had been discovered. On June 16, the courtroom was hushed as the defense dropped a bombshell. "Larry Weisberg is the one who committed this crime," she said in her opening statements.

For months Marjorie's defense attorneys had hinted that was the card they intended to play, cross examining Larry and other witnesses on the stand about his behavior during the investigation. While the prosecution expected this defense, for the jury and other courtroom observers it was shocking. This was the first time in five years that Larry Weisberg had been publicly accused of the murder.

In a calm and steady tone, Varcoe explained that Marjorie had no motive to want her husband dead. They had an amicable, platonic relationship. Marjorie had an allowance and never wanted for anything. Then, in the summer of 2004, Larry Weisberg entered the picture. Marjorie felt abandoned by Jay's constant road trips and longed for companionship. "She was a lonely woman and she saw something in Larry Weisberg," Varcoe said.

Varcoe theorized that before Jay left for his trip to Florida, he was aware of Marjorie's affair. Larry gained access to the Orbins' garage using a remote Marjorie had provided him. When Jay, who traveled with a loaded .357, came home, he was surprised to see another SUV in the garage. There was a confrontation in which Jay was killed.

After the murder, Varcoe said Larry shifted attention away from himself and on to Marjorie. "He did this by dismembering and dumping Jay Orbin's body like trash and leaving it virtually at Marjorie's doorstep."

The defense began their case by attacking the state's strongest witness: Sophia Johnson. According to the defense, Sophia had benefited because of her testimony against Marjorie. Both Levy and Barnes had argued on her behalf during the hearing in which Sophia was released from jail. Months later, Sophia's case went to trial and she was convicted on charges of custodial interference. At her sentencing, Levy and Barnes again testified on Sophia's behalf and she wound up receiving the minimum sentence.

Three and a half years later, Sophia was released from prison. While Marjorie was locked away, Sophia claimed to still be in fear of her former cellmate. Because of her concerns, Sophia was housed in protective custody at a Phoenix motel throughout January and February. Following her initial testimony in February, it came to light that she had not disclosed the fact that she had spent those two months in witness protection.

On June 17, Sophia was called back to the stand. The defense tried to use this omission, and the benefits she had received, as the motivation for her to lie about Marjorie's confession. The attorneys claimed Sophia had learned information about Marjorie's case by reading her files and concocted the story to receive favorable treatment. Sophia, however, said she didn't view her situation as a benefit.

"This whole thing has not been beneficial towards me at all," Sophia said. "It has been a nightmare."

Later, the defense fought to compel Barnes to testify. He was called back to the stand where he asserted his right to not incriminate himself—pleading the Fifth Amendment to every question other than his name. This was on the advice of his attorney who didn't want him testifying until the scope of the warrant was revealed. Barnes later said it was the lowest point of his career. For his last five years in homicide, Barnes had dedicated his life to bringing murderers to justice. Now he was the one being treated like a criminal. "I put four to five years of my life into this case and I never got to see it through," Barnes recalled years later. "It was hard to take."

The judge later ruled Barnes could not take the Fifth Amendment and ordered him to testify concerning Sophia Johnson only. In front of the jury, Barnes revealed the same information—Sophia was placed in protective custody because of fear for her safety. It was the only aspect of the case to which Barnes would ever testify.

Months later the search warrant was unsealed and the scope of the charges against Barnes was revealed. He was being investigated on charges of felony computer tampering and misdemeanor property theft. Barnes, however, would never be indicted on those charges. He was later indicted on two counts of perjury and harassment, unrelated to the Orbin case.

Marjorie's only character witness throughout the trial was Michael J. Peter. While Michael testified that he hadn't seen Marjorie in more than a decade, he had known her since she was eighteen and did not believe she was capable of murder. "She wouldn't kill a spider," he said.

Michael testified that during the summer of 2004 he started to question his life. At that point he was in his mid-fifties and had never been married. Of all the women in his past, Marjorie was the best he'd ever had. Michael said he begged Marjorie to come back to him, but she refused. "Her answer to me was, 'There was nothing I would rather do, Michael, than be with you again, but Jay is a good man. I would never take the father from the child or the child from the father.' "

Michael said he would happily have taken Marjorie back and supported her financially. He also admitted to funding her defense. The defense used Michael's testimony to dispute her motivation for the crime. Marjorie had no reason to kill Jay, Varcoe said. "When Marjorie and Michael were together, they lived the high life," she explained. "She could always go live with Michael Peter."

On August 3, the judge announced that the trial would be postponed for one month. Initially the case had been expected to conclude by May. Because some of the jurors had prior obligations, the trial was postponed until the end of August, during what the judge referred to as a "summer vacation."

On August 23, the trial resumed. The defense took just six more days to present their case, which focused primarily on Larry's character. Larry was portrayed as a hunter with a violent temper. The defense pointed to hunting knives and a taxidermied deer head discovered in his house.

A photo from Larry's sparsely furnished home was also shown to the jury. In the spare bedroom Larry had a futon mattress. The defense claimed this was the same mattress found wrapped around the tub in the desert. However, there was never any forensic evidence linking that mattress to Larry or his home. Much was made about Larry's violent encounter with SWAT officers and the plastic sheeting found in his vehicle, which was consistent with that found with the torso.

Most compelling in the defense's case were the expert witnesses. One expert testified that the dismemberment could not have occurred with the short blade of a jigsaw. Instead, the dismemberment was conducted with a reciprocating saw by someone with a high knowledge of anatomy, the expert said. Another expert testified that it would not be possible for a 135-pound woman to dispose of the body of a 260-pound man, claiming, "It would be virtually impossible that she moved that tub."

Noticeably absent in their case was anything to explain Marjorie's behavior after the killing. The defense seemed to concede that Marjorie wasn't entirely innocent, although the attorneys never said that Marjorie had known Jay was dead. While they implied that Marjorie helped with the cover-up, there was no testimony concerning either the cleanup of the garage or the cell phones bouncing off the same towers. Additionally, they didn't argue that a blonde woman fitting Marjorie's description was seen near the Ford Bronco.

As for the tub, there was no disputing that Marjorie purchased two Rubbermaid storage containers just days after her husband's death, but she had dozens of tubs in her garage, all different colors and sizes. Larry could have easily used those tubs to frame Marjorie for the murder.

But if Marjorie's story was true and Larry killed Jay in the garage of their home, why didn't Marjorie report the crime? Why had she lied to Jay's family and friends after the disappearance? There were so many questions only Marjorie could explain. On the stand, Marjorie would need to give the performance of a lifetime. Throughout the case, she had intended to take the witness stand and Alcantar was confident she could believably explain herself to the jury.

The defense viewed Noel Levy as an ineffective prosecutor and felt Marjorie could confidently handle herself on the stand. But when Treena Kay took over, their strategy changed. If Marjorie took the stand, Alcantar thought she would get buried on cross-examination. They encouraged Marjorie not to testify and she agreed. Marjorie would never explain herself to the jury. On August 30, the defense rested.

CHAPTER 33

On September 8, 2004, Jay Orbin returned to Phoenix for what should have been a forty-fifth birthday celebration with his wife and son, Treena Kay said in her final statements. "No birthday cake for him," she said, her voice unwavering. "He had another surprise waiting for him on his birthday."

Kay dramatically recounted her theory of the crime. The motive for the murder: greed. The defendant, Kay said, had a million reasons for wanting her husband dead. When Jay came home early on September 8, Marjorie saw an opportunity. "She got his gun, she took it out of his briefcase, and she killed him."

Kay then detailed how Marjorie Orbin had painted over the garage floor and began running up tabs on Jay's credit cards and draining his bank accounts, even buying a grand piano. "She did buy him some gifts for his birthday: two fifty-gallon plastic tubs," Kay exclaimed. "She wrapped him up like little presents in plastic and tape."

The defense's claims were ludicrous, Kay said. There was no evidence ever discovered that tied Larry Weisberg to the murder. He was just another man for Marjorie to manipulate. "There is nothing in this finger-pointing defense that ties Larry Weisberg to the murder of Jay Orbin."

The defense disputed Kay's version of events. In Herman Alcantar's closing argument he asked: How could a 135-pound woman lift Jay's 260-pound body by herself? The real killer, Alcantar said, was Marjorie's bodybuilder lover, Larry Weisberg.

Alcantar also reiterated arguments that Marjorie could never have accomplished the dismemberment with the short blade of a jigsaw. According to the defense experts, Jay's body was dismembered with a reciprocal saw. Alcantar also hinted that perhaps Marjorie realized at some point that her husband was dead. Regardless, he maintained that this did not amount to first-degree murder.

Marjorie may have made some bad choices in trusting Larry, but she did not kill her husband, Alcantar said. He also implied that Marjorie and her son had been threatened by Larry and that Marjorie was in fear for the life of her son.

On September 1, the case went to the jury for deliberation. Both sides were confident that they had proven their case. The defense, however, admittedly had some concerns. Throughout the trial Alcantar had argued that Marjorie was too petite to dismember a body. But in her five years in jail Marjorie had put on more than fifty pounds. When she stood with her attorneys, Marjorie towered over both Varcoe and Alcantar. She no longer looked too delicate to dismember a body. "Here we're arguing that this little woman couldn't do all of this," Alcantar recalled. "Here she's looking like a linebacker. She looked pretty husky."

In addition, Alcantar recalled, Marjorie's demeanor hadn't exactly endeared her to the jury. Throughout the trial she often appeared angry and emotional. Alcantar worried about how the jury had perceived Marjorie. "I felt confident that we had raised reasonable doubt, but I wasn't confident that the jury was going to buy it," Alcantar recalled. "Only because by that time, it had become pretty clear that they did not like her."

For her part, Marjorie was positive that the jury had seen "the truth." For eight months she had sat and listened to damning testimony, but she was convinced she was about to be vindicated. "They don't know when Jay died, where he died. They don't know his cause of death or the manner of death, there is no murder weapon, no crime scene evidence, and no witness to the incident," Marjorie recalled. "How can they profess to know who caused Jay's death beyond a reasonable doubt?"

Over the next two days, the jury deliberated for six hours. On Friday, they broke for the weekend. The following week, a juror was out sick and deliberations were delayed for one week. As the weekend passed, the Orbins fought to keep their anxiety at bay.

That Tuesday, September 8, marked the fifth anniversary of Jay's death. Jake Jr. took Noah to the park to celebrate what would have been Jay's fiftieth birthday. They shared happy memories, laughed, and tossed a football. In preparation, Noah had also written his father a letter. Noah dug a shallow hole in the dirt and buried the note so his dad could read it from heaven. From atop a mountain trail in the park, Noah also released a fiftieth birthday helium balloon attached to a scroll that read, *I miss you Dad*. As the balloon sailed off, Jake Jr. and Noah both felt Jay was watching them from heaven.

A week later, on the afternoon of September 14, the jury reconvened. After just one more hour of deliberation, there was an announcement. Word spread through the courtroom and hallways: The jury had reached a verdict. The Orbins filed solemnly into the courtroom. Jay's family and friends crowded the wooden pews and spilled over to the defense side of the courtroom. Jake Jr. held his wife's hand. Jake and

Joann sat in the front row along with several of Jay's close friends.

Marjorie wore a button-down collared shirt, a black sweater, gray slacks, and her thick-framed glasses. Her long brown hair was wavy, and cheap, dark pink lipstick glossed her lips. She appeared positive and at ease as she stood for the jury's decision.

"Have you reached a verdict on all counts?" the judge asked.

"We have, Your Honor," said the jury foreman.

A manila folder was passed to the bailiff. Marjorie's breath quickened. Her eyes darted quickly to the jury and back to the bailiff.

"We the jury do unanimously find the defendant . . ." The bailiff paused for several seconds. "Guilty."

Marjorie shut her eyes for a moment, but otherwise she didn't react. The Orbins were overcome with relief. Shelly dropped her head and quietly sobbed. Jake and Joann embraced. For Jake Jr., it was the moment he had waited for for five long years. "A guilty verdict is what we expected all along," he recalled. "There was no doubt in our minds. There was so much evidence against her, we couldn't envision it going any other way."

That afternoon, word of the verdict reached David Barnes, who was at home on paid leave from the police department. He felt relieved to know that, despite everything, justice had prevailed. But the news also triggered an unexpected twinge of sadness. "I wish I could have been there for the verdict," he said later.

But the jury still had to decide Marjorie's fate: life in prison or death by lethal injection. The next day, the jury reconvened to decide the sentence. For the first time, the family got to tell the jury about how Jay's loss had affected them.

Jake Jr. addressed the court and read a prepared statement. "Words can't express all the pain our family has endured since Jay's murder," he said, his eyes glistening with tears. "No one will understand the fear we felt when we heard he was missing. How we couldn't sleep thinking we were not doing enough to find him; meanwhile his body was here all along. No one will ever understand the pain my parents and I felt when we were told that part of Jay's remains were located. It was hard enough hearing confirmation of our worst fears—but to then learn that he was dismembered. It was almost more than my parents and I could take."

Jake Jr. said that since the day that Jay's partial remains were found, his parents had aged a decade. His father had become bitter and angry; his mom struggled to keep from crying all the time. There was no longer a light to guide their family, only grief and pain.

Jake Jr. told the jury about Jay's life: his goofy side, his wilder days, his generous nature, and his love for his son. He explained how Jay had built his business from scratch. At the time of his death, Jay was planning to use the technological advances of the Internet to expand his business. He wanted ultimately to retire early to spend more time with his son. "Jay would have deserved that."

For the past five years, Jake Jr. said, his family has struggled. Milestones like Christmas, Jay's birthday and the anniversary of his death, had been the hardest. While his entire family had struggled with the loss of Jay, it had been especially difficult for Noah. "Our family is broken . . . losing Jay has changed our lives forever," he said, his voice cracking. "We will have to live the rest of our lives with only our memories of Jay. There won't be any new photos, no more hearing Jay's laughter at any family events, no more late night e-mails, no more parties, holiday celebrations, or any family activities with my brother." Instead, he said as he showed a picture of Jay to the jury, they now live in the past—reminiscing about Jay when they look at old photos. "This reminds me of exactly the type of person Jay was—happy, smiling, outgoing, and so alive."

* * *

No one spoke in person on Marjorie's behalf. In a written statement, her sister Colleen wrote about growing up with Marjorie in Florida. In another letter, Marjorie's old boss from Church Street Station, Porter Freeman, recounted what a hard-working employee Marjorie had been nearly two decades earlier.

Treena Kay then argued for the jury why Marjorie deserved nothing less than death for her crimes. The Orbin family had been devastated by the loss of Jay, she said. The way that Jay was killed and the recovery of his remains were callous and unthinkable. "When we talk about Noah, this is a young boy who is becoming a young man, who now is at the age where normally he would be looking to go to his father for someone to explain to him growing up, how to be a man, and teaching him about these types of life lessons. He no longer has that ability because this defendant took his father from him," Kay argued passionately. "He does have, obviously, a very loving family, a very supportive family around him, but it never will be the same for him. This family has suffered extreme emotional harm."

Robyn Varcoe delivered her own persuasive speech. Sentencing Marjorie to death would leave Noah an orphan, she said. He would grow up with the knowledge that his mother was put to death for killing his father. "He lost his father," Varcoe said to the jury. "Don't take away his mother."

After her final statements, Varcoe sat back at the defense table, emotionally spent. Marjorie leaned toward her and quietly whispered, "Well, that was weak." Varcoe didn't respond.

Two weeks later, on September 30, the jury handed down their decision.

The bailiff read the sentence: Life in prison.

Marjorie's face contorted with emotion. She took a short, shallow breath. Her eyes went red as she glanced up at the ceiling. Her life had been spared.

For the Orbins, it was a relief. They had never wanted the death penalty. Despite everything she was still Noah's mom. They didn't want her to lose her life. "Our family always believed that if she was found guilty she deserves to wake up every day in prison, knowing she's going to spend the rest of her life there," Jake Jr. said. "I think that's more of a punishment than the death penalty."

More than three months later, on January 15, 2010, everyone gathered in the courtroom one final time. According to Arizona law it was for the judge to decide whether Marjorie would ever be eligible for parole or if she would spend the rest of her natural life in prison.

For the first time, Marjorie addressed the court. She wore black-and-white prison garb, her hands cuffed in front of her. With no indication of remorse, Marjorie continued to profess her innocence. She spoke directly to the judge for the first time.

"Just a couple of things," Marjorie stated matter-of-factly. "There is a lot I would like to say but through this experience I have learned that there is really not much point in that. All that has happened here is a group of people have been convinced of something that is not true."

With that said, Marjorie continued, she just wanted to move forward with the sentencing so she could proceed with the appeals process. There was not much the defense could say in support of their client. Herman Alcantar could only argue that Marjorie had no felony record. "I'm not going to belabor the point," Alcantar said. "Obviously, I have an obligation to request a minimum."

It was time for the Judge Arthur Anderson to deliver his ruling.

"Ms. Orbin. I think it's true that you loved your boy and spent a lot of time with him," Anderson began. "I think the fact that you care so much about your boy cuts both ways."

The judge admonished Marjorie, stating that if she

loved her son and had ever loved Jay, it was unfathomable that she had let police scurry around trying to figure out what happened while she knew her husband was dead.

"Why you didn't seek help, if any of the arguments that you make are even remotely true . . . and you dismissed these, frankly, as bad choices. These aren't bad, ma'am. Your position is absurd and that's because I don't believe one bit of it, frankly," the judge said sternly. "Because if you cared at all for Jay Orbin, if you cared at all about your boy and this business about Weisberg being responsible for this, you would have told police, because you had ample opportunities, you were alone with them in interviews, you had ample opportunities to get your boy into a safe haven and you did none of it."

The judge acknowledged that Marjorie was a good mom. With Noah, the judge said he believed her love was sincere. The judge also believed that for a period of time she genuinely cared about Jay. "But prior to those days, it seems that cracks begin to show. The testimony was you were becoming unhappy with this marriage and you sought, for your personal gratification, a teenaged boy to a man in his sixties. You did that for your own selfish reasons," he said. "Your dark side started to come out until that day that you killed him. That's the jury's finding, ma'am. You are a murderer and I don't believe for one moment you posture yourself as a victim. That's just not true in my view."

The judge said that while he understood Marjorie's position, he didn't give it much credibility.

"What you did to him is hard to imagine anyone doing to another human being," he said. "And I don't know how anything is appropriate but natural life for you. You can't be trusted in our society today because when that dark side is unleashed, it's about as dark as it gets."

The cutting judgment resounded with bleak finality as Marjorie was unceremoniously led away from the courtroom in shackles. Barring an appeal, Marjorie would live out each day for the rest of her natural life in a jail cell. Imprisoned with her was something far more tragic for the Orbins—the truth. Throughout it all, Marjorie never revealed the missing pieces that could have brought the family some sense of solace. By the end of the trial, after a seemingly endless gambit of testimony, the Orbins had come to realize that they would never be bringing all of the remains of Jay home to rest.

Somewhere out there in the barren Sonoran desert, the skull and bones of a loving father were smoldering under the scorching Arizona sun, likely sealed in that second, undiscovered Rubbermaid container. The whereabouts would remain unknown.

High Heels and Low Lifes:
My Life as a Dancer

A Novel by Marjorie Orbin

CHAPTER 34

The first time I got a glimpse of Marjorie Orbin, she was shackled in the courtroom jury box, surrounded by a dozen other inmates. Dressed in frumpy black-and-white prison garb, she bore little resemblance to the glamorous blond showgirl I had seen in photographs. But despite her substantial weight gain and darkened locks, I recognized her right away—she was still a striking beauty.

Each morning before trial, Marjorie sat shackled in Judge Arthur Anderson's courtroom while he spent the morning sentencing convicted felons on unrelated cases. On my first day in court I arrived early, sat in the back row of the spectator pews, and observed Marjorie from across the courtroom. One by one, each inmate approached the bench as Anderson handed down sentencing ranging from probation to decades in prison.

Toward the end of the morning session, the judge called a nineteen-year-old boy who had spent six weeks behind bars on petty theft charges. The boy's parents asked to speak on his behalf. To the judge, his mother told a moving story about how her son had a college scholarship and a bright future but had just gotten mixed up with the wrong crowd.

"He's a good boy, Your Honor," the mother cried. "He deserves a second chance, please."

As the mother pleaded with the judge, I glanced over at Marjorie and noticed a single tear glistening on her cheek; her face looked flushed with emotion.

For me, it was chilling.

By that time, I had already covered the case for years as an editor for a local, Phoenix-based magazine. Throughout my research, I had become well versed in the thousands of pages of police reports and interviewed Jay's friends and family members.

It was utterly jarring to witness this woman moved by the plight of a stranger—a woman who all evidence indicated was capable of a brutal murder and dismemberment. It further fueled the mystery that was Marjorie. Throughout her remarkable life, Marjorie had experienced some of the best things that the world had to offer. As a dancer she had performed all over the world, and with Michael J. Peter she had lived a lifestyle most people could only dream about. But in September 2004, she seemed to throw it all away for reasons I still can't quite comprehend.

Over the next several months I sat through the trial, listening to testimony painting Marjorie as a dangerously calculating woman who would stop at nothing to get everything she wanted. With her friends and lovers, Marjorie lied and schemed. And by her own admission, she fooled Jay's family for a decade into believing their relationship was more than it was.

It was amazing to me how she was able to influence so many people. Jay Orbin, Larry Weisberg, Michael J. Peter, Todd Christy and countless other men who over the years fell victim to her charms.

What was it about this woman? I wondered. *How did she have this power over people?*

I wouldn't truly understand until much later.

* * *

Weeks after the jury had spared her life during the initial sentencing phase, I drove down to the Estrella Jail to interview Marjorie Orbin.

The heavy clank of the steel doors clamored behind me as I was led into a drab, fluorescent-lit room filled with inmates conversing with their loved ones. Inside a smaller room, I eased onto a metal stool and waited for Marjorie to be escorted from the secure lockdown wing where she was being held. I heard the clanging of her ankle cuffs resonate down the linoleum hallway as she approached. Suddenly, the door opened and Marjorie entered the tiny interview room. Separated by the metal cage, I was face-to-face with Jay Orbin's convicted killer.

Fluorescent pink handcuffs confined her wrists. The prison garb she wore was dull and faded; the white stripes had turned gray from years of wear. Marjorie's brown wavy hair fell thick around her face. As she had through the trial, she wore pink lipstick with black makeup lining her almond-shaped eyes.

Marjorie smiled pleasantly as she situated herself on the stool. Throughout our interview she was charming and polite, even as she lambasted me for my prior coverage of the case, quoting particular passages that irritated her. "I know you," she said. "I wrote you the nastiest letter." I reminded her that she had declined prior requests for an interview until after her recent conviction. But for the next four hours, I placed all judgment aside and listened quietly to her stories, asking few questions.

That afternoon, Marjorie and I talked about many things—her childhood, her seven ex-husbands, her unusual marriage with Jay and the affair with Larry. We covered in great detail nearly every aspect of her life over the past forty-three years, up until the night of Jay's murder.

As our interview concluded, Marjorie invited me back to hear the rest of the story. Intrigued, I returned one more time, just weeks before she was transferred to the state prison. During our final interview, Marjorie slid me a stack of papers through a three-inch gap in the metal cage that separated us.

"Here it is," she said. "That is the meat of the story. It's all in there."

Printed neatly in pencil on the first page were the words, *High Heels and Low Lifes: My Life as a Dancer.* Below the title she had written, *A Novel by Marjorie Orbin.* With a tiny jailhouse pencil, similar to what you would find at a golf course, Marjorie had printed her version of events on 161 pages of white legal paper. By giving it to me, she said she just wanted an opportunity to finally tell her side of the story.

The following is the story she never told police or in court. This is Marjorie Orbin, in her own words.

"I do realize that the most tragic part of this whole thing is Jay's death. But I have never really considered that the greatest offense that has taken place," Marjorie wrote. "I believe that intent weighs the greatest in measuring culpability and I know that no one intended to cause Jay's death. The greatest offenses I see here are really those which resulted in Larry letting me take the blame for what he inadvertently did, having no regard for what he has done to me."

Marjorie's story began in the summer of 2004. She was lonely and depressed. Emotionally, her relationship with Jay was wonderful—they had a respectful partnership based on their mutual love for Noah. Physically, however, they hadn't been intimate in years and Marjorie was desperate for companionship.

Then one day at the gym she met Larry Weisberg. Instantly, she found him attractive, but she wasn't the one to make the first move. Instead, Larry approached her. According to Marjorie, Larry was aware that she was married but was undeterred. Over the next few weeks he pursued her aggressively. Marjorie became overwhelmed with desire and gave into her passion. "He touched me and it began affecting me in ways I wasn't prepared for and I didn't want to admit. I began to want him."

Their affair was intense and passionate. After just a few months together, Marjorie and Larry were talking about living together. Marjorie envisioned a better life with her new lover and was ready to separate from Jay. "By July, I was seriously considering leaving Jay."

Jay, however, was completely unaware. According to Marjorie, he never knew of the affair.

As their relationship progressed, Marjorie saw another side to Larry. She learned that he had lied to her about his steroid use and his age, originally claiming he was in his early fifties. Then one night at Marjorie's house they had a disagreement. Larry later told police that the argument stemmed from when he had asked her what she planned to do with her life and she replied, "I'm going to be a soccer mom." Marjorie, however, said the fight was actually because she told Larry that even if she separated from Jay she planned to continue helping with his business, "Because as far as I was concerned, this was our son's legacy."

Larry began to become jealous and possessive. If Marjorie didn't call him first thing in the morning, Larry would become frantic and say things like, "I was worried that he found out."

"Larry began making comments to the effect that he cared for me more than Jay did," she wrote. "As August wore on, my feeling began to chill a little bit."

Still, their romance continued throughout that summer.

Early on the morning of Jay's forty-fifth birthday, the phone rang. It was Jay. He had just left his hotel in Tucson and was headed back to Phoenix. In preparation for his birthday, Marjorie had purchased a carrot cake and she and Noah had bought and wrapped several presents including a laptop with wireless capability so that Jay would have access to his e-mail and client lists on the road. In addition, Noah had picked out some rare collector comic books for his father's extensive collection of memorabilia.

But the day before his birthday Marjorie had become ill with a sore throat. The following morning, Jay's birthday, Noah also claimed he was not feeling well.

When Marjorie spoke to Jay, she voiced her concerns that she and Noah might have strep throat. Not wanting to get sick himself and because of all the sales he had lost due to the hurricane, Jay said he was going to stop by the warehouse, contact some of his clients, and make plans for a detour trip.

"I'll make some calls and let you know," Jay said.

Marjorie and Noah went through their morning routine. After breakfast and a shower, Noah seemed fine and had no temperature. She sent him off to school. After dropping off Noah at Copper Canyon Elementary, Marjorie went to the grocery store and picked up ingredients for her "famous chicken noodle soup." When she spoke to Larry she told him, "Jay's not coming home as planned." Larry did not mention stopping by the house.

That afternoon, when Marjorie picked up Noah from school he said that he was feeling worse. They returned home and Noah went to his room. Marjorie fluffed his pillows, brought him a snack tray with Gatorade, and set up the vaporizer by his bed. Marjorie always doted on Noah when he was sick. "Jay always used to tease me that I was going to turn Noah into a hypochondriac because I made being sick such a wonderful, pampered experience. I always thought it was a mom thing."

While Noah sat in his room watching movies and playing video games, Marjorie made the soup and popped in a load of laundry. Jay called from the warehouse and confirmed that he was planning to go to Utah or El Paso to try and make up the sales.

"Do you need anything?" Jay asked.

"No," Marjorie said. "We're fine. Don't worry. We'll celebrate your birthday when you get back."

"I love you guys," Jay said. "I'll talk to you later."

According to Marjorie, it was the last time she ever heard his voice.

Bang! Bang! Bang! Bang!

It was around six p.m. and Marjorie was sitting on the edge of Noah's bed when four shrill blasts reverberated through the house. Marjorie sprang off the bed, closed Noah's door behind her, and sprinted across the foyer. She approached the laundry room. The garage door suddenly flung open. Larry exploded through the laundry room in a panic. Marjorie shrank back, gasping with astonishment. Larry looked disheveled. He was breathing heavily; his brow was dripping with sweat.

"What are you doing here?" she asked, perplexed. "What's wrong?"

"It was an accident!" Larry yelped. "It was an accident!"

A car accident? Marjorie thought.

"Hold, on, let me check on Noah," Marjorie said.

"Oh, my god! Noah is here?" Larry balked.

Marjorie went to Noah's room and looked in on him. Unfazed, he was playing video games. The vaporizer was humming. Marjorie added more vapor fluid and told Noah to stay put in his room so that the steam could help cure him.

Marjorie went back to the laundry room off the garage, but the door was closed. She tried to open it, but something was blocking the door.

"What the hell?" she muttered to herself. She forced it open, pushing a pile of clothes out of the way. Marjorie scanned the small laundry room, which was covered with debris. Everything from the shelves had been thrown onto the ground and her purse had been dumped. Clothes and laundry powder were strewn across the floor; cell phone chargers, Walkmans, sunglasses, and the contents of a change jar littered the tile.

Suddenly, Larry burst into the laundry room through the garage.

"What is going on?" Marjorie asked perplexed.

"It was an accident! It was an accident!" Larry clamored repeatedly.

"Hey, calm down," Marjorie placed her hand on his shoulder. "Whatever it is, we'll figure it out."

Larry grabbed Marjorie by the arms, dragging her to the master bedroom. Trembling, Larry stumbled into the bathroom. As he splashed water on his face, Larry began to sob. "Why did you say he wasn't coming home?"

"Wait." Marjorie jolted up. "Jay's here?"

She brushed past Larry and headed toward the garage. Larry grabbed her around the waist and wrapped his arms around her. Dropping his head on her shoulder, he sobbed hysterically. Marjorie tried to pull away, "I have to see. Is he hurt?"

"It's too late. It's too late," Larry whimpered. "It was an accident."

"Let me go!" Marjorie broke free of his grasp and headed toward the laundry room. Larry followed steps behind, reaching for her.

"Don't," Larry bawled. "It's too late. You don't want to see."

Marjorie approached the laundry room. Stumbling over the debris, she reached for the door to the garage.

Grabbing the handle with her left hand, Marjorie pushed her shoulder against the door. It was wet and sticky. Marjorie looked down at her hands. They were covered in blood. She fell backward, shrieking, "Oh, God! Oh, God!"

Backpedaling through the mess on the floor, Marjorie fell into Larry. He picked her up, carried her to the bathroom, laid her in the shower, and turned on the water.

As the water rushed over her, Marjorie cowered in the

corner of the shower, crying. The blood on her hands turned the white tiles on the shower floor red; the murky water swirled around the drain. *This can't be real,* Marjorie thought. *This can't be happening.*

Larry returned. He stripped off her clothes and sneakers, depositing them in a trash bag. He left Marjorie alone, naked, in the shower. She hugged herself, shaking in disbelief.

Suddenly, Marjorie's thoughts turned to Noah. Hurriedly, she dried off, threw on some dry clothes and rushed to Noah's room. In the hallway, Marjorie could see Larry had barricaded the laundry room door with the couch. Marjorie approached Noah's room, slowly opened the door, and tiptoed inside.

Noah was asleep. Marjorie stood over him, silently shaking and crying. She turned off the television and vaporizer and left the room. In the kitchen, Marjorie found Larry. They fell into each other, crying.

"What are we going to do?" Marjorie asked.

Larry pulled back. "You can't tell anybody about this! They'll think we did this on purpose."

Haltingly, Larry explained what had happened. Earlier, he had called the house, but Marjorie hadn't answered. After work, believing Jay wasn't returning home as expected, Larry decided to come by the house and check on her. He pulled his Tahoe into the garage, using the garage door remote Marjorie had given him. He got out of the car and entered the house through the laundry room, pressing the garage door button on the wall. Suddenly, the garage door reversed. Startled, Larry jerked around and was confronted by Jay Orbin. They tussled for a moment in the laundry room. During the struggle, a gun went off and Jay was killed. Marjorie wasn't sure which gun, but she assumed it was the pistol Jay carried with him in his briefcase.

"The most tragic part of all this is a thought that haunts me always. Jay very likely lost his life believing that he was protecting both Noah and I from an intruder. He probably died worrying that Noah and I may be harmed. This is one of the difficult things that stays with me always," Marjorie wrote. "Jay's death was a horrible, unforeseen accident which took place during a confrontation between him and Larry Weisberg. There was no premeditation. Neither of them were expected at my house, much less both of them at the same time. I came onto the situation after the fact. I had no part in causing Jay's death. I never saw his body or knew what had been done to it until much later."

In the kitchen, Larry concocted a plan, Marjorie wrote. He told her to stay put. "Just give me a little time so I can figure out what to do."

He went through the sliding glass doors that led out to the backyard and around to the side door, which opened onto the garage. Marjorie remained in the kitchen, numb, her arms wrapped around herself. Jay was dead; her mind was reeling.

After a few short moments, Marjorie went to the foyer and stared out the long windows on both sides of the front door. She saw Larry back his Tahoe out of the garage. He got out of the truck and pulled Jay's Bronco inside. Several moments later, Larry rushed back into the house through the sliding glass door. He headed directly to the kitchen, poured himself a water glass full of tequila, and downed it in several gulps.

"Okay, you said he wasn't coming home," Larry said as he slammed down the glass and poured another. "Just stick to that. If anyone calls, tell them he's still on the road. I need a couple of days to figure out what to do."

Larry instructed Marjorie to act as if everything was normal. Go shopping, make phone calls, and no matter what, don't tell anyone that Jay had come home, Larry said. He took Jay's cell phone, which he had retrieved from his body, and dialed the house number. When the number came up on the caller ID, he said to Marjorie, "See. Jay just called home."

Larry told her to make several more phone calls from Jay's cell over the next few days. Stay on the phone long enough for the number to stay on the caller ID, Larry told her. In addition, she needed to regularly check his e-mail. Marjorie did as she was told. A few moments later, Marjorie went into the home office, signed into Jay's e-mail, and scrolled through his messages. Most of the e-mails were automatic messages from the Republican Party. She clicked on a few links. Years later, in court, the prosecution would try to use that evidence to show that Jay returned home the night of his birthday and checked his e-mail from the house. In her writings Marjorie admitted that was not true. "Jay was no longer alive at that time," she wrote. "It was not Jay on the computer, it was me."

At a little past eight p.m., Larry entered the office and told her he was leaving in Jay's Bronco. "I'll be back in a while," he said.

Marjorie felt drained. For the next few hours, she wandered aimlessly around the house.

After ten p.m., Larry returned. He seemed manic. "Did anyone call?" he asked.

"No." Marjorie shook her head.

Larry moved the furniture that was barricading the laundry room door.

"Where is Jay?" Marjorie asked. "What did you do with him?"

"The less you know, the better," Larry snapped.

He reiterated the plan: "Jay never came home." If Marjorie didn't do as she was told, Larry threatened that "I could have ten people say I was somewhere else tonight."

Once again, Larry left in his Tahoe. Marjorie was afraid. She called Charity McLean but she was too scared to tell her anything that had happened. It was just comforting to hear her voice. After awhile, she went back around the house through the backyard. The side door had been left propped open. As she approached the garage, Marjorie was struck by the smell of gasoline. She slowly entered the garage and flipped on the light. There was nothing to see. The garage was empty. Both Jay's Bronco and Larry's Tahoe were gone.

How'd he move both vehicles? Marjorie wondered. *Had someone helped him?*

Missing was some plastic sheeting and a purple and green rug that had been situated in front of the refrigerator. "I stood there, imagining Jay, having been rolled up in the rug and plastic and then taken away in the Bronco."

CHAPTER 35

When Marjorie opened her eyes the following morning, reality came flooding back. Jay was dead. A million frightening images rushed through her mind. *How is this going to affect Noah? How am I going to take care of Noah?*

It was Thursday, September 9. Noah's throat was still sore, so Marjorie called him out sick from school. She spent the morning making breakfast and cleaning the house.

Marjorie went into the laundry room and began putting things back together. Among the items she picked up from the floor were Jay's credit cards. Marjorie carried several of his credit cards and had used them with his authorization over the years. In the mayhem, she didn't even realize that these were the cards Jay had had with him at the time of his death.

That day, Larry called constantly.

"Stick to the story," he said. "Go about business as normal as possible."

"What did you do with him?" Marjorie asked timidly.

"Nothing yet," Larry said. "I haven't figured out what to do."

Marjorie was anxious and uncomfortable around the house. That afternoon she shopped at Target. While a lot of the items she purchased were cleaning supplies, Marjorie said those were all for common household chores and not for cleaning up blood. "I just remember roaming around aimlessly for a long time, just for something to do rather than go home." That afternoon, Marjorie cleaned the house and shampooed the carpet.

For the next few days, she did as she always did—cleaned and organized. Prior to Jay's death, Marjorie had planned to epoxy coat the garage. In preparation, she had purchased concrete stain and several storage bins, cabinets, and plastic totes. Larry instructed her to go forward with the project so as not to draw attention to the garage. Marjorie said there was never any blood on the garage floor.

On September 10, Marjorie returned to Lowe's and purchased two more fifty-five-gallon tubs, which she said were intended to store her two-part, pre-lit Christmas tree. They were never intended for Jay's remains, she said. Over the next few days, Larry helped her in the garage, organizing items in storage boxes. "If the tub really is the same one that Jay was found in, I don't know for sure, I never really believed so, that was after the fact."

In the ensuing weeks, it was as if Marjorie were in a trance. She made a lot of purchases, but she shopped simply to be out of the house and stay busy.

Larry came by the house. He said the Bronco was parked two blocks away and she needed to "get rid of it." The following Monday, after dropping off Noah at school, Marjorie went searching for the vehicle. She drove aimlessly around the neighborhood but could not locate it.

A few days later, Larry took her to where he had abandoned the vehicle. Marjorie drove the Bronco a few blocks before it died outside an apartment complex. She walked back home. That's where the vehicle remained until it was later reported to police.

At first there was no unusual reaction to the story she told about Jay being on the road. Over the next few weeks, however, the situation escalated. "More and more people were asking about Jay. More and more lies were being told.

Larry was hounding me more and more, giving me the third degree, asking about every conversation I had and everything I did. Noah began asking about his father. It was awful."

As Jay's loved ones began to ask accusatory questions, she became increasingly defensive. "I could tell people were beginning to question what I was saying."

Marjorie told Larry that she couldn't keep fending these people off.

"Let's just tell the police it was an accident," she said.

According to Marjorie, Larry would have none of it. He told her to keep quiet and stick to the story.

Marjorie began to tell people Jay was returning on September 20, so she could use that as the date that Jay had failed to return home.

By September 20, many people were calling for Jay. Marjorie continued to pretend to be awaiting his return. It was becoming overwhelming. That day she used Jay's cell phone to make it appear as if he was still alive. "It is true that I had Jay's cell phone after September 8, 2004. It is true that I was dialing numbers and disconnecting so that his cell phone number appeared on a few people's caller ID to make it as though Jay called."

After finally reporting Jay missing on September 22, Marjorie began to pull out of shock. She started to figure out how to handle things with Jay gone. At the warehouse, Marjorie retrieved Jay's "in case of" letter. Everything that happened next was according to Jay's instructions. She retrieved his computer and the valuables from the safe as she prepared to continue conducting Jay's business from the house as per his instructions.

Concerned that the bank accounts would be frozen, Marjorie started to withdraw cash and set it aside in case it was needed to put gas in the car or buy groceries. Marjorie maintained that she was always honest about the finances because she felt she was doing nothing wrong. "These were our assets that we worked for, for over ten years," she wrote. "Anyone thinking I was not entitled to Jay's assets is having no respect for Jay's wishes which he made very clear and in writing. No one but Jay had the right to make those decisions, and obviously Jay trusted me to handle the estate."

Meanwhile, the phone rang incessantly as Jay's loved ones became increasingly concerned about his disappearance. "Everyone had a million suggestions as to what I should be doing and an attitude if I didn't jump on each one. There were so many with ideas it left no time for anything. Meanwhile Larry is ragging me to death between every other call. All the while I am pretending to be concerned for Jay when I know it is all for nothing because he is already dead . . . So I am lying my ass off and, to my credit, very poorly."

With Jay's parents it became increasingly difficult to feign concern. Jake and Joann went over various scenarios which Marjorie knew had nothing to do with the truth. She found it aggravating. "I am trying to act appropriately emotional, but at this point I have been dealing with this overwhelming situation now for over twenty days and am wrung out," she wrote. "I was terribly concerned about the pain they would endure when Jay's death was revealed. And yes I had compassion for that but I was just drowning and exhausted and at my wits end."

Through it all, Larry was no solace. Every time she told him about a new development, he would become panicked. Larry began to believe surveillance cars were following him. One night he stormed down the street chasing after a car.

Then, on September 28, police served a search warrant on Marjorie's house. The SWAT team busted through the house and Larry was tased in her foyer. "These couple of minutes were the most traumatizing of my entire life."

When Detective Jan Butcher questioned her, Marjorie

confessed about the affair but stuck to the "cover story" concerning Jay. In contrast, Larry lied when he told police that he didn't believe Jay and Marjorie were a couple, she said.

That evening, Larry was allowed to leave.

"His Tahoe with blacked-out windows was in my garage. Anything could have been in it. Nobody searched it. They gave him his keys and he was free to go," she wrote. "He threatened officers, resisted arrest, assaulted officers, and was heard yelling at me not to cooperate with police . . . Does this sound like the actions of someone who has done nothing wrong and knows nothing?"

Marjorie hired an attorney and for the next few weeks she went about business as usual—focusing on what needed to be done to move forward with her life. The situation, however, was becoming increasingly traumatic. "I am helping cover up a murder, lying to police and everyone else, being interrogated by Larry, worrying about my son, doing everything myself, trying to figure out how to do the work of two people, stressing over how to keep a roof over our heads, terrified about how all this is going to turn out. If the phone rings one more time, I'm going to lose it."

In October, she agreed to meet with Joann at the park so she could see Noah. By this point, Larry had become extremely paranoid. He told Marjorie he was coming with her for her protection. The park was very close to Jodi Weisberg's home, and he concocted the idea of bringing his grandsons. To Marjorie, it made no sense. She knew it would seem suspicious but she went along with the plan.

"This has to go in the *Guinness Book of World Records* of 'what the hell was I thinking,' " she wrote. "I have to say that I was definitely not myself and I was in a very vulnerable, fragile, traumatized frame of mind. I was very fearful and pretty paranoid myself. What was going on was very serious and frightening."

When Marjorie saw Joann at the park, she felt like her heart was about to fall out of her chest. She looked distraught. "I'm standing there facing her and I don't know what to say. She is shaking and devastated and clearly fearing the worst and I am here and I know that her son is never coming back and that sooner or later her greatest fears are going to be confirmed. It was horrible."

Marjorie told her not to worry and made a remark that was meant to be consoling, not ominous. This had nothing to do with not being able to collect insurance for seven years if no body was found. "I said a couple of things to her like, 'don't worry,' 'they'll find him,' 'we'll figure this out,' with no more meaning or intent than if I said, 'there, there,'" she wrote. "Just something innocuous and consoling. I didn't know what to say to her. It was just a really horribly sad situation."

A week later, on October 28, Detective David Barnes informed Marjorie that a body was found that they believed to be Jay. Marjorie was surprised but prepared for the discovery. But she was not prepared to learn that Jay's body had been dismembered. When Barnes told her the condition that they found Jay's body in, she couldn't quite comprehend. "I couldn't breathe. I couldn't understand. I didn't want to believe it. My head was spinning. I could not wrap my mind around this," she wrote. "I could not believe what police were telling me about a dismembered body."

Reeling from what she had learned, that evening Marjorie directed her attorney to take her to Jodi Weisberg's house. She wanted to confront Larry, but he was emotional and his daughter and son-in-law would not let them speak. "The dismemberment was pretty hard for me to wrap my mind around. But I have to believe it was just a panic-driven, desperate act out of fear."

The following day was Marjorie's forty-third birthday. Her attorney picked her and Noah up at the motel where they had slept and brought them home. That afternoon, Larry came by. He seemed furious. He stormed into her house and started yelling about how she had caused a scene at his daughter's house. But Marjorie was more focused on what police had told her about the dismemberment.

"They're wrong, aren't they, Larry?" Marjorie said. "That's not Jay, right?"

"What did you expect me to do?" Larry said, sobbing. "*We* couldn't think of anything else to do."

Marjorie specifically recalled Larry using the word "we."

"How could you do that? That was Noah's father!" Marjorie cried.

Sobbing, Larry confessed. "I had to get rid of it!"

That's when Marjorie said she learned what had been used to dismember Jay's body. It was not done with the small blade of a jigsaw, Marjorie claimed. The dismemberment was conducted with a chain saw.

"How could you do that?" Marjorie screamed. "You're crazy!"

"Shut up!" Larry slapped her across the face.

"You're crazy!" Marjorie shrieked, pushing him away. "Get away from me."

Larry grabbed Marjorie by the hair and dragged her into the kitchen, hitting her in the face. Violently, he pulled her arms behind her back.

"It would be that easy." Larry snapped his fingers. "To snap Noah's scrawny neck."

Marjorie said she knew right then that Larry was a psychopath. He was threatening the life of an eight-year-old boy. She knew she had better keep her mouth shut. "I will never forget that statement or the look on his face. I knew then he was totally crazy. He left. I just sat on my kitchen floor crying. I didn't know what to do . . . I never wished Jay was there more than at that moment," she wrote. "On Jay's birthday in 2004, he lost his life. On my birthday that year, I got beat up—both at the hands of Larry Weisberg."

After that incident, Marjorie and Larry no longer spoke. But she said she still felt his control over her. In the middle of the night, she began receiving strange calls. The voice on the other end would say things like, "I'm watching you."

It was too late to come clean to the police. She had already lied repeatedly. Marjorie was just hopeful that Larry would be arrested. "I really thought that the police would figure out what happened."

On November 13, Marjorie was arrested at Circuit City. In the interrogation room, Detective Barnes showed Marjorie the color photo of Jay's dismembered torso. Marjorie was disgusted. It was the first time she had ever seen his corpse. "I freaked out. The picture looked odd. It was sort of yellow and didn't look real but I knew it was."

After her release from jail, she called Michael J. Peter. He sent her to attorney Tom Connelly. With Connelly, Marjorie said she was honest. "I told him the whole story. The real story, about Larry."

Then on December 6, Marjorie was arrested for first-degree murder. "I was home alone with Noah and they arrested me. My little eight-year-old boy saw me taken away in handcuffs." It was the last time Marjorie ever saw her son.

AFTERWORD

January 15, 2010

More than five years after the murder of Jay Orbin, the desert swath where his grisly dismembered torso was found remained vacant. It had once been slated for development, but the devastating crash in the housing market had since ground Phoenix's urban sprawl to a halt. The now tranquil desert bore no trace of the ghastly crime. The Rubbermaid tub had long since vanished. Yellow police tape no longer fluttered in the chilly October breeze. The fresh scent of cactus blossoms had replaced the piercing odor of death.

The day of Marjorie's final sentencing, I went to the desert to experience the spot that had once served as a graveyard for Jay's plastic casket. As I wove carefully through the thorny brush, I marveled at the ability of nature to erase such a terrible memory. I closed my eyes and pictured what the landscape must have looked like on October 23, 2004, in an attempt to understand the brutality behind the crime.

From the moment I first learned the details of Jay Orbin's death, I was drawn to this compelling murder mystery that had occurred in my own North Phoenix neighborhood. Jay's dismembered body was discovered just miles from my home. His home was a few blocks from where I lived. And the arcade where Noah celebrated his eighth birthday was a place I frequented with my husband.

For years, I had written about Jay's murder, without ever being able to speak with Marjorie. At times it was bewildering. There were a thousand unanswered questions only she could answer. After her conviction, Marjorie finally consented to an interview. During our lengthy jailhouse visits, I found myself intrigued by Marjorie. She was charming, persuasive, intelligent, and well-spoken. As I listened to her version of events, I began to wonder. *What if the story she was telling was true? What if Larry Weisberg had murdered Jay?*

I wanted to believe Marjorie. It was more comforting to think that Jay was murdered by his wife's lover than by the person he trusted most in the world. But there were too many holes in her story: Namely, why hadn't she reported the crime?

"Why didn't you tell them about Larry?" I asked.

"I don't know." She sighed. "Have you ever been in an abusive relationship?"

"No," I said.

"Well, umm. This wasn't really an abusive relationship," she stammered. "There have been steps all along the way that put me, or I allowed myself to be put into, or I got myself into, situations where my frame of mind was . . . I don't know."

Marjorie trailed off. Her answer was so convoluted that I asked the question again.

"I don't know. I don't know," Marjorie replied. "I don't have a way to make it make sense. I don't have a reasonable explanation."

During our interview, Marjorie ultimately admitted that Jay's death was a result of her tangled web of lies. "Jay is dead because I was having an affair," she said. "I did not cause it or intend for it to happen but that's something that I'll have to live with forever. Even if I was found not guilty and got out, it's still a fact that I would have to live with forever."

When she told me that, she appeared to be crying, although I never saw any actual tears. After our final interview, I returned home with Marjorie's manuscript in hand, anxious to read her story. As I flipped through the pages, I was astonished. While she denied the killing, it was the first time she had openly revealed her tremendous level of culpability in the cover-up. Marjorie's account of Jay's death was detailed, meticulous, and convincing. It seemed reasonable that Jay might have been killed during an accidental confrontation. Meanwhile, Larry had consistently turned down requests for interviews. He maintained to the police and in court that he was in no way involved in the murder or dismemberment.

While it is certainly possible that Larry committed the murder, I don't believe it is very plausible. In Marjorie's story, she portrayed herself as a victim. She claimed that, in an incredible coincidence, both Jay and Larry arrived unexpectedly and simultaneously. Afterward she just happened to epoxy coat the garage floor and buy the tub his body was found in.

For me, it didn't add up. But it was not for me to judge. A jury of Marjorie's peers had already decided they didn't buy her story. Regardless, I proceeded as I told Marjorie I would and added a new ending to my book to include her version of events. But the story didn't stop there. In the weeks following our final visit, Marjorie sent me dozens of letters adding almost a hundred pages to her manuscript. These supplements covered everything from her hair extensions to Jay's weight and the size of his penis.

In one chapter, she even claimed that her eyebrows added to her conviction. "I think the high arch sort of creates a look a littler meaner than reality is. There is nothing I can do about it. But I do think it adds to an unfair misconception and the perception of being angry or meaner than I really am. It's unfair."

Mostly, however, she disputed the claims of every witness who testified against her. Anyone who claimed she hated Jay was lying. "In ten years nobody who was around Jay and I can ever say that they heard or saw anything wrong between us," she wrote. "I never hated Jay and never said anything of the sort to anyone."

Her letters dripped with venom as she tore apart everyone involved with her trial. Marjorie claimed that Detective Jan Butcher had lied when she stated that Marjorie would be unable to collect insurance payments for seven years unless the body was found. As for Noel Levy, she called it "karma" that he fell ill.

Concerning the tie-rod, Marjorie wrote that she believed it had been sabotaged, but not by her in 2004; she claimed that Jake Orbin Jr. had sabotaged it in 2008 to secure a first-degree murder conviction. For the record, Jake Jr. called that statement ludicrous.

"The other primary offenses in this whole thing are by those who lied in my case, those who had something to gain by my conviction, which could have caused my death," Marjorie wrote. "To me those acts were intentional attempted murder. Those offenses were committed by: Sophia Johnson, Sharon Franco-Rueckert, Jake Orbin and even Jan Butcher. Those people have committed far greater offenses in this case than I did. Those were done with forethought and intent."

Included with Marjorie's supplements were several personal letters to me. She told me how much she enjoyed meeting me in jail and appealed to me to take a more compassionate approach with her in my book. "I like you very much and I felt a positive connection with you and I thought that maybe you would be more fair to me."

Bizarrely, she wrote about how happy she was that I was writing a true crime book about the murder of her husband—for which she was the convicted killer. "I'm excited about your project, I guess that sounds inappropriate," she wrote, after which she drew a smiley face.

Other letters were personally complimentary toward me. "You are a very beautiful and impressive young lady and you have something about you that is difficult to describe," she wrote.

As a journalist, I found that highly unusual as well as very uncomfortable. But over the next few days I began to feel an odd sense of sympathy toward Marjorie. She was going to spend the rest of her life in prison. While I believed her to be a killer, I realized that she was also once a loving mother. It seemed so sad. I wanted to return to the jail one more time to say good-bye before she was transferred to the state prison. But something stopped me. I began to wonder why she was being so kind toward me.

That's when it hit me. I had often wondered throughout the case why so many people had fallen victim to Marjorie's charms. Now I began to realize that it wasn't because she was so beautiful, intelligent, and magnificent. It was the way she made other people feel about themselves. Marjorie was trying to influence me from behind bars with insincere flattery. Despite my brief flash of sympathy, I decided it was not wise to visit Marjorie again. My contact with her had an effect on me, if only momentarily. Despite knowing the details of her crime, even I was not immune to her charms.

Through my research I have come to believe Marjorie was the sole person responsible for Jay Orbin's murder. The notoriously fickle Marjorie was weary of Jay and ready to move on with her life. But unlike her previous marriages, Marjorie could not just walk away from this one and start anew. Noah was her everything. She was unwilling to lose even partial custody of her son. Jay had to die. When his trip to Florida was cut short, I think she saw an opportunity. He arrived home at about six p.m. on his birthday. In the garage of his home, Marjorie shot and killed him. There, I believe, his body was brutally dismantled like one of her construction projects.

As Marjorie said herself in her manuscript, the dismemberment was a desperate act. Jay was too heavy to move, so I believe she hacked him apart into manageable pieces and deposited him in the Rubbermaid tubs. But what I don't think Marjorie accounted for was the outpouring of concern from Jay's loved ones. As the questions became increasingly worrisome, it was difficult for Marjorie to feign concern. She wanted everyone to know what she already knew—Jay was dead. She picked out the least incriminating piece of his body and dropped it in a place where it was almost certain to be found.

Marjorie was a skilled liar and a master manipulator. She thought she would be able to convince everyone that she was innocent. But after the body was discovered her web of lies quickly came unraveled.

Like the hurricane that altered Jay's plans and brought him unexpectedly back to Phoenix on his forty-fifth birthday, Marjorie was a violent, destructive force leaving anything that crossed her path in ruins.

Marjorie stole the life of a good man—a man who by her own admission was a kind, generous soul and a wonderful father. While only one person died, the actual casualty count in this case is much higher. For, in murdering Jay, Marjorie destroyed the lives of countless others. She selfishly robbed Noah of his father and in the process took away his mother. By doing so, she also stole his childhood. Noah has had to spend the last five years in counseling. Despite everything, he has adjusted well in the now permanent custody of his uncle and aunt. Gradually, he has learned to face life with the disturbing knowledge that his mom killed his dad.

The Orbins and Jay's large network of friends will never be whole again because Jay is no longer in their lives. With no more new memories, they live in the past, haunted by their fading recollections of Jay. Having had fatherhood thrust upon him, Jake Jr. spends everyday with a constant reminder of the little brother he will never see again. While he tries his best to do everything a father should, he knows in his heart that Noah wishes it were his dad throwing the football or helping him with his school projects. Jake and Joann have been devastated by Jay's death. Now in their late seventies, they will live out the last years of their lives in unimaginable agony.

The ripples of Marjorie's actions trickled through many lives. Jessiah Rueckert will never achieve his dreams of becoming a police officer because he lied about his affair with Marjorie. Todd Christy spent eleven months in jail and received a felony on his record for foolishly stealing from Jay's estate. While both men were responsible for their own actions, neither of those incidents would have occurred if not for Marjorie.

In an indirect way, the careers of Detective David Barnes and Prosecutor Noel Levy were left crumbling in Marjorie's wake. While David Barnes's own criminal charges had nothing to do with Marjorie's case, his career was left in shambles in the middle of her trial. The felony charges he had been facing for perjury and harassment were ultimately dismissed. However, he was fired from the police department. As of 2010, he was appealing the dismissal.

Nearly one year after he recused himself from the Marjorie Orbin case, I spoke with Noel Levy at his Tempe home, which is ironically decorated with the same Southwestern art and decor Jay had once sold. Now officially retired and still dealing with medical issues, Levy has come to terms with not being able to finish his final case. He read about Marjorie's conviction in the newspaper. The following day he sent his replacement, Treena Kay, a congratulatory e-mail.

If Marjorie is lying in her own twisted version of events, as the jury ruled, and as I believe, she also ruined the life of Larry Weisberg. If he is truly innocent, Larry will spend the remainder of his life cast in the shadow of suspicion—forever labeled a murder suspect. His grandchildren will grow up wondering if he did what he was accused of doing in court and in the media.

Through my encounters with Marjorie Orbin, I suspect none of these casualties weigh on her conscience. I expect only one loss truly bothers her—her own. For in murdering Jay, Marjorie nearly lost her own life and most certainly destroyed her future.

Marjorie is appealing her conviction. However, despite all of the legal issues at her trial, it seems unlikely her appeal will ever be granted. Thus, there is a high probability she will spend every day of the remainder of her natural life in a grimy prison cell. She will be there until her hair turns gray and time has erased all trace of beauty from her face. In the end, she will die behind those bars a lonely, elderly woman, her body buried in a cheap pine box in the prison graveyard.

That fate is a loss, I suspect, that even Marjorie will view as a tragedy.

ACKNOWLEDGMENTS

For my first book, I can't imagine selecting a more complicated murder mystery. Sorting through the varying ver-
sions of events was often exasperating. Many of those
involved with Marjorie Orbin were left scathed by their
encounters and scared to talk. Consequently, I had to com-
pose several portions of this book using police reports and
trial transcripts. I attempted to be as thorough as possible,
cross-checking my research with multiple sources. Any er-
rors or inaccuracies are unintentional.

I am very grateful to so many people who led me through
the labyrinth of this complex case. First and foremost, I
would like to thank David Barnes for sharing with me the
stories behind the police reports. Barnes and I spent countless hours at the bookstore coffee shop reviewing each detail of the complex investigation. Those interviews brought
the story to life. One day I hope he will be vindicated as an
honest detective who was unjustly punished for doing what
he believed was right.

In addition, I'd like to express my appreciation to Jan
Butcher, Noel Levy, and the dozens of other police officers,
detectives, and prosecutors who were involved in Marjorie's
arrest and conviction.

I also want to thank Jake Orbin Jr. and Jay's many

friends who took the time to meet with me. I have tremendous sympathy for your loss and my condolences are with you and your loved ones.

I owe a very special thank you to my literary agent, Sharlene Martin, for taking a chance on an unknown writer. Without her dedication and passion, I believe this project would not have been possible. Additionally, my gratitude goes out to my superb editors at St. Martin's Paperbacks, Allison Strobel and Charlie Spicer.

I also want to thank Steve Strickbine, my magazine editor and publisher, who first let me delve into this case as the features editor for the Phoenix-based *Times Publications*.

On a personal note, thank you to Eric Hendrix and Ryan Hendrix for your editing advice. To my beloved Mimi, Carol Hogan, as well as my Great Aunt Phyllis White for being my first readers—I send my love and gratitude. Sadly, my Aunt Phyllis passed away in 2010 before this book was published. She will be greatly missed. To my entire family, namely my parents Dann and Debbie Hogan as well as my mother-in-law Joann LaRussa—words cannot express my appreciation for your support of my career.

Lastly, I want to add a very special thank you to Matt LaRussa—my wonderful, adoring husband and love of my life.